To begin with—
This place you've come to see called Hiroshima
is no one place.
There are many places, each bearing that name.
One is located in the past.
One in the present.
One in the future.
Understand—
The legendary place that you seek
is not located on a map.
It is a state of mind.

BETTY JEAN LIFTON
A Place Called Hiroshima

Nagasaki Spirits, Hiroshima Voices

Making Sense of the Nuclear Age

WALTER ENLOE
RANDY MORRIS

HAMLINE UNIVERSITY PRESS
Saint Paul, Minnesota / 2003

Hamline University
1536 Hewitt Avenue
Saint Paul, Minnesota 55104
www.hamline.edu

Copyright © 2003 by Walter Enloe and Randy Morris
All rights reserved

First printing 2003
ISBN 0-9723721-1-3
Library of Congress Control Number 2003101574

Editing and project management by Stacey Lynn
Book design and layout by Green Sand Press, Tucson, Arizona
Production management by Susan Carr, Carr Creatives

Printed in U.S.A.

For Isaac, Serene, and my love and soulmate, Kitty
—W.E.

For Anna and Daniel, my hope for the future
—R.M.

CONTENTS

About the 2003 Edition — ix

Preface and Acknowledgments — xi

From the Mayors of Hiroshima and Nagasaki — xvii

Part I. Meditations on the Bomb
Randy Morris

Introduction — 3

1. Beyond Despair: An Imaginal Odyssey — 9
2. Nuclear Nightmares — 22
3. The Dream Peace Project — 26
4. The Psychology of Extinction: Inquiries into Anxiety — 45
5. Reveries on Martin Luther King's Birthday — 64
6. Reveries on Hiroshima and Education — 68
7. Education for Apocalypse: A Depth Psychological Approach — 72
8. Liberating Psyche in the Aftermath of 9/11 — 96

Part II. Stories of the Journey
Walter Enloe

Introduction — 117

9. Mama's Birthday — 127
10. Ground Zero: Nagasaki Spirits, Hiroshima Voices — 134
11. A Thousand Paper Cranes — 143

12. Hiroshima and the 1000 Cranes Club	146
13. Winged Messengers	156
14. Bringing Constructivity to the Classroom	161
15. Folding Ourselves into a Nonviolent Society	170
16. A Powerful Youth Movement	180
17. Young Peacemakers	185
18. Two Hiroshima Stories	191
Bibliography	199

ABOUT THE 2003 EDITION

MUCH HAS CHANGED ON THE WORLD STAGE SINCE the publication of our previous book *Encounters with Hiroshima: Making Sense of the Nuclear Age* in 1998. The fears of Y2K and the turn of the millennium have come and gone. Nuclear war between India and Pakistan seems to have been averted for now, but the fallout from the terrorist attack of 9/11 is still swirling about us. As of this writing in December 2002, the Bush administration is hungering for war with Iraq, along with the rest of the "axis of evil," and a senior administration official has been quoted as saying, "Our message is be afraid, be very afraid." As civil liberties are being eclipsed in the name of national security, it becomes more important than ever that we look back to the lessons that history has to teach us. Whether it be a study of government cover-ups during the Vietnam War or the worst excesses of the McCarthy era or the carnage inflicted upon civilians with the dropping of the atomic bombs on Hiroshima and Nagasaki, we have an obligation to remember the past. To do so reminds us that our best intentions as a nation carry with them a shadow side of unforeseen consequences that have profound effects on the future.

The premise of this book is that remembering Hiroshima and Nagasaki carries with it a special ethical obligation. Our memories of those events shape our imagination of the future. Will we literalize what the atomic bomb wrought and see the future as flame and destruction, or will we heed the warnings and change our course so that future generations might see the light of day? Furthermore, there are the educational questions: what soul capacities do we need to nurture in our students that will give them the flexibility to deal with the heightened fear that surrounds them without being incapacitated by psychic numbing? How can we seize this historical opportunity to open the heart in love and enhance our students' powers as choice makers? What choices can we encourage in our students that will make future generations look back and say, "Thank you. You saved our lives!" In this new edition of our book we have added important essays in response to these questions that supplement our earlier thinking.

We have retitled this book to include the city of Nagasaki in order to make several important acknowledgments. The atomic bombing of Nagasaki is one of history's great ironies. As the only portal of entry to Japan during the long Shogunate period, Nagasaki was the most Western of all Japanese cities and included a large Christian population. Ground zero in Nagasaki was Urakami Cathedral, the largest Christian church in Japan. Furthermore, Nagasaki was only a secondary target to Kokura, the original site. The vagaries of cloud cover obscured Kokura while providing a brief window over Nagasaki. Perhaps this combination of Western consciousness, Christian sensibility, and fate is what led a Jesuit priest who had lived for many years in Hiroshima before moving to Nagasaki to remark, "In Hiroshima they got angry; in Nagasaki they prayed." We acknowledge the spirits of Nagasaki as they have helped us to make meaning of what happened there, and we acknowledge the power of prayer as an important tool in the creation of a viable future. Our awareness of the theological implications of the bombing of Nagasaki has been greatly enhanced by the work of Dr. Takashi Nagai, whose many books, including *The Bells of Nagasaki*, continue to inspire a Christian interpretation of the redemptive power of Nagasaki's suffering.

A second reason to include Nagasaki in our title is to recognize the oldest sister-city relationship between Japan and the United States, that of Nagasaki, Japan, and St. Paul, Minnesota. It also honors the new sister-university relationship between Hamline University in St. Paul (Minnesota's oldest university, celebrating 150 years in 2004) and Kwassui University in Nagasaki (Japan's oldest university for women). Both universities are affiliated with the United Methodist Church.

And so our lives continue to be affected by our encounters with Hiroshima and Nagasaki. Our quest to make sense out of what happened there continues to inspire our best efforts to be of service to both the present and the future. We thank the readers of our previous book and hope that they will find the new material in this edition to be of interest. We invite new readers into a meditation on the continued relevance and revelatory power of Hiroshima and Nagasaki.

PREFACE

WE ARE ALL RELUCTANT WITNESSES TO HIROSHIMA. The authors of this book are no exception. And yet there is something about growing up in the 1950s and 1960s in the shadow of the bomb that demands our attention. If we ignore it, the image of the bomb will slide underground to haunt our dreams. We all have a responsibility to come to terms with the symbolic power of Hiroshima—what it has to say about who we are as Americans and global citizens, about technology and power, about the nature of evil and human destructiveness as well as the power of redemption and healing. Hiroshima symbolizes a particular time in history, the end of one age and the beginning of another.

This book is the result of journeys undertaken by the authors as educators, liberal artists, and human beings to make sense of the nuclear age. Our unique vantage point is that we lived in Hiroshima for many years, time enough for the psychic landscape of the city to speak to and through us. This book is an attempt to report on what we have learned and how we have been motivated by the power of Hiroshima's legacy. We hope that it will stimulate others to deepen their thinking about this crucial time in human history.

The authors of this book first met as graduate students at Emory University in Atlanta, Georgia. We found ourselves at the Graduate Institute of Liberal Arts studying epistemology. Our common interest and consuming passion was to understand how we can make sense of the world, how we can "know" anything at all. This led to a long collaboration centered on the work of the great constructivist epistemologist Jean Piaget. We wanted to understand the deep meaning in the title of one of Piaget's seminal works, *The Child's Construction of Reality*. How *do* children construct reality? To study that question we needed to be near children. First Walter, then Randy, migrated to a nearby experimental community called the Paideia School, a perfect epistemological laboratory where we both worked for many years, eventually teaching every age group in the K-12 school. Later, armed with doctorates and teaching experience, we found ourselves in Hiroshima. How we got there requires knowing something of our background.

Walter was born and raised in rural Louisiana and then Atlanta. He first went to Japan in 1961 as the son of Presbyterian missionaries. By the time he was fourteen, his family had moved to Hiroshima, where his parents conducted missionary work for almost thirty years, establishing a center for rehabilitative medicine and numerous churches. Walter attended high school at the U.S. military base at Iwakuni near Hiroshima and also at Canadian Academy in Kobe before returning to America to graduate from high school while his father studied at Princeton. He then attended Eckerd College in St. Petersburg, Florida, where he was active in student government, sports, and the study of "Humanities and Social Action." He decided to follow the suggestion of his college mentor Robert Detweiler to pursue work in human studies at the Graduate Institute of Liberal Arts at Emory University. He enrolled in American Studies, in large part because of his Japan experience and participation in social movements: he was an active resister during the Vietnam war and a four-year tutor in the Upward Bound program for college-oriented disadvantaged high school students. He was president of the Student Association at Eckerd during the civil turmoil in the aftermath of Kent State and was a Rhodes Scholar nominee, Danforth Fellow, and recipient of the college's award for outstanding leadership; his efforts to build forums for dialogue between college students and older citizens were quite successful.

In his first year of graduate work at Emory, Walter was invited to join a group of fellow students who had received an N.E.H. grant to make a nine-program TV series for PBS stations titled "World of Choice." The series would showcase the schools that had been established as alternatives to public education in Atlanta from 1965 to 1971. These included free schools, an international Montessori School, segregation academies, Christian Schools, and a Black Panther school. The "open" Paideia School was in its first year, and Walter fell in love with the school's philosophy and community spirit. He began that spring in 1972 to work several hours a week as a volunteer aide and the next year became a full-time aide in the half-day kindergarten program, teaching K-12 there until he moved to Hiroshima in 1980. He was beginning his third year of work when first-year graduate student Randy Morris moved in next door.

Randy Morris was born and raised in Richland, Washington, a government city established in 1943 to house the workers at the Hanford nuclear reservation, site of the creation of plutonium for the Manhattan Project. Randy's father taught at Columbia High School in Richland, home of the "Bombers," whose logo was a large mushroom cloud. Displayed on school letter jackets, the water tower over the athletic fields, and the parquetry floor in the entrance hall, the logo was living proof that the A-bomb ethos was alive and well. Living in Richland was fine for a child of the 1950s, although there was a lingering cloud of suspicion in the air, fueled no doubt by the combination of air-raid drills at school and the fact that most kids either did not know or could not talk about their parents' work.

Randy spent four years at the Episcopal High School in Alexandria, Virginia, before returning to the West Coast to attend Whitman college, where he studied biology and the humanities. At somewhat of a loss about what to do after graduation in 1972, Randy ended up on the East Coast with some high school friends, working as a crab fisherman in Beaufort, South Carolina. From there he migrated to Atlanta, Georgia, to paint houses. He decided to return to graduate school to pursue his passion for learning when he discovered the perfect program at Emory University. Randy had an admissions interview with a professor by the name of Robert Detweiler and was accepted on the spot. A few weeks later, while looking for student housing, he moved in next door to Walter and Kitty Enloe.

The Institute of Liberal Arts at Emory University was a great place to be a student in the 1970s. Emory's self-directed Ph.D. program allowed a great deal of latitude and had attracted an interesting intellectual community. Walter and Randy threw themselves into a seven-year intensive reading program. Walter completed his studies with doctoral examinations in three areas: Piaget's Theory of Knowing and Activity, the History of Progressive Education, and Human Science Methods: Structuralism and Phenomenology. His dissertation was titled *An Open Systems Approach to Jean Piaget's Life Work*. Randy completed his studies with doctoral examinations in developmental psychology and phenomenological philosophy and a dissertation titled *The Contributions of Jean Piaget and Erik Erikson to a Philosophical Anthropology: A Phenomenological Approach*. Both Randy and Walter are indebted to Robert Detweiler and the Institute of Liberal Arts for an excellent educational experience.

After graduating from the Institute of Liberal Arts, Walter spent two years teaching humanities and social studies at the Paideia High School. He was then invited to apply to be the principal and a teacher at the Hiroshima International School in Japan for a two-year stint to help the school through an accreditation process. When Walter left for Japan, Randy took his position as social studies teacher at the Paideia High School. Two years later, he was offered a job as a middle school teacher at the Hiroshima International School. Walter and Randy worked together at HIS from 1982 to 1985. Randy returned to the States and eventually ended up as a core faculty member at Antioch University in Seattle. Walter returned to the States in 1988 after establishing the international school as a nonprofit foundation and building a new school facility. He became Senior Fellow in Global Education at the University of Minnesota and now is Associate Professor at Hamline University.

Ours has been a long and fruitful journey, and the articles and essays collected here record a small part of it. In the end, this book has three aims. First, we want to try to make sense of the nuclear age by combining the clarity of the intellect with the conviction of the heart. The writing herein represents our best thinking about the state of our culture and the way in which the Hiroshima event serves as a cipher for understanding late twentieth-century America and the possibilities for a global culture. Second, we want to demonstrate our long-held conviction that knowledge of the world is constructed by an individual in ever more complex webs of understanding. We accept Jean Piaget's notion, a corollary to his constructivist epistemology, that the intellectual life of a human being tends to be dominated by a single idea that differentiates over a lifetime into a tapestry of elegance and sophistication. For this reason, we have organized our respective sections of the book chronologically so that the reader can see the progression of our thinking. It is our hope that this strategy will serve as a mirror, helping readers to question and discern within their own lives the shape of the idea that seeks understanding through them. And finally, we aim to model through our own actions the myriad possibilities each human being has to become a peacemaker. We present our stories as a catalyst for others to become self-conscious about their own unique contributions to peace on Earth. Certainly, it has been one of the great gifts of our lives to be called to a meditation on the image of Hiroshima, and we pray that this book may be one small contribution to a "necessary hope" for future generations.

ACKNOWLEDGMENTS

This book was created because of many wonderful people. It is written in memory of the Reverend Kiyoshi Tanimoto, minister, pacifist, and peacemaker; and in honor of the lifework of Ichiro Kawamoto, *hibakusha* (A-bomb survivor), Christian pacifist, day laborer, and friend of Sadako. Ichiro is to some a fanatic, to others the A-bomb zealot-saint, and to others the unassuming adult leader behind the building of Hiroshima Peace Park's Children's Monument. He was a modest school janitor and a humble founder of the Folded Cranes Club. We have also learned much from the life work of Takashi Nagai of Nagasaki. Dr. Nagai worked tirelessly on behalf of the bomb victims and children while he suffered the misery and slow death of the A-bomb disease.

This book is also written in appreciation of the faculty and our peers at Emory University's Graduate Institute of the Liberal Arts as well as the communities at the Paideia School in Atlanta and the Hiroshima International School, who taught us the art of peacemaking. It is for the children, citizens, and sojourners of Hiroshima; to future peacemakers; and to future generations.

Walter gives special thanks to his parents, Winton and Mary Katherine, who first introduced him to Japan and whose lives exemplify love, respect, and peacemaking. He also thanks the Hamline University community, especially his colleagues in the Graduate School of Education.

Randy acknowledges his mother, Virginia, and her ancestors, who taught him that the purpose of knowledge is to serve compassion. Thanks also to his colleagues at the B.A. (Liberal Studies) Program at Antioch University/Seattle and to the many students it has been his privilege to serve.

This book is the fruit of a long collaboration between Walter and Randy as well as the many people who have affected their lives. In particular we want to acknowledge Ms. Shibama, teacher at Jogakuin Methodist Girls' School and peace activist, who motivated the senior students at Hiroshima International School to begin their quest to make sense of living in Hiroshima. We also deeply thank the Rev. Kiyoshi Tanimoto, a friend of our families who was minister of Nagarekawa Methodist Church in Hiroshima, and the well-known activist of the No More Hiroshimas movement. The story of Reverend Tanimoto's heroic efforts on August 6,

1945, have been immortalized in John Hersey's account of that day, *Hiroshima*. An alumnus also of Emory University (Chandler School of Theology in 1939), Mr. Tanimoto was sponsored by the Methodist Missions Board and gave more than a thousand presentations to audiences throughout the United States in the late forties and fifties on Hiroshima, reconciliation, Christian love, and universal peace. He and his family motivated us and our students to take on the work of peacemaking as found in the stories collected here. We also thank International School colleague and friend Mayumi Yingling, who supported our encounter with Hiroshima's culture and people. And we wish to acknowledge our many "outsider" friends who contributed to our learning and peacemaking in Hiroshima: Elizabeth Baldwin, Lonnie Wiig, Carol Miki, Steve Leeper, Don Nilson, Phil Lewin, and Charles and Julie Fleming. Thanks also to David Miller, Mark Mudge, and especially John Rehlin. And, finally, thank you to Stacey Lynn, Harrison Shaffer, and Green Sand Press.

From the Mayors of Hiroshima and Nagasaki

NAGASAKI PEACE DECLARATION 2001

Having entered a new century, we offer heartfelt prayers for the repose of the souls of those who died in the atomic bombings and for all the victims of war in every country, calling to the world for peace from the atom bombed city of Nagasaki.

We the citizens of Nagasaki have continuously appealed for the realization of the twenty-first century as an era free from nuclear weapons. Notwithstanding, no fewer than 30,000 nuclear warheads remain in existence on the surface of our planet, and the nuclear threat is now on the verge of expanding into space. Fifty-six years ago, it required only a single and relatively primitive atomic bomb to instantly transform our city into hell on Earth.

The twentieth century was an age of great progress for humankind in terms of science and technology, as well as awareness of human rights. At the same time, however, the twentieth century gave birth to nuclear weapons, instruments capable of destroying all of humanity. The nuclear weapons states have refused to give up these instruments, even with the passing of the Cold War, and a nuclear superpower is now insinuating that it may renege on international commitments in the area of nuclear disarmament. We are vigorously opposed to these movements, which could negate previous efforts for the elimination of nuclear weapons.

The agreement on "an unequivocal undertaking to accomplish the total elimination of their nuclear arsenals," expressed in May of last year at the 2000 Review Conference of the Parties to the Treaty on the Non-Proliferation of Nuclear Weapons, should not be allowed to become an empty promise. We shall continue to raise our voices in unison with the peoples of the world to actualize this undertaking.

We urge the Japanese government, representing a nation that has suffered nuclear attack, to play an active and befitting role in the elimination of nuclear weapons, and to call for the convening of an international assembly to enact a treaty for their prohibition. Japan must uphold the peaceful ideals of its constitution, build relations of trust with neighboring countries by squarely facing its history of aggression, and work for the establishment of a Northeast Asian nuclear-weapon-free zone that will enable Japan's withdrawal from the "nuclear umbrella." Accordingly, the threefold non-nuclear principle must be drafted into law.

We also urge greater levels of care and assistance for all of the atomic survivors, both in Japan and abroad. The passage of fifty-six years has not at all alleviated the physical and mental anguish of the atomic bomb survivors who are growing increasingly elderly. In fact, their anxiety and discomfort are mounting year by year. At the same time, the Japanese government must not forget those who suffer similarly, despite residing in districts in and around Nagasaki that have not been officially designated as being affected by the atomic bombing.

It is heartening that young people in Nagasaki are voluntarily devising peace-related programs and are engaged in various efforts and activities. For example, a group of high school students is now undertaking a petition drive seeking 10,000 signatures in support of the elimination of nuclear weapons, and we are proud to think that a new generation of youth is rising up to take action and initiative. Also, the City of Nagasaki is creating the Nagasaki Peace Education Program, which encourages young people to discuss and learn about the atomic bombings, peace, and human rights in a cross-generational context. In this way, we are working to develop human resources for the active pursuit of peace.

In November of last year Nagasaki hosted Japan's first-ever event linking local governments and NGOs, the Nagasaki Global Citizens' Assembly for the Elimination of Nuclear Weapons. This event confirmed our belief that the united actions of ordinary citizens can indeed move the world. Recalling that worldwide grassroots activities brought about a treaty for the international prohibition of anti-personnel land mines, we shall further strengthen our links with NGOs and municipalities around the globe, standing at the forefront of efforts to abolish nuclear weapons.

Nagasaki must forever remain the last place ever to have suffered nuclear attack. We, the citizens of Nagasaki, hereby pledge to exert every possible effort to insure that the twenty-first century is an age of peace, free from nuclear weapons, and from war itself.

MAYOR ITOH OF NAGASAKI
August 9, 2001

HIROSHIMA PEACE DECLARATION 2001

On the first August 6 of the new century, we, the citizens of Hiroshima, living witnesses to the "century of war," hereby declare that we will do everything in our power to make the twenty-first century one of peace and humanity, free from nuclear weapons.

We believe that humanity means our willingness to listen to the voices of all sentient beings. Humanity also means nurturing children with loving care. It means valuing reconciliation in creating the human family's common future. It means rejecting violence and reaching peaceful agreements through the power of reason and conscience. Only humanity can assure the abolition of nuclear weapons. Only humanity can insure that nuclear weapons, once eliminated, are never reinvented.

In the twenty-first century, Hiroshima intends to soar to new heights as a city of humanity. We intend to create a spiritual home for all people, a home with compassion, a source of creativity and energy for our planet's children and youth, a city offering a personal place of rest and comfort for all, young or old, male and female.

However, the calendar end to the "century of war" has not automatically ushered in a century of peace and humanity. Our world is still darkened not only by the direct violence of local conflicts and civil wars, but also by innumerable other forms of violence including environmental destruction, violence-promoting publications, images, and games. Now, through advanced science and technology, some are trying to extend battlefields into space.

We need our world leaders first to look at this reality humbly and unflinchingly. They must also possess a strong will to eliminate nuclear weapons, sincerity in abiding by their agreements, which are crystallizations of human wisdom, and finally, the courage required to make reconciliation and humanity top priorities.

Many *hibakusha* (survivors of the A-bomb) and their kindred spirits, feeling called upon to shoulder the fate of the entire human race, have sought the abolition of nuclear weapons and [the promotion of] world peace with a will strong enough to cut through solid rock. For hibakusha, the living hell suffered fifty-six years ago remains vivid and present even today. This—communicating in living form to coming generations the hibakushas' memories, their sense of responsibility, and their unrelenting will—is the most dependable first step toward survival through the twenty-first century and on to the twenty-second century, connected by a bridge of hope.

To that end, the city of Hiroshima is investing in the revitalization of peace education, in the broadest sense of that term. We are striving, in particular, to establish Hiroshima-Nagasaki peace study courses in major universities around the world. The basic framework for such courses will be constructed from the accomplishments of the Hiroshima Peace Institute and similar institutions where academic endeavor based on unalterable fact has brought humankind closer to the truth.

This week, the citizens of Hiroshima and Nagasaki are hosting the World Conference for Mayors for Peace through Inter-City Solidarity. The conference has been organized for the expressed purpose of abolishing nuclear weapons and realizing world peace through truth-guided solidarity among cities, the entities that will carry most prominently the torch of humanity in the twenty-first century. It is no mere fantasy to believe that in the future, member cities of the conference will lead other municipalities in expanding the circle of nuclear-free authorities until ultimately the entire Earth becomes one solid nuclear-free zone.

Hiroshima calls upon the national government of Japan to play an active role as a mediator in Asia in creating nuclear-free zones and implementing confidence-building measures. We further expect that, as a matter of national policy, Japan will initiate an effort to conclude a global treaty that prohibits nuclear weapons forever. We demand that our government properly value the contributions made by hibakusha, wherever they may live, which should culminate in improved relief measures that respect their rights. Finally, we demand that our national government forge the will to abolish nuclear weapons and, in accordance with the preamble of our constitution, work with Hiroshima in the effort to create a century of peace and humanity.

On this first August 6 of the twenty-first century, it is by vowing to spread the peace of this moment through the entire twenty-first century and throughout the world that we pay our sincerest respects to the souls of all the atomic victims.

Mayor Akiba of Hiroshima
August 6, 2001

**Nagasaki Spirits,
Hiroshima Voices**

PART I

Meditations on the Bomb

RANDY MORRIS

INTRODUCTION

Take these teachings: that we are all brothers and sisters, the children of one father and mother; that all human beings are interconnected; that we share many thoughts and feelings that we imagine about the world, about the future, about each other; and that the images and dreams we hold in our minds and hearts do matter. Treat children and animals with kindness, and pass this wisdom on to the generations yet to come, and I assure you that there will come a time when our grandchildren, or our great-great grandchildren will live in a world of beauty and harmony. And they will hear a far-off music, a beautiful, cosmic music, that will lift them beyond all fear, all suffering and limitation, into a universal brotherhood, beyond this little world and its fearful dreams. That music will draw closer and yet closer with its message of hope and becoming. That music is the Song of the Stars. Indaba....

A song that I sing with the sangomas says, "There shall arise out of the ashes of man, a newer man who shall rule the far stars, carrying with him the seven laws of love; and that the first and the greatest law of God—doing unto others as you would have them do to you—will be the law of that time." This, too, is the "Song of the Stars"—that humanity can stand fearlessly and joyfully before the Universe, with love in his heart, and be welcomed home as a long-lost child.

I have no message more important than this: All people, all nations, must seriously work for peace on the Earth....I know that many have made this futile call, but I shall also make it: That there should be an end to all war and all conflict on Earth. More than this I cannot say.

Vusamazulu Credo Mutwa
Song of the Stars: The Lore of a Zulu Shaman

How *does* one compose a life of the mind? I remember the first time I asked myself this question. I was twenty-one years old and the year was 1971. I was traveling through Scotland by myself, reading a book of short stories by Borges as well as the recently released *Pentagon Papers*. I was riding on the luck of a high draft number and a few remaining dollars from my stash. Waiting for a ferry on the Isle of Skye, I climbed the nearby mountain and sat to wait for a few hours. It was then that the solitude, the clean fresh air, the tumbling clouds, the magnificent vista, and the ideas from the books I was reading constellated into a vision. I became hyper aware of my consciousness and realized, for the first time, that I was an individual living in freedom. I was suddenly aware that I was capable of making a vast array of choices, many of which I had never before considered. I could choose to think about anything I wanted to. A second question fell quickly upon the first: What is *worth* thinking about?

In a way, my contributions to this book are a response to these two questions. These essays were written in a variety of contexts and for different purposes, and it was only upon organizing them for this book that I was able to see just how appropriately they were answering my two questions. One composes a life of the mind by following the scent of curiosity into matters that are close to the heart. Typically, it is only in retrospect that one can discern the thread of Ariadne that links the various themes that have engaged the thinking heart. For me, this has meant digging deeply into the sentiments that arose from being raised in the 1950s in an odd town where secrets were held close to the chest. It has meant dealing with the ambivalence of being a college student during the Vietnam war when thinking with conviction seemed unpatriotic. And it has meant diving into the terror of nuclear war. It seems that the worthiest things to think about are also the deepest, the things that bring us to the borderlands between the human and the inhuman. I feel blessed that I have been given the opportunity to navigate these deep waters and to share them with an audience such as you.

Most of the articles in this section have not been published before. I tend to write when the spirit moves me, making a few copies to give out to colleagues and students and keeping the rest for later. I am grateful to my friend Walter Enloe for pushing me into this public display. I begin my contribution with an essay written to commemorate the fiftieth anniversary of the atomic bombing, *Beyond Despair: An Imaginal Odyssey into the Soul of Hiroshima*. I remember Walter telling me to write something for this occasion, but the weight of daily responsibilities prevented me from doing so. But then I was called to jury duty in the winter of 1995 and realized I was being presented with a golden opportunity. I sat down with a yellow pad in the jury waiting room and the essay seemed to pour out of me. I had only to change a few words in my editing. There was something about being with all those fellow citizens, folks like me, who were giving their time on behalf of justice. I was inspired by the setting. The essay is a good introduction to my work because it will inform readers about my own biography and some of the stories it has been my privilege to live. The essay employs a style of writing that I have come to call "reverie," based on Gaston Bachelard's idea of reverie as the fusion of memory and imagination. The style seems to agree with my desire to express the thought of the heart.

The rest of the essays that follow are arranged chronologically, beginning with a short letter to the editor of an English language newspaper in Japan entitled *Nuclear Nightmares*. When I first saw the letters about nuclear nightmares mentioned in the article, I wanted to seize the opportunity to think a bit more clearly about what the dreams were saying. I had already been collecting nuclear dreams and had spoken about dreams in a series of talks at the World Friendship Center in Hiroshima, but I had not yet committed myself to writing. The short article represents the beginning of my formal thinking about this topic.

The Dream Peace Project evolved out of my interest in dreams and my desire to penetrate deeper into the heart of the nuclear issue than the rather superficial political rhetoric allowed. The group of people who were constellated around this project were an interesting mix of Japanese citizens and expatriate Americans. We met for over a year to discuss our dreams and figure out a way to talk about the psychology of peace. One initiative that was inspired by our dreams was the "Peace Picnic for Future Generations," a nonpolitical family march that celebrated the real reason we work on behalf of peace: to ensure the possibility of future generations. I understand that, in a slightly altered form, this Peace Picnic has become a festival and is still celebrated in Hiroshima. While all this was going on, one of our members had a particularly interesting nuclear dream and we decided to turn that dream into a story requiring a conclusion. Many of the original members wrote their own versions, as did several participants in a workshop conducted in Nagasaki. I include four short stories here to give some idea of the variety of responses. I would like to thank the World Friendship Center for extending their hospitality and goodwill to this project.

The longer I lived in Hiroshima, the deeper my thinking became. Somehow, my work was brought to the attention of Dr. Mikihachiro Tatara, a professor of psychology at Hiroshima University who had worked with Erik Erikson in the United States. Dr. Tatara graciously asked me to contribute to a forum on psychology, an invitation I readily accepted. So I labored away on a lecture that summarized the ideas with which I was working and produced *The Psychology of Extinction: Inquiries into Anxiety in the Nuclear Age*. The only psychologist whose books I had much access to and who saw the deeper implications of Hiroshima was Robert Jay Lifton. I was lucky because I still believe that Lifton's formulations provide a good road map into the psyche of Hiroshima. The essay is somewhat didactic in style but provides a good overview of Lifton's work and how it can be made relevant to teaching in the nuclear age. It represents the culmination of my thinking while living in the city of Hiroshima.

Upon returning to the States after three years of living in Hiroshima, I eventually landed a job teaching adult students in a liberal arts program at Antioch University in Seattle. By the time I wrote the short piece entitled *Reveries on Martin Luther King's Birthday*, I had discovered the rhetorical possibilities of the reverie style. The year 1989 marked the sixtieth anniversary of the birth of Martin Luther King, a man who continues to inspire me in so many ways. I wanted to honor his imaginal presence in my life, so I tried to commit my feelings to paper. I am pleased to submit this short meditation to the memory of Dr. Martin Luther King, Jr.

Reveries on Hiroshima and Education was written at the request of Walter Enloe, who once again encouraged me to be more public with my Hiroshima experience. We traded drafts back and forth, then submitted the essay to the *Holistic Education Review*, who published the essay in 1990 to commemorate the forty-fifth anniversary of the bombing. It is published here with permission. Soon thereafter, Walter was badgering me about writing something for the fiftieth anniversary too, resulting in the aforementioned essay *Beyond Despair*. Thanks again, Walter.

By this time I thought I had exhausted the theme of Hiroshima. All of my best stories had already been told and even though my audience was small, it seemed that I was done. But then I began work on another project having to do with spirituality and adult education. This project was inspired by a dream in which Mother Teresa appeared to me and said, *"Randy, the point is not to save people. The point is to create the conditions for the possibility of Grace."* The call to "create the conditions for the possibility of grace" has inspired my teaching ever since. In the summer of 1997 I drove my family from our home in Seattle to Walter's house in Minneapolis. While the kids were at a Japanese language camp, my wife and I hung out with Kitty and Walter. Once again, Walter's encouragement convinced me to write a concluding piece for this very book. I wanted to dovetail my interests in adult education, spirituality, and the theme of apocalypse into a single essay. I decided to dive into the subject matter using the intellectual tool that I had been honing for the previous decade—depth psychology. In a space of three days, while vacationing in an old musty cottage somewhere in upstate Minnesota, I wrote *Education for Apocalypse: A Depth Psychological Approach*. Once again I chose to use the image of apocalypse as a doorway into what I think is most important to think about: the future of our species and the destiny of humanity.

And then came September 11, 2001. While many pundits said that after the events of 9/11 nothing would ever be the same, I tended to view those events as simply a wake-up call to what was already present. When I was invited to give a lecture at Antioch University/Seattle as part of a series titled "Toward a Humane Future: Emerging Issues in the Aftermath of September 11," I wanted to make my case that the events of 9/11, like the events of Hiroshima and Nagasaki, are opportunities for the psyche to undergo an initiation, a dying of old patterns of thought and the birth of a new imagination of sustainable culture. I agree with one of my spiritual mentors, Joanna Macy, that we are now in the time of the "Great Turning" as we move from an industrial growth society to a sustainable society. I aspire to be a warrior on behalf of this Great Turning, and "Liberating Psyche in the Aftermath of 9/11" is a contribution to this work.

With the completion of this final essay I am prepared to gather my work together for public consumption. I have kept covenant with that original vision that came to me on the Isle of Skye when I was twenty-one years old. I continue to live a life of the mind and I know what is most important to think about. But my fantasies of having exhausted the Hiroshima theme were cut short when just a few weeks ago I was informed by mail that I qualified for a special dispensation. As a person born between 1949 and 1951 in a three-county area downwind from the Hanford Nuclear Reservation, I am eligible to be part of a cancer research study on the long-term effects of radioactive iodine-131. The state of my health is now of interest to those besides my loved ones, and I get to study the psychodynamics of nuclear radiation up close and personal. Events like these suggest to me the possibility that perhaps we do not compose a life of the mind, but rather *we* are composed by *it*. My task, and yours as well, is to stay alert to the possibilities of what is happening.

And now, I invite you into the domain of my understanding.

1

Beyond Despair

An Imaginal Odyssey into the Soul of Hiroshima
1995

Oh, Hiroshima!
   You cry out
To my reluctant heart.
Must I enter your flaming tori
   gate once more,
Ride past lit lanterns floating
   on ink dark seas
To gaze upon seared flesh
   and the skulls of the dead,
Water wells fouled by inhuman thirst.
Must I suffer once more
   the indignity of my God's face
Bubbling in neutron tars.
   Must I wonder anew?
Yes, I know. The dead
   demand their due.
Our ancestors seek
   their own redemption
Through us, their only means.

My fears pale beside
    the perversity of incandescent
Arrogance. The mind
    loosed from all constraint.

Bodies melt before the throne
    of abstractions, Where Eros
Is barred, where kind words
    and promises made
Veil evil pride.

I hear your call, beloved
    of my soul.
Orpheus sinks
    to meet your embrace.
For redemption's sake,
    mine and yours.

FINDING THE DOORWAY

My relationship to the bomb as image begins with my birth in 1950 in Richland, Washington, home of the Richland High School Bombers, where cheerleaders still wear the logo of a mushroom cloud across their chests. There I grew up among my friends and their parents, workers at the Hanford Nuclear Reservation, the birthplace of the plutonium bomb (later dropped upon the city of Nagasaki, Japan), an incendiary device that killed 70,000 human beings. It never occurred to any of us that by virtue of living in this stark desert land by the mighty Columbia River we were becoming "downwinders," passive recipients of massive radiation leaks from the Hanford Reservation.

    My dance around the bomb continued through the age of air-raid drills ("Get back under that desk, young man!") and bomb shelters ("Mom, will we let our neighbors in or not?"). Later, while attending a boarding school outside of Washington, D.C., I had a dream in which a huge B-52 was flying over the capitol. In the dream, bomb bay doors open and a man who is partly me straddles a bomb as it falls to the earth. It lands near my dorm.

There is a huge flash of light and I can see the veins behind my eyelids. I wake up in a panic, knowing I have but thirty seconds to live. Sure enough, there is the huge boom that rattles the windows and walls. But survival is a powerful instinct. I jump out of bed and dash for the closet to grab some clothes and head for the basement, expecting at any moment to be annihilated. Frantically I dig in my closet as my mind begins to split and separate the phenomenal world from the dream world. When the process is complete, I am left standing in my underwear, clothes a jumble, listening to the sharp rain of a thunderstorm clatter against the window.

Circumambulating the bomb as image continued when, in 1981, Ph.D. in hand, I prepared to have a cross-cultural experience in Hiroshima, Japan, home of the Hiroshima International School, where I had secured a teaching position. A month before I was to leave I had a dream in which I was one of four people in white coats working skillfully but feverishly around a table. Lying like an anesthetized patient on the table is a cylindrical bomb, its innards exposed, wires sticking out, waiting to explode. To defuse this device requires a great deal of controlled passion. The fate of the world rests on our shoulders, and sweat pours down our foreheads as we try to keep our hands steady. Five…four…we almost have it! We're going to make it! Three…two…Wait! Wait! Just another few seconds! One…*kaboom!* In disbelief at my failure, in anger at not having enough time, I am subjected to the full experience of nuclear annihilation, first the flash of light that lifts and peels the skin, then the explosion that expands and shatters the body, the last sensation memory can sustain.

This was the dream I held in my mind as I first orbited ground zero near the *Hondori* of downtown Hiroshima. It was as if that place, 600 meters above a hospital door, were an aperture from one world into another. But from what kind of world? Would I ever understand what passed through that door? Would I be required to pass through it myself? Later that day my friend took me to Peace Park. "So this is it!" I thought in ego-based wonder. "What is that pretty green mound over there, the one with incense trays before it?" "Oh, that is the Memorial Mound for the Unknown Dead. Inside it are tens of thousands of boxes of human remains, most of them unidentified, waiting to be claimed by relatives." To my surprise, I felt hot tears well up spontaneously in my eyes. An unseen hand gripped my chest and squeezed without mercy as sobs rumbled clumsily from my center. I bent my head, half in acknowledgment of the dead, half in shame for my lack of control. It was only then, with that first awakening to the well of grief, the first time I ever recall crying in public, that I began my descent into the soul of Hiroshima.

OVER MY HEAD

Having been awakened by the images of death that lie etched in monuments throughout the city, barely discernible beneath the hustle and bustle of a modern Japanese metropolis, I resolved to do my part for peace. But what could I do? I had no desire to join the political posturing, mostly because I felt that the opposing powers would enact their wills anyway, that power has no use for peace. Neither did I feel I was mature or talented enough to create any of the unique and beautiful works of art that have already been lovingly dedicated to the city. An idea occurred to me based on my naive belief that I knew something about dreams. After all, I had studied some dream theory in graduate school and had the benefit of a few years of analysis. I had already come to the conclusion that dreams were an epistemological problem worth meditating upon for a lifetime. How *could* we be both the author and the audience of our own dreams? Why *are* dreams so revered in religious traditions? Why do I find myself so moved by certain images in dreams? Perhaps I could change the outcome of my nuclear nightmare by moving more *into* the dreams.

I decided to collect the dreams of *hibakusha*, or A-bomb survivors. Wouldn't it be interesting, I thought, to see how the unconscious has come to terms with that event? If there were some new mythology to come out of the A-bomb experience, surely it would appear in the dreams of the hibakusha. But who would share their dreams with me? Brief forays into the field quickly turned up a daunting fact for any dream researcher: the folkways of Japan say that it is a sign of ill health for one to recall dreams, certain exceptions being allowed for dreams that appear at the new year. But with the enthusiasm of youth, I did not give up. Then I was introduced to Tomoko (not her real name), a Japanese hibakusha with extensive facial scarring who had dedicated her life to the making of peace. In her somewhat breathless and matter-of-fact way, her English accented and delightful, she offered me this dream story:

Ah, Randy-san. I will tell you this dream. You see many years ago I went to America to talk of peace and every night I had this dream, sometimes two or three times a night. I couldn't get any sleep. We traveled all around the country giving talks and I was very tired. Finally I couldn't stand it any more and I came back home. I didn't leave again for twenty years because I feared this dream.

You see in this dream I was twelve years old again and I woke up on a fine morning. I was walking to school when this big bomb exploded all around me. I was screaming and my dress was on fire, as was the land all around me. People were yelling and running every which way. I tried to make it to this bridge that would lead me back home. As I crawled over the bridge I heard my name being called: Tomoko! Tomoko! I looked into the water where all these bodies were floating. And there I saw my friend Akiko. She was still alive, slowly turning in the current. 'Save me, Tomoko, Save me!' Ah, but Randy-san, you see I was too weak to do anything. I couldn't save her. I turned away and walked on, walked on. And then I wake up feeling terrible! This dream kept happening to me, over and over and I couldn't get any sleep.

Listening to this dream, I felt the familiar chill that alerts me to the presence of forces larger than myself. Yet even while I was full of the grief of the dream I thought to myself that finally I had the dream of a hibakusha with which to work. Then Tomoko turned to me, her eyes burning in her lovely, flawed face. She whispered in a low voice full of memory and pain,

You see, Randy-san, that is what really happened to me. I dream about what actually happened. I cannot escape. I wish I could have saved my friend Akiko, but, you see, I was too weak and was barely able to help myself. I never saw her again.

Of all the reactions that one could have to such a powerful story, I was surprised to feel shame begin to spread like a crimson tide over my torso until it reached my smooth, inexperienced face. A voice demanded to know who I thought I was, asking people to tell me their most personal inner experiences. No wonder people would not speak to me about their dreams. The secrets of the bomb as image cannot be penetrated so easily, especially by one who was just awakening to the full extent of the suffering soul of Hiroshima. Clearly there was a region in the collective psyche of this city that relived the apocalypse on a nightly basis, in all its particularities, thirty-five years later.

Did I really understand how posttraumatic stress syndrome creates a purgatory of repetitious psychic events? Could I understand the magnitude of this suffering? And what about all the nuclear nightmares I had heard from non-Japanese people? Doesn't the experience of apocalyptic terror that is revealed to us in a dream make symbolic hibakushas of us all? Could it be that the terror *is* the wake-up call, the revelation itself? Could it be that this is the meaning of apocalypse in its original sense, "to reveal"? And finally, begrudgingly, how many more lessons in pride awaited me before I could claim any wisdom at all?

WE ARE ALL PARENTS OF FUTURE GENERATIONS

My favorite place in Hiroshima City from which to view the bomb as image is the Buddhist reliquary on the top of Mt. Futabayama. Sitting at the base of the silver-lined *stupa,* inside of which resides the Buddha's knucklebone, one looks out upon the stunning natural beauty of the Ota River delta, surrounded by mountains and emptying into the sea. To the left is Mt. Hijiyama, the sacred Buddhist burial grounds. That is where the U.S. Army in its post-bomb inflation chose to place the Radiation Effects Research Facility (RERF). Behind that hill one can see the brown wooden buildings that represent the only prewar structures left standing in the city. A quaint sight indeed, until one realizes that the neutron fire storms released by "Little Boy" (as the army affectionately called the uranium bomb) swept rapidly outward from ground zero to consume everything in their path, impeded only by this hill of graves. The quaint old buildings stand because they were protected by the graves of their ancestors. It is just one more irony in the soul of Hiroshima, an irony that lies like shrapnel imbedded in a human body. Below and to the left and right, one can see the small valleys in the mountains where survivors fled, some of them unscathed but already dying from "A-bomb disease." And there are the beautiful stone-lined tributaries of the river, once clogged with the bodies of the dead. The silence of this place is deafening.

I was lying against this silver dome on a brilliant sunny day, the hum of the city below, reading a book that had just been published at the height of America's nuclear fear during the early 1980s. It was called *The Fate of the*

Earth and was written by Jonathan Schell. I was disturbed. The vision that Schell paints of post-apocalyptic existence is overwhelming in its detail, all of it based on the latest research into nuclear war. Schell is masterful at exposing the ironies and inconsistencies in our thinking about nuclear conflict. While reading him in the reflected light of the silver stupa, I realized that I was sitting on a Buddhist reliquary on Mt. Futabayama in the year 1982 imagining life after nuclear war. More specifically, I was imagining life after the extinction of the human species. But then it occurred to me in a flash of insight: nuclear war eliminates the very possibility of imagining anything. The Bomb will eliminate the human consciousness that gave it birth, nurtured it to fruition and pushed the button. I had to agree with Schell that extinction, like death, is felt not when it has arrived, but before, as a deep shadow cast back across the whole of life. It is we the living who experience extinction as it slowly saturates the deep recesses of our psyches.

Depressing, indeed. But then a familiar counterreaction set in, reminding me once more of the numinous quality of the shadow cast by nuclear extinction: The awareness of what changes when consciousness is no longer extant awakened me to the power of consciousness itself. Like a fish discovering that it is swimming in water, I realized that I was a carrier of consciousness and that consciousness was the means by which creation looked upon itself. The threat of extinction had awakened me to the God-spark within, to the "myth of consciousness." But the revelation did not end there. Another idea of Schell's, a logical extension of the threat of extinction, kept knocking at my door. He said that whether we have children or not, the possibility of human beings choosing to extinguish themselves makes us all parents of future generations of humankind. After Hiroshima, humans must actively choose *not* to destroy themselves. To make the choice to live is an act that makes future generations possible. The wonder of this idea washed over me and began to sink into my body. I realized that it was investing my actions with dignity and responsibility. I resolved to do something for future generations. I took this image to the World Friendship Center, a Quaker peace organization in Hiroshima. From there we developed it into an ongoing community event called "Peace Picnic for Future Generations," a quiet walk from Peace Park to the graveyard on Hijiyama and a celebration with games and music for the generations of children yet to be born.

That moment on Mt. Futabayama was like an egg cracking open on my head: the idea that we are all parents of future generations has slowly worked its way into everything that I think and do. I see the threat to future generations to be at the psychic root of many of our cultural ills: the neglect of children and the aged, the absence of spiritual rites of passage for our adolescents, the culture of narcissism that mocks our democratic institutions, and much more. The psyche, true to its nature, is throwing up healing counter-images to this threat, searching, probing for humanly attainable solutions. I believe the revival of indigenous spiritual traditions with their strong ties to the earth and ancestors to be a key psychic response to the threat to future generations. I believe the current political debates on multiculturalism are psychically based in a desire for our own ethnic stories to be told and heard. Doing so resurrects the imagination of our ancestors and links us, through them, to generations yet unborn. Cultivating the image of future generations in its profundity is a conscious act with moral consequences. To see one's self as a link, as a choice-maker in the continuity of generations, is to invest one's choices with *mana* or spiritual power, a power grounded in the love of life itself.

"I MUST TAKE RESPONSIBILITY FOR WHAT HAS HAPPENED HERE"

In the spring of my last year in Hiroshima, during the festival of *Hanami*, when the aroma of warm sake and blizzards of cherry blossoms drench the stone-lined pathways of the Ota River, I boarded the *Shinkansen* bullet train to Kyoto to attend the fourteenth annual meeting of the International Transpersonal Association. I was eager to connect with the world of ideas generated by the concept of the transpersonal. Besides, there is no city on Earth like Kyoto in the spring. It is the ancient spiritual heart of Japan. Making my way through the crowds of people, I noticed a brightly dressed, portly black man in traditional garb telling an African folktale. Intrigued by his voice, and then his demeanor, I paused to listen. Soon I was mesmerized by the lilting tone of his British English and the huge and scintillating images that he was conjuring with his words, images that were redolent with the smells, sounds, and textures of South Africa. I quickly discovered that this man's name was Vusamazulu Credo Mutwa and that he was a witchdoctor from Soweto, South Africa. But I already knew him as the greatest storyteller I had ever heard or was ever likely to hear. After following him around for several days, just to soak up his stories and to be near a large soul, I was both shocked and delighted when I was asked to lead Credo, his wife, and a small entourage through Hiroshima's Peace Park.

During our ride south on the Shinkansen, I sat next to Credo, a striking figure in his African *dashiki* against the backdrop of Japanese faces. He wore around his neck a heavy, beaten brass yoke, from the collarbone of which hung two carved wooden masks. Credo explained that one of the masks was Father Sun, the other Sister Moon. A chain below their mouths linked them both to a large Coptic cross that rested upon Credo's ample belly. Turning his eyes to me, blurry behind thick spectacles, Credo explained that the cross was the child of Father Sun and Sister Moon. "And that…?" I asked, pointing to a stunning emerald-green stone, the exact size and shape of a human heart, that rested over Credo's own. "It *is* as you *see*," he replied cryptically. He went on to explain that the African headband he was wearing was given to his grandfather by Mohandas Gandhi when the Mahatma was experimenting with Truth in South Africa. All in all, Vusamazulu Credo Mutwa was the most impressive spiritual presence I had ever encountered. I knew our trip to Peace Park would be extraordinary.

Indeed, my walk among the memorials to the dead with the South African witchdoctor *was* memorable. The Peace Bell with its hidden image of Africa upon it, Sadako's dome resplendent with a hundred thousand folded paper cranes, even the ever-present pigeons—they all shone forth in a new way on that spring day as Credo Mutwa cast his humanity and wisdom upon them. But even as this walk drew to a close, I was not, nor could I ever be, prepared for the single most illuminating moment during my three years in the International City of Peace.

The small group I was leading paused near the entrance to the Peace Museum. Stretching before us was a pathway, stepping stones to the Cenotaph Memorial upon which is written "Rest In Peace, For We Will Not Repeat The Sin." Each year on August 6, more names of those who have died from the effects of A-bomb disease are added to the stone box tucked beneath the canopy, eternal flame burning brightly nearby. I explained to my small band of guests that this is the most sacred spot in the entire park. I added a few more words in a quiet voice as we prepared ourselves emotionally for our encounter with the Cenotaph. But then I heard a loud tapping noise and noticed that Credo had turned from our group and was walking slowly and deliberately toward the Memorial Cenotaph. The tapping came from the large black walking staff, with a huge brass eagle attached to the top, that Credo carried in his right hand. In the sound of the walking stick against the stones, we could hear the sound of anger and pain, of power and determination, as Credo walked toward this monument of warning, remembrance, and death.

From the other side of the doorway that lies suspended 600 meters above the hospital entrance, a force descended upon our group and enveloped the unfolding scene. Like an electrical field, spiritual energy constellated about us and the moment slowed to a liquid crawl. Credo reached the stone steps before the Cenotaph. I silently groaned as he crashed to his knees. Two pigeons on the Cenotaph roof, their still images vibrating from the heat waves of the eternal flame, etched themselves into my memory. The air was thick and undulating. I saw Credo bend over in prayer, his back huge and curved, like the wooden statues of the weeping Buddha. After some time, who knows how long, I saw him remove his African headband, that family heirloom linking him to Gandhi's Truthforce, and lay it gently, lovingly into the ashes of the altar.

Then he struggled laboriously to his feet. Slowly he turned to face us and even from a distance I could see that his eye sockets were full of white, his pupils turned into his head, lost on the other side of Hiroshima's door. Involuntary, tears welled into my eyes, and the now familiar hand squeezed my chest yet again. Oh, the suffering! I could feel its immensity coursing through the solitary body of Vusamazulu Credo Mutwa. Louder now, his walking stick crashing against the stones, threatening to split open the earth beneath his feet, Credo walked toward us wrapped in mystical fire. He began to speak and I strained to hear his words. Unmistakably he said to me, to us all, "I *must* take responsibility for what has happened here! I *must* take responsibility for what has happened here!"

These words, like an arrow cloaked in mystery, pierced my heart deeply, and there they lie festering today. How can a black South African accept responsibility for a bomb dropped by Americans on the Japanese? What kind of man is it who accepts such responsibility? What is responsibility if it is something that can be accepted in this way? Credo's statement challenges my familiar notions of guilt and responsibility, challenges my ideas of God and redemption, and calls me deeper, ever deeper, into the soul of Hiroshima.

BEYOND DESPAIR

Spiritual revelation is more common than we often imagine. The hard work is bringing consciousness to the revelatory experience and then converting it into ethical obligation. It has been more than ten years since that spring day in Hiroshima, and I struggle with Credo's words like a Zen practitioner would with a *koan*. I am closer, but I am not there yet. I do know that soon after returning to the States, I was overwhelmed by reading Jim Garrison's book *The Darkness of God: Theology After Hiroshima*. In this text of theodicy, the first to adequately address the profundity of Hiroshima from my own Christian spiritual perspective, Garrison sees the hand of God at work in Hiroshima.

The phenomenology of the bomb is the same as the phenomenology of God—annihilation and judgment, white light, incandescent fire, ultimate concern. While God remains a mystery rooted in antinomy, the bomb is clearly a god-image, an *imago dei*, that is calling for new responses from the human spirit. To dance around the bomb is to dance around God. Garrison also gives voice to my experience that Hiroshima has "humanized the eschaton," has placed in the sphere of human choice the future of the created order. To bring consciousness to this new responsibility, a responsibility that could not even be conceived by the human mind prior to Hiroshima, will require a deeper, more holistic education than that currently practiced. I have dedicated my professional life to elucidating an adequate educational response to the terrible beauty/suffering of Hiroshima. I proceed using the principle of Mahatma Gandhi, each new teaching moment an "experiment with truth," searching and re-searching for the transformative teaching moment when insight is converted into ethical agency.

Fortunately, I am not alone in my quest. I speak here not of my numerous friends and colleagues who are responding to the call of their own muse just as I am, but rather of the spiritual resources that surround us. I speak here of what Thomas Berry, in his essay *The Dream of the Earth: Our Way into the Future*, refers to as "genetic guidance." Berry points out that under normal historical conditions we turn for guidance to our cultural traditions; but when cultural traditions are insufficiently imaginative, they are themselves obstacles to healing transformation. In such cases we must turn to our genetic coding for guidance, the spontaneously creative and mysterious impulses that originate in the same instincts through which the Earth itself came into being. The closest I have been able to get to my instinctual source, to my "genetic guidance," has been through my dreams. I pay close attention to them, especially those that illuminate the dark and destructive forces in my own psyche, aware that if the end comes through nuclear war it will be because some *individual* could not sustain the tension of those very same dark and destructive forces. *Every individual psyche is a field of discovery for genetic guidance.* Following the advice of the dream is to exercise my moral obligations.

One night, in a particularly vivid dream, a well-respected United Nations leader, in a poignant moment of remembrance for all those who have given their lives in service to peace, broke into a spontaneous speech in which he said, *"We are all, myself included, held in bondage by forces we must begin to identify and break free of, give form to and consume. The time is now for huge international shifts of consciousness."* On another night I was visited by Mother Teresa, who gifted me with my teaching mantra: *"Randy, the point is not to save people. The point is to create the conditions for the possibility of Grace."*

Recently I held a dream conversation with social activist Joanna Macy. I have admired Joanna's work in waking life for some time because it begins with the most honest emotional response we can have to the nuclear threat: complete and total despair. She is able, through a great deal of inner work, to sustain the presence of abject despair both in herself and others. She has learned how to sustain the gaze of Hiroshima's terror. The point of her work is to break through psychic numbing and denial, to liberate the imagination into its natural state of sympathetic participation with other and world so that the heart and will can be moved toward their ethical obligations. In short, despair awakens and liberates the moral imagination. It is clear that to break out of our current predicament, we must drink deeply from the well of grief. In my dream,

> *Joanna and I lie on separate mattresses, a small glowing pile of gold coins between us. We are immersed in a discussion about the problem of evil as illuminated by Hiroshima. Then our attention turns to a question that troubles me still: Why wasn't the nuclear threat sufficient to awaken consciousness in the culture?*

I awoke before the dream revealed its answer, but on a subsequent night Joanna's spirit returned to talk at great length about meditation practice and techniques of compassion. In one of life's delightful synchronicities, I chanced to meet Joanna Macy in waking life only three weeks after my dream while on a kayak trip to a remote island in British Columbia. We sat together overlooking the salt water and time stood still for me as we continued our conversation on this side of the doorway. Through such experiences, imaginal and physical, the genetic guidance system of the Earth lures us to our own healing. Experience reveals to me that there is a symmetry between the inner and outer worlds, a balance that suggests that political agency and spiritual insight are like Brother Sun and Sister Moon: the product of their union is the redemption of humanity, a humanity which is now, since Hiroshima, co-creator of the Earth.

I end my imaginal odyssey with this scene: I am standing with Vusamazulu Credo Mutwa on the boarding platform of the Shinkansen bullet train. I know it is the last time I will see him on this Earth. I had been wanting to make a request of him since our ride down from Kyoto, but I was uncertain and indecisive. Finally, however, my importunity wins out. I ask Credo if I can hold the emerald-green heart stone that lies on his chest. He looks at me intently and nods his permission. My hand slowly closes over that stone, surprised by its heat, humbled by the extreme intimacy implied by such an act. I shut my eyes and there, among the surging and rumbling tones of this living rock, I perceive a doorway. Darkness lies before its path, but it is slightly ajar and through a crack in the door a ray of light penetrates the gloom. How many, I wonder, are willing to face the darkness, to enter that door and return with rays of hope? How many can drink deeply from the well of grief, can sustain the gaze of Hiroshima's terror? How many are willing to penetrate the dark heart of this city, to extract its wisdom, so that Hiroshima's healing balm may be spread upon the Earth?

With respect to the soul of Hiroshima, I slowly begin to comprehend Credo's words, "It *is* as you *see*."

2

Nuclear Nightmares

1983

I AM AN AMERICAN SOCIAL SCIENTIST living in Hiroshima and teaching at the Hiroshima International School. As a psychologist specializing in the interpretation of dreams, I was particularly interested in two letters in the August 7th and 17th issues of an English language newspaper here in Japan. Each described a nuclear nightmare. The first read:

> To the Editor:
>
> I am a mother...
>
> ...And one night, I had a terrible dream.
>
> I am with my child and we see a huge mushroom cloud rising in the sky. I know it means the end. I hold my child close and I try to run away. I know it is useless and so I pray for instant death.
>
> This is a real dream. It was so real that I couldn't even tell my husband why I was crying.
>
> I couldn't say a word. I am sure there is a mother in Russia, just like me, who dreams this terrible dream, who holds her child close...and prays for instant death.
>
> If neither of us want it to happen, then *who* is it that does?
>
> A Mother
Tokyo

The second letter was published a few days later:

> To the Editor:
>
> Recently I also had an unusually disturbing dream of a mushroom cloud, and there was the same certainty of it being the end.

But the part of the woman's account that struck me, and compelled me to this response, was her comment on her dream: "This is a real dream. It was so real that I couldn't even tell my husband why I was crying. I couldn't say a word." The day before my dream, I would have reacted to this statement by thinking, well, yes, she must have had a very graphic, realistic dream. But it was precisely this "real" quality to my own dream that spooked me, and that made the dream so difficult to communicate to others. It was real, at least as real as today feels. Oh well.

At any rate, I'm glad I had the dream/experience, because the idea of a nuclear disaster had, I realize now, become a dangerously distant, abstract one to me. (I wonder if other people anywhere are having this type of hyper-vivid holocaust dream. Could it be some kind of collective survival mechanism to come as close as possible to experiencing, in order to reject, our self-destruction?)

Here's the dream, as recorded the next day, in the hope that at least it may show "A Mother" that she's not alone:

I am driving along a winding mountain highway, and in the field up ahead and to the right a giant mushroom cloud is forming. As I come within its shadow, I know at once that nothing is alive anywhere. The very air is dead or gone. The lighting is a strange mustard color, and it all feels like some giant indoor fluorescent environment. The only sound is a kind of middle-pitched synthesizer drone. I feel lonely. When I look down, I see that the skin on my arm is bubbling.

Jeffrey Dann
Tokyo

For the last year I have been collecting such dreams from hibakusha and Japanese and foreign residents of Hiroshima. Furthermore, I have been leading a dream workshop at the World Friendship Center in Hiroshima to discuss just such dreams as these letters describe.

I was originally inspired to study this field while a teacher in the U.S. There I listened to the dreams of American children in which nuclear imagery played a significant role, giving vivid expression to the group anxiety that pervades our cultures concerning the threat of nuclear war. As a psychologist interested in peace, I have been looking at these phenomena as a mental health issue of unprecedented proportions. Whether we have a nuclear war or not, the very threat of war (usually perceived as a nuclear explosion from which there is no escape) is causing a great deal of anxiety in our populations, especially among children and adolescents whose image of a nuclear future tends to blunt their initiative to work towards the future. Why invest one's time in education and work apprenticeships if there is no future in which to live? Why not indulge oneself in the present, through sex or drugs or just "hanging out"? Of course this "Live for today, for tomorrow you die" philosophy has always confronted adolescents and overcoming it (i.e., finding a meaning to one's existence) represents one of the main tasks of growing up. But today's youth are, I believe, considerably more pessimistic about their future than their elders and I would attribute a substantial part of this fact to the threat of nuclear war.

The question remains, as it always does, What can we do about it? I was very impressed by the insight offered in Jeffrey Dann's letter. He asks, "Could it be some kind of collective mechanism to come as close as possible to experiencing, in order to reject, our self-destruction?" To this question I would respond with an emphatic "Yes." There have been many extravagant claims concerning the nature of dreams for thousands of years, but one claim that remains fairly consistent is that dreams are pictures or images of emotions and therefore give us direct access to what we are "really" feeling. It is well known to psychologists working in the field of peace studies that one of the main obstacles to a worldwide rejection of nuclear weapons is the inability of average citizens to admit to themselves the horror of nuclear holocaust. This common psychological mechanism, known as "repression," is one way in which the mind protects itself from unpleasant or terrifying truths. Given the fact that every person dreams four or five times a night, and given the climate of fear about nuclear war, it is not particularly remarkable that nuclear imagery populates many of those dreams. What is remarkable, even astounding, is that more and more people are *remembering* those dreams, admitting them to conscious awareness and being emotionally moved by the message those dream images contain.

Some dream theorists posit a part of the human mind common to all human beings. I believe that nuclear nightmares represent an impulse on the part of this collective psyche to confront directly the horror of nuclear war, literally, to "imagine the unimaginable," and by so doing to take the first step toward healing this festering rupture in the family of humanity. These dreams, as expressions of pure emotion, have the power to motivate people to work in new ways for the peace movement. The context of the dreams themselves and the characters we perceive in them are all parts of a personal message which can be deciphered and used to influence the actions of the dreamer.

Without denying the unique and terrifying experience of the hibakusha of Japan, the fact remains that anyone (and there are many) who has suffered the vivid and intense imagery of a nuclear nightmare are themselves hibakusha, survivors of an atomic bomb experience. As such, they have the same right, indeed the same duty, to speak out on behalf of peace from the perspective of one who has survived the horror of nuclear annihilation.

I am continuing my study of these dream phenomena and would greatly appreciate anyone who has had a nuclear nightmare, or any kind of dream involving nuclear imagery, to send me copies of their dreams with a brief note describing themselves. Strictest confidentiality will be observed; anonymous dreams are also welcome. The message of these dreams *must* be heard.

3

The Dream Peace Project

Re-mythologizing Nuclear Peril

1984

PURPOSE

In 1983 a small group of concerned Japanese and American citizens at the World Friendship Center in Hiroshima, Japan, began working on ways to harness the power of dreams and imagination to further the cause of peace. Everyone in this group except Randy, the leader, was a complete novice to dreamwork and creative writing. But all of them were interested in exploring any new approach to peace, agreeing with Mahatma Gandhi that truth is not a given but must be achieved by experimenting with one's life.

Our seminars began as an introduction to the imagery of dreams and how to use images in our personal lives. But gradually, as we shared our dreams and waking lives, a pattern began to emerge that assumed the characteristics of a myth, story, or fairytale. We began to realize that this format could be a powerful tool for communicating the insights of our imagery. After a bit of experimenting, we decided upon a format that anyone could follow, provided the person was sufficiently motivated. And our motivation was high. As residents of the first city to be obliterated by a nuclear weapon, we were constantly reminded of the reality of the nuclear peril and our vantage point on the politics of the greatest threats to peace in our time—apathy, disunity, and misunderstanding. These are very human reactions to the threat of incomprehensible destruction, and everyone interested in working for peace must confront them; they imperil us.

Our myth writing project offers all who join a chance to do something, to make a contribution, to exercise their imaginations in a creative and vital way. Our basic thesis is that humanity's capacity for disciplined imagination is both the source of and potential solution for nuclear peril. Technological imagination has led us to the edge of extinction, but a more balanced and wholistic imagination can be a source of renewal and change, and can eventually liberate us from the nuclear shadow. This project is an attempt to re-mythologize the nuclear peril, literally to imagine our way out. At the very least, participants in this writing exercise will deepen their understanding of their fears, strengths, and hopes. We invite you to join us.

PROCEDURE

Participants write three pieces in this project. The first piece is the myth, the second is a reflection on the experience of writing the myth, and the last piece is an autobiography. The pieces should be written in that order.

The instructions for writing the myth are simple, and they are subject to change according to the creativity of the author.

1. Begin with the first section of our myth, "The Beginning." All participants share this part of the story.
2. Imagine that you are there at the restaurant and that you experience the nuclear peril described in "The Beginning."
3. Begin writing. Make a resolution to go on a long journey to find the answers to your questions. Describe your thoughts and feelings as you leave the restaurant to embark on your journey.
4. Describe your travels.
5. While you are on your journey, meet a wise person. This person may be anyone, living or dead, a figment of your imagination, even your own grandfather.
6. Ask this person one or more difficult questions about peace and how you can help actualize it. Then have your wise person respond to these questions in a meaningful way.
7. Near the end of your dialogue, have the wise person give you a gift. At this point you do not understand what it is or what it does.
8. Leave the wise person to return to the restaurant, satisfied that you have accomplished your task.
9. Along the way you are attacked by dark, evil forces. Describe these forces and the ensuing battle in some detail. You are almost killed, but then you remember the gift. Open it. The gift saves you. How?
10. Return to the restaurant. Summarize what you have learned.

THE REFLECTIONS

The movement from the active imagination of myth writing to a critical reflection on that experience is an abrupt transition in modes of thinking. You should not attempt to reflect on your experience until the myth is completely finished. The purpose of this section is to help you expand the underlying meaning of your own story. You do not need to analyze every nuance. Just write about where some of your ideas came from and how you managed to organize them into a coherent story. How difficult was it to write this story? Why? In what social and physical environment did you write the story? If you had to do it again, how would you change it? What do you think of your final product? Remember, this is not a college writing assignment. Anything you write is all right and helpful to the project as a whole. Be as relaxed and conversational in your style as you wish.

AUTOBIOGRAPHY

This section should be a brief review of who you are, where you have lived, how you spend your time, your relationship to peace work, and so on. The purpose of this section is to provide a living context of our understanding of the myth. It may be long or short, heavy or light. Above all, it should be enjoyable to write.

WRITING TIPS

Writing the myth can be difficult, even for those who have had experience with creative writing or active imagination. You will find that myth writing requires a contemplative, quite attitude in which you allow the images of your stream of consciousness to wash over you. It is very important that you be nonjudgmental and uncritical of the images that appear. Some of the images will stand out more than others; they will feel more important, more alive than others. See if you can make these special images conform to the format outlined above. You may find the language you are using to describe these images to be quite audacious and bombastic. That's normal. Just let it flow and write it down.

    Some people in our group have found that when they incorporated images from their dream life into the myth that the emotional power of the writing experiences was increased. If you choose to do this, don't be limited by the entire narrative of a particular dream. You may pick and choose images from various dreams to make your story more exciting and powerful. It would be helpful if you could use a footnote in the myth to acknowledge a dream image and then include the complete dream under a footnote at the end of the story.

The story should not be limited to the written word. Creating other kinds of imaginative forms will deepen the meaning of the story for you. Please feel free to include any other artistic products that you make while writing the myth, including illustrations of the story itself.

The rules for writing the myth are not etched in stone. They can be changed by the myth writer if s/he feels the urge, though if the author's story becomes too tangential to the original format, it will be difficult to resolve the myth with the other contributions.

Last, but not least, you should realize that anything you contribute—long or short, well written or poorly written, correctly punctuated or not—is a valuable resource for our project. Expressing feelings is not the final product but the self-process that went into its creation. Clumsy attempts are gladly accepted and especially appreciated. The only requirement is that you care.

CONCLUSION

When you complete your project, please mail all writings and illustrations to the following address:

> The Dream Peace Project
> c/o Randy Morris
> Antioch University/Seattle
> 2326 Sixth Avenue
> Seattle, WA 98121-1814

Now we invite you to read the following introductory story and to join us at the restaurant, an imagined gathering place that marks the beginning of a sojourn in peacemaking.

THE BEGINNING

A woman and her two children were walking together through a familiar neighborhood of their old hometown. They began to walk up a hill on the broken cement sidewalk. This was not a "good" neighborhood in the economic sense, but it was quiet, with a little traffic, and the family was comfortable with the familiar surroundings. The boy was the first to notice a small dot in the sky traveling at a high speed over the horizon. As it came closer, they could recognize the elongated, lethal shape of a rocket. It was headed directly for them. They looked at each other, eyes wide, and knew there was nothing they could do. It is a horrible feeling knowing that one has but 45 seconds in which to live in the presence of loved ones. The woman and her children hugged each other, but mostly huddled. And then it hit.

Nothing happened. The family was all right. With barely a sigh of relief, they started to walk, to run, toward the direction of the downed rocket. It was very dark. Suddenly, they bumped into something soft. They looked closely at the shadowy figures before them. Only by looking closely could they discern that they were hundreds of Japanese students, all dressed in black uniforms, walking very silently.

But no time to think about that. They hurried on, over the hill, and there a startling scene was revealed. The rocket had hit a car and smashed the left front door, the driver's side. The scene was illuminated with bright light. A group of people were there. Perhaps they were bowlers or maybe factory workers. They were all very angry. The police had come and were yelling and ordering people about. They wanted people out of there because of the nuclear bomb. With no further explanation they ordered the crowds to disperse. They wanted the car because it was radioactive. The people started screaming obscenities at the cops, telling them to bug off. They started rocking the car to turn it over. There was a short woman in the crowd; she appeared to be loud, stupid, and tough. She was with many people and they all looked the same. The car overturned. The family stood, gaping at the scene, filled with horror and numbed by the implications of what they were experiencing.

It was later and in a restaurant. One by one, people filed in through the door and sat in chairs. The looks on their faces were of bewilderment and fear, but these people were different from the earlier crowd. Within their wide eyes were also looks of concern and compassion. Upon entering the restaurant, they carefully folded their jackets and laid them down. Everyone was aware that their outer clothes had become radioactive, that somehow they were all contaminated by the preceding events. No one spoke, but as if by a silent agreement, each arranged their chairs until a circle was formed. These people had never met before, but they were drawn to each other in an unknown way by an unseen force. A glance around the circle revealed an equal number of men and women, of Eastern and Western features. An air of expectancy hung over the gathering.

Just then, the woman looked at her hands and noticed that her index finger was gradually being eaten away. It was not ugly, and neither did it hurt. The finger just started to disappear. This extraordinary event gave her the courage to speak first.

"We have to educate stupid people," she said. It was a rough beginning, but her voice contained a note of urgency and conviction and her comment served to stimulate and focus the thoughts of her companions.

"I have no enemies, least of all the citizens of my own hometown; but those people out there were angry at the wrong things and for all the wrong reasons. Now I am losing my hands, my principal form of livelihood and the source of all my creativity, because of the inability of my fellow human beings to perceive the real threat to our existence—ignorance. I remember Three Mile Island. Because the people there couldn't see the radioactivity, they didn't believe it was there. If we could color nuclear waste or radioactivity, maybe we could make people understand; but what they can't see, they won't believe."

A murmur of assent followed these remarks, but no one rose to add a rejoinder. Each person was lost in thought. How could this have happened? But, more important, what can we do about it? Always this last question, what can we do about it? Without an answer to it, one remains a pawn of invisible, dark powers. With an answer at least one could die in a nuclear holocaust with the satisfaction of having tried. But no one spoke because no one had a response to this difficult question. What can we do about it?

The restaurant was tense with the energy of inexpressible yearning and suffuse hope, yet none could speak. The air was rife with the conflict in each person's heart between the easy road of apathy and the difficult road of omitted action, yet none could speak. As the air crackled with energy commingling with the intense emotion generated by human hearts, a threshold energy was exceeded and a loud report was heard. The atmosphere cleared and a voice was heard:

> *"You question deeply for difficult answers. It is a beginning, but it is not enough. The balance of the world sways in the wind, yet it bends toward truth. Seek out this truth. You will find it first beyond the darkness of your own heart and then in the collective spirit of your group endeavors. The path is long and difficult, but your hope shall make you strong."*

Then the voice was gone, to be replaced by a collective sigh of released tension from the people who had witnessed this event. A young man stood up and spoke the thought that everyone was thinking:

"Now we have a purpose. Let us disperse, each to our own path, to find its meaning. We will know when the time has come to meet again."

The group was silent, absorbed in their thoughts and feelings. But gradually their minds opened to include the thoughts and feelings of their fellow human beings, drawing strength from each other's presence, giving strength in equal measure. Without a word, the group stood up and walked out the door to confront the task before them. Darkness came to the empty restaurant, save for the dull glow of their discarded, radioactive jackets.

The End of the Beginning

I. *The following story was written by a Japanese woman who attended a Dream Peace Project seminar given in the city of Nagasaki in the spring of 1984. Her story is translated from the original Japanese.*

By the time I left the restaurant I had settled down a little, but deep within me I still felt uneasy. As I walked, the uneasiness became stronger and stronger and heavier and heavier and I had to stop and take a deep breath. The pain from within became so strong that I clutched my chest and started shaking. I walked through a field of grass that was up to my head. There was no trail. I had to spread the grass apart to walk through. I tried to look into the distance but couldn't see hills or mountains. From time to time as the wind blew, I seemed to be in a wave. I continued walking and fighting the fear that was overwhelming me.

I live in Nagasaki. Five years after the end of the war I came to live here. I was in the fifth grade at that time. In my new school I took notice of a boy, but since he was in another class I didn't know his name. The upper half of his face was shining from scar tissue caused by burns. His eyes were always opened wide as if he were constantly in a state of surprise. When he laughed he looked even stranger. I knew I wasn't supposed to stare at his face, but at recess I couldn't help following him and staring at him for the sake of seeing something scary.

So, as I was walking through the grass, his face suddenly appeared in my mind. He wasn't smiling. His face showed pain and suffering. The frightfulness of his face was increased by purple spots over the scars. I saw another face, that of Chieko. When we entered eighth grade Chieko didn't come to school one day. Several days later she died. Her face was in the newspaper and the article said she died of leukemia due to radiation from the atomic bomb. She had round, black eyes and was a bright, cheerful girl. Her death was unbelievably sudden.

I recalled the face of Miss Takeda. She was a beautiful, petite girl who was good at tennis. After graduating from high school I never saw her again. At our twelve-year school reunion I heard she died at the age of twenty-eight, leaving two children behind. She died of leukemia. She was well until one day she became fatigued. Her hair started falling out. Her gums started bleeding. Twenty-three years after the atomic bomb experience, she died with the same symptoms as those who died right after the bomb. In my mind she was running around the tennis court with her white, pleated skirt blowing in the wind.

With the surprise and fear of the experience a few hours before, the insecurity and solitude of being alone in the tall grass, and the visions of my friends who were atomic bomb victims, night came. It was pitch dark outside. I couldn't see anything. My tired body was automatically moving my arms and legs through the grass. All I could do was continue walking. After a while it started to rain. I was getting soaking wet. I couldn't open my eyes. I staggered aimlessly. I asked myself, "Could this be the black rain?" The fear built up. The pain in my chest increased. I felt like vomiting.

When the atomic bomb exploded, the sky was covered with black clouds and it started to rain suddenly. I heard the rain was black. It was filled with radiation. The rain soaked the wounds of the burned atomic bomb victims. The black rain fell over a large area, not only at the "hypocenter," but in the suburbs as well. The black rain stained the white walls of people's homes and their laundry hanging in the summer sun and dirtied the crops of the field. Could the rain falling on me now be the black rain? I wondered if it would stain my arms, chest, and face with black dirty spots. It was too dark to tell.

The fear, solitude, and insecurity formed a lump that started to choke me. I threw up, but my stomach was empty and nothing came out. I still felt something hard in my throat. I wanted to free myself from the fear and the darkness, but my body couldn't move as much as I wanted. I continued walking, but it was as much as I could do to remain on my feet. I finally lost consciousness.

I opened my eyes feeling something warm on my cheeks. I was surrounded by bright sunlight. I was still in the tall grass. Through the grass in front of me I could see a building. The wind brought the sounds of a car going by and people's voices. I didn't know how long I had been there. Even though I was hungry, my spirits picked up. My whole body stung. "The black rain!" I was struck with fear. When I looked at my arms and legs, they were covered with scratches and cuts. It seemed I had been cut with the blades of grass the night before. I examined my white dress carefully but found no black spots, although it was soiled with dirt. The rain was an ordinary rain. I sighed with relief and stood up and started to walk. Cheerful children's voices became louder and louder as I walked toward the park. Soon I was able to see them. The scene before me was an ordinary one. People were sitting on benches in the shade of trees and older people were walking. I felt strong security and peace. I walked to the water faucet and quenched my thirst and washed my hands and legs and my spirits became higher. There was a young mother sitting on a bench several meters away from me. She was reading a book. In the carriage next to her was a ten-month-old baby. Its back was to me so I couldn't tell if it was a boy or girl. The baby was holding a small hammer in its right hand and hitting a pink, tray-shaped object in its left hand. When I looked carefully I realized it was something like a sugar candy, and the baby, without getting bored, continued to amuse itself by hitting it. The mother stopped reading the book and pulled a radio from her bag. As she put the radio to her ear, she turned on the switch and the music started to flow. It was Mozart, written for a clarinet quintet. I felt dizzy for a moment from the soft sound of the clarinets and the strings. The early autumn afternoon, with the lively sounds of children, the young mother and child and the music created a peaceful scene. My wish was for this beautiful day to last forever.

The lump in my chest had disappeared without my knowing it. This day gave me the courage to overcome my fears. "I may be able to do something. I should find something that I can do. I should go back to the restaurant one more time and see someone. I'll find out what 'that' means. I'll start from here."

The music finished. I heard the announcer speaking on the radio. I started to walk back toward the field. I had come through.

II. *This story was written by a woman from Hiroshima who actually experienced the bombing of her city. Since then she has worked tirelessly for peace, but not without doubt and sacrifice. The story is translated from the original Japanese.*

Since I was born and bred in Hiroshima, I know what happens when an atomic bombing takes place. But, upon leaving the restaurant, I did not know what I could do nor how I could contribute to the total abolition of nuclear weapons and world peace. I left that place having fear and despair because I felt I was powerless in the matter. The cold night air let my confused mind refresh.

Where shall I go? At first I wanted to find a good place to rest my mind and body. I hit upon a good idea! I shall go back to the house that I had lived in when I was a little child.

"Hi, Kazuko! Sit at the table in a hurry. It's getting late." After I enjoyed playing outside all day long and having dinner with my family, my kindhearted grandmother said in her usual sweet voice, "Let's go to bed."

"Grandma! It is so good to see you!" I go toward her bringing my small pillow. I lie by her side and she pats me on the back gently.

I am in my childhood home, a rude barracks with its back against a small patch of woods. It is long and slender and almost ten times as large as a typical Japanese-style room. It was built by my uncle after the destruction by the atomic bombing. My uncle's family and my family lived together in it, so there were eight people in all. My uncle and my mother worked outside and my aunt did needlework at home for our living. We were poor. We were extraordinarily poor. But the adults cherished a desire for the children's healthy growth. We children lived a happy life, accepting adults' love to the full. We used to share even little things, not only with my family but also my neighbors. We used to share happiness and sadness.

I woke up and I was very surprised to find that I was standing by the A-bomb dome. The barracks had suddenly disappeared. I stood gazing vacantly at a man who eagerly muttered away to himself. I moved on toward him. I could hear his words:

> *Give back fathers.*
> *Give back mothers.*
> *Give back the aged.*
> *Give back children.*

I didn't know him by his face but I know this poem. I asked, "Are you Sankichi Toge?" He nodded but continued saying his poem.

> *Give back me.*
> *Give back all people*
> *Who are connected with me.*

"Why are you reading out the poem standing here?" I asked. But he didn't reply to my question.

> *Give back peace*
> *Which won't be destroyed*
> *As far as human beings exist on earth.*
> *Give back peace.*

I wanted to ask him what I should do for peace, but he seemed to ignore me. He raised his voice and shouted:

> *It isn't too late!*
> *It is the very time for you*

> *To summon up your real power.*
> *For you experienced the flash of the atomic bomb,*
> *Which attacked your eyes*
> *And reached to your retinas.*
> *And if you still shed tears even now*
> *Because of the heavy blow to your mind*
> *By the atomic bombing,*
> *Summon up your real power!*
> *If you hate wars so very much,*
> *You can realize the idea toward peace*
> *Which people in Hiroshima must have.*

Then he began to stare at the ground silently, making faces due to agony, not saying a word. After a while he looked up and gazed at me. "This is my answer for you. Could you catch what I meant?" His eyes appealed to me. His figure disappeared just as I wanted to utter words in response.

I suffered hell on earth by the atomic bombing, but my agony and grief had almost vanished from my mind over time. They had become only a piece of knowledge in my head. I have often felt my sympathy for the non-nuclear movement waver in spite of myself while I was living a good life. So I can easily despair of my lack of power. I found that I had lost the idea that was told to me by this brave poet. I refreshed myself with prayer and meditation. I am going to think about nuclear weapons with my refreshed mind. I am going to summon up my real power.

Oh, what time has passed since I left the restaurant? Has everyone gone back to the restaurant? I will tell them about the encounter with Mr. Toga. I will bring back his attitude of mind, which he showed to me at last, as a gift for them. I began to walk toward the restaurant. It seemed to me the beautiful trees in the park looked full of life, as if the people who were killed by the atomic bombing rose again from the dead.

III. *This story was written by an American woman who was teaching English in Hiroshima and who wanted to contribute to peacemaking by participating in the Dream Peace Project.*

I left the restaurant with a warm feeling of community; this was a community of people who could rise above the terror of the moment, people who cared both about the things they couldn't see (the spiritual things) as well as about the problems and injustices they *could* see. I felt the power that being in such a community can bring. Having heard the voice tell me I should seek answers I felt a sense of purpose, but this began to wane and led to a feeling of helplessness as I set out on my own. What was I supposed to do? Where should I go? My brisk walk turned to a shuffle as I began to feel more and more alone. I was determined to keep moving somehow, partly to take my mind off my fears, and partly because I couldn't return to the restaurant without *something* to offer. I found myself walking intuitively toward the countryside, away from the madness of the city. There with nature, I thought, my mind will be clearer and I may be able to communicate in silence with the Higher Spirit, hopefully receiving some insights.

Having made a decision, albeit a small one, I felt lightness return to my steps. Having faced death so powerfully just hours before, I felt a sudden joy in merely being alive. The sky looked like the crystal blue waters of the Caribbean, and the puffy white clouds contrasted sharply against it. The trees on either side of the narrow road were green, green, green. The old Japanese houses I saw, with their thatched roofs, looked the way I had always hoped and expected Japan to look: quaint and clean. I looked down from the road and saw a forest path which said to me, "Please enter.... You will find peace here." The forest was a deep green, with lots of moss on the ground, and I found it irresistible. After walking for awhile, I saw and heard a small waterfall with clear water and lots of stones. The air was cool, and the only sound I heard was that of the water falling. I sat down on a large rock in the middle of the stream. I closed my eyes and began to present many questions to God: Why had the bomb been dropped on Hiroshima, of all places? Why didn't the bomb explode this time and what should we do about the radioactivity? What would the future bring for me, the rest of the world, and future generations? Why do we allow ourselves to be manipulated by our politicians and military "experts"? Why does the U.S. Air Force get away with its slogan, "Peace is our business"? Why can't we live together in love and respect, instead of emphasizing our differences to the point of stereotyping nations as "good" and "evil"? What can I, as one person, do to promote peace in my community and in the world?

I became overwhelmed by these questions and began to cry with big, breathless sobs. I became paralyzed with fear about my hands and the rest of my body as the reality of the radioactivity settled into my consciousness. Would I be like so many of the 1945 survivors, adjusting to my handicaps, happy to at least be alive, only to die later from radiation sickness? I didn't want to die! I loved life too much! I could no longer be at peace at the waterfall.

Then I knew I was not alone. I turned around and saw the face of a man, a dark-faced man. I was not alarmed, because the face was so serene, obviously not there to hurt me. The face was familiar, but at first I could not place it. Then I knew it was the face of Kahlil Gibran, whose book *The Prophet* had been a source of comfort to me on many occasions. How grateful I was for his presence! He did not speak, and his demeanor indicated to me that he wished to meditate with me. I was thus able to continue in my silent prayer. It was as if he, as a fellow human being, shared my questions, but as a *spirit* he was closer to the answers than I was. I felt that perhaps he had shared the bombing experience with me.

Together we shared a worship and answer-seeking time. The energy we gave to each other's searching was very powerful. He gave me a special gift, the gift of support in prayer. But I received another gift from him. I became unaware of the passage of time, but when I turned around after awhile, he was gone. A simply bound book, with my name on the front and with no other markings, lay on the moss beside the stream. After a few moments I picked up the book, but with an uncharacteristic lack of curiosity, did not open it. I carried the book with me as I began to walk down the path out of the forest.

I began the return trip to the restaurant with a sense of renewal. I knew that somehow the answers which were knowable were within my heart, even though I wasn't able to verbalize them yet, and that I could learn to live *without* the unknowable answers. I felt that the God within me was alive and well, and I was relieved to have this feeling. It had eluded me to a large extent since I had left America for Japan several months earlier.

As I was walking down the road toward town, I met a male friend who was unaware of the morning's events. I explained about the bombing and my intention to return to the restaurant. My friend became quite agitated, and could not understand my resolve to accept the reality of the bomb with a level head and a silent inner core. He mistook my attitude for apathy. Still, he insisted that he too wanted to go to the restaurant, and I agreed. As we walked the miles, he continued to babble, ask silly questions, and blame the police as the others had. As we grew closer to the city we suddenly saw a plane overhead, and I immediately recognized it as an American bomber, based on recent photographs I had seen in a news magazine. Suddenly my hard-earned inward peace was threatened, as I was once again confronted with a senseless death. The Americans, realizing their first bomb hadn't exploded, had returned. I knew it was coming any minute, and I had the horrible premonition that the bomb would be dropped right over the 1945 hypocenter. To make matters worse, I was to be killed by my own countrymen, with a bomb purchased with my taxes, and the soldiers wouldn't have changed their well-laid plan had they known of my presence in Hiroshima.

The man and I began to run away from the city. I had never run so hard in my life, over fences and through yards with clothes lines, which made me think for one crazy moment that I was back in the U.S. For the first time I realized there was snow on the ground. I was absolutely terrified. We hit the side of a building, hoping for cover, and argued over who would shield whom. Suddenly I heard my own shrill voice and felt very guilty about my behavior. I was disgusted with my selfishness and the hopelessness of the situation. I just didn't care to run anymore, to fight this battle. I felt a compulsion to remain where I was and to open, for the first time, the book Gibran had given me. My friend continued to run, urging me to follow him, but I was strangely content to remain where I was, closer to the hypocenter. I opened the book and read:

> *Your pain is the breaking of the shell that encloses*
>   *your understanding.*
> *Even as the stone of the fruit must break, that its heart*
>   *may stand in the sun, so you must know pain.*
> *And could you keep your heart in wonder at the daily miracles*
>   *of your life, your pain would not seem less wondrous*
>   *than your joy.*

After reading these words I spied a large drainage pipe to my left. I jumped into the pipe, and a millisecond later heard the bomb hit the hypocenter, miles away. The sound was deafening and I was blinded by white light, even though my eyes had been facing toward the floor of the pipe. I was alive, dazed, and somewhat amazed at the fact, and most grateful for the pipe and the book which had kept me close to it. I began the walk to the restaurant, or whatever remained of it, book in hand. I wanted to discuss with the group the fact that sorrow and pain are perhaps an inevitable aspect of the human condition. We could wallow helplessly in our pain, become destructively enraged by it. Or, we could use our pain as a creative impetus as we sought to at least *alleviate* it for ourselves and for future generations through our antinuclear and peace efforts. Only then would our suffering have meaning. I was anxious to explore possibilities with the remainder of the group. I hoped they were all still alive.

IV. *This story was written by a retired Methodist minister and a peace activist who was living and working at the World Friendship Center in Hiroshima.*

A tale that is told...

The day was totally without reason—strange smells annoyed my total being. The faces around me seemed frozen into stares of nothingness. My world was gone: the world's world was gone. I must leave this horror that lay so heavy on my soul. I must escape the fear that so surrounds my dumbness. I struggle to say, "I still am!" and leave the restaurant...leave that world that is no more, now desolate and dark with doubt. Only one course remains, the search. I plunge into the darkness of my unholy quest. My thoughts dash ahead of me. The words that childhood taught come tumbling out of my numbed mind...

> *Time has no turning—*
> *since there is no unlearning*
> *the bridge is down behind*
> *We must go on from here...*

But where and why? The call to search is silent and strong—the leap forward is uncertain but it has begun. The bridge is down, but I am on my lonely way—to seek, to doubt, to become the world's loneliest skeptic, determined to deny that whatever is, is not!

I step into the dark night. The woods beside me are black and haunting, the sky dark and threatening, heavy with tears, wanting to weep. The sounds that caress my ears are not familiar. The road I travel twists and turns. I twist and turn and stagger and stumble and all around me is empty silence. I recall the harrowing words—"lonely were the wastes I traveled"…would that my travels would quiet my doubts, would that I could find the truths that seem to evade all who search for truths.

And then out of the total and vast silence a voice breaks through the silence in a whisper and the whisper sears the silence with words I don't want to hear…

"What if, my friend," he asks, "your God does not exist?"

Anxious, frightened, I think, "If he does not exist, how absurd the whole journey is." With the little energy I have I utter, "But who are you?"

And the answer comes back, "I am David the Unknown." And then, as if he is reaching out to instruct the whole universe, he says, "Hear me, hear me, all you who doubt and lament. A thousand years is like yesterday, already gone." And I feel myself slipping off into darkness again and his lonesome voice trails past me on the wind whispering, "None of us last. We last no longer than a dream. We are like weeds that wither. We are like frail wind, children of the Universe—laughing, rollicking, talking today and tomorrow like the dust returning to the earth from which we come…."

And I am once again fleeing down the endless corridors, my head pounding, my heart throbbing, my soul running to become free—searching, seeking, questing where my body chooses not to go. Who will hear my sobs? Who will quiet my fears? Who will summon up the courage to tell me the ultimate truth to questions still unanswered? Who will choose to rise above our floundering humanity?

…And then, without warning, I am caught in the winds that sweep even the frailest into eternity. As I ride these winds, the phrase keeps repeating and repeating, "The longest journey is the journey inward."

And then *his voice*—also riding the winds of eternity—quietly possesses my mind and my inner being begins to warm to this one who was born in the nineteenth century in a quaint little village in Germany. As his accent penetrates my conscious being, I know that this one, with much wisdom, has suffered the heartache of terrible prejudice. He too is searching, even in death, for the lonely answers that could free all mankind.

As I listen to that soft, gentle soul he says, "It is plain that we exist for all persons. We are destined to be members of one great humanity which directs our material and spiritual existence from the cradle to the grave." Slowly he continues, "The most beautiful thing we can experience is the mysterious. It is the true source of all art and science. He to whom this emotion is a stranger, who can no longer pause to wonder and stand rapt in awe, is as good as dead, his eyes are closed…"

And as this great man of destiny, this citizen of the world community, begins to fade and hearing becomes scant, I press my mortal ear to his immortal whisper and I hear him, like a soft breeze on the border of the Universe, utter so faintly, "I am convinced that, left alone, people would not hate each other. If they were not stirred into hating each other, they would live together in harmony forever."

My answer for peace in the world had been given without my asking…and as I turned to go my way, there in my trembling hand was a gift. And as I gazed downward I was gripping in my fist the *theory of relativity*. I clasped it closely to myself and drifted off into the middle of nowhere, once more striding forth into a dark and relentless night. Forty paces down the path I was to begin the strangest battle of my life as the sound of the roaring sea suddenly beat against my ear drums and then swept in upon me. I was tossed like a small craft up and down. As the sweeping continued, large black holes developed within the surging water and an incessant black rain was pouring down upon my weathered body. I was alone, helpless in the bosom of a roaring sea, thrown first up into the pelting black rain and then downward into the depths of black holes that sought to squeeze the very life from my now almost lifeless frame. In this torrent of black water from above and blacker water from beneath, I knew no path of escape. As I was once more swept to the height of the wild surf and then mercilessly pounded deep into the black and watery hold, I felt the impulse to thrust my hand upward and cry to the black waters of the earth, "Within my grasp I have the greatest theory known to all humanity, a creative act of genius worthy of our kind. It is time to put it to good use, to use it for the making of one great universe. O waters of the universe—be calm! And know that in a compassionate universe we are destined to find the key to mankind's final purpose."

And with my plea the black rain stole silently away and the black surging waves and bottomless black holes became as peace on earth….

I docked the small piece of driftwood upon which my frail body now was at rest. I walked down the dock, down narrow streets, past narrow buildings—to a restaurant where there was no beginning and no ending. It seemed as though I were becoming another self—destined to no beginning and no ending…only a forever that is built on the theory of Love, which has no beginning and no ending—only endless days and nights. Endless as Eternity!

4

The Psychology of Extinction

Inquiries into Anxiety in the Nuclear Age

1985

WE LIVE IN A SELF-CONSCIOUS "AGE OF ANXIETY" and much of our professional life as psychologists is spent understanding and confronting this malaise. Recent developments in world politics, however, have heightened our awareness of a new kind of anxiety associated with the threat of nuclear war, instilling in us and our clients a special kind of dread of the unknown and uncontrollable. This anxiety is unique because it contains within itself the threat of extinction—not only of ourselves, but also of our species as a whole. Given the urgency of this threat, two questions arise: what is the nature of the psychology being shaped by the threat of extinction, and what is our responsibility as helping professionals to act on behalf of mental health? This essay is an interdisciplinary response to these questions utilizing categories of understanding derived from the disciplines of biology, psychology, and existential philosophy. Only through such a general approach can we hope to encompass the full range of issues posed by this fearful topic.

Let us begin with an image of health and vitality. Consider the image of the Earth as viewed from the moon. I believe that this is the most significant image of the twentieth century, showing in a graphic way the global interdependence of man and nature. The significance of this image lies not in the ethical behavior it has evoked from the citizens of "spaceship Earth," but rather in the ethical behavior it *ought* to evoke. The blue-green colors of the Earth's biosphere beckon to us, proclaiming the sanctity of life and illustrating the interconnectedness of living things and the *ecos* they inhabit. This image of global interdependence is the most significant image of the twentieth century because it provides us with a moral imperative, a controlling image of health, vitality, and strength around which we can organize human behavior.

Consider now an image of disease, literally "dis-ease." The English word *anxiety* is derived from the Greek *anxere* meaning "to choke" or "to hurt." In the Greek worldview, the spirit or soul was in the *pneuma* or breath, which left one's body at death. Anxiety, therefore, has the connotation of a choking of the soul, a slow squeezing of vitality, a draining of the spirit. Thus, anxiety is an apt image for the insidious way in which modern life sucks away our vital juices until, unbeknownst to us, we are merely a husk of flesh and bone, living in our routines, separated from our soul, our center lost.

THE PROBLEM

The image of a healthy, harmonious, and interconnected Earth is threatened from many directions. These threats are experienced as either direct fear or vague anxiety, fear without a clear object. Of course the threat posed by nuclear weapons is not the only problem confronting the Earth and its inhabitants. Pollution, world hunger, and the problem of disenfranchised third world nations are other significant issues that come to mind. However, the threat of nuclear war, and therefore of extinction, is psychologically unique for a number of reasons. Consider that if a nuclear war were to happen, destruction would be immediate, unlike other world problems in which we would be warned by signs of progressive decay. The feeling that we should continue to live our lives in a normal way, knowing the possibility of instantaneous destruction, instills in us a sense of foreboding. The mere possibility of apocalypse erodes our trust in the continuity of the Earth. Consider, too, that as we try to visualize the consequences of nuclear war we see that the destruction it will cause is relatively complete. But our imaginations cannot encompass the totality of the destruction because images require a subject to imagine them. Just as no one can really imagine his own death, so no one can really imagine the holocaust, because in imagination the subject always survives. Consider also a 1982 survey in Britain of 15- to 18-year-olds, 70 percent of whom thought nuclear war was inevitable. Even more surprising, one-third of those polled did not know that atomic weapons were used against Japan in World War II. There is no doubt that we are dealing here with widespread fear and ignorance, but what are its consequences?

And finally, consider that our participation in world events forces us to join in a nuclear debate that is rife with conflicting theories and false feelings. Indeed, the current negotiating strategy of the United States and the Soviet Union—mad, or mutually assured destruction—forces us to place our trust in terror, an aberrant form of emotional investment that requires us to separate our morality from our thinking.

The rhetoric of this kind of "mad" reasoning, the very purpose of which is to maximize fear, can reach ludicrous proportions. Consider the front page of a local newspaper on September 7, 1983, soon after the downing of a Korean Airlines jumbo jet by the Russians. On one side of the front page President Reagan denounces the Russians as "inhuman." He says: "The attack on the airliner was an act of barbarism, born of a society that wantonly disregards the rights of the individual and of human life....But we shouldn't be surprised by such inhuman brutality." On the left-hand side of the same page are comments by a Russian spokesperson: "We can compare the White House with Nazi Germany, accusing it of sacrificing people for its own aims. When the Hitlerists made an attack they placed women and children in front of them. I do not think this comparison is too strong. I think it is just right."

This is strong rhetoric indeed, capable of instilling a great sense of insecurity in the people who must listen to it and whose fate is being decided by it. While this rhetoric frightens most people, it should also pique the curiosity of the psychologist in us. The deep structure of this language is a tangled web of fear, anger, projection, aggression, repression, conscience, evil, and a host of other psychological issues. There is no doubt that the language warrants a psychological analysis, but the problem is how to begin to untangle the knot. Clarifying the mess is only part of the problem, however. We must also use our skills as healers to confront, re-order and renew the lives that are being affected by this "disease." Furthermore, we should provide the foundations for an education that is psychologically adequate for citizens of the nuclear age.

As we embark on this task, it is appropriate to remind ourselves that as healers, we too are wounded by the very afflictions we try to heal in others. In healing ourselves, others are healed: "Physician, heal thyself."

THE SELF-PROCESS

How then do we access the circle of nuclear thinking? How can we get to the heart of the problem? Let us return to a fundamental issue in psychology and expand our awareness from there. Consider the self. The history of psychology is filled with various attempts to grasp this elusive concept. For our purposes, the definition used by Robert Lifton, an important writer on nuclear issues, will suffice. Lifton (1967) defines the self as "the person's symbol of his own organism" while the self-process is "the continuous psychic re-creation of that symbol." Using his definition as a stepping stone, let us bracket the issue of nuclear war. Let us pretend the nuclear threat does not exist and observe how the self-process works in a nuclear-free environment. We immediately discern that while the self-process has its strengths, it is also assaulted from many sides. Let's examine in more detail the virtues of the self-process as well as some of the threats to its inherent vitality.

The self-process is a marvelous extension of biological regulations embedded in the natural world. To be sure, the environment presents us with constraints or "coefficients of resistance" to which we must respond or die, but the success of our species as a whole lies precisely in the flexibility we have demonstrated in adapting to a changing reality. Flexibility within constraint, then, is a hallmark of the self-process.

Because the self-process is a natural extension of organic regulations, it is subject to the fundamental principle of living things: hierarchical organization. In other words, the psychic re-creations of the self-process cannot proceed in a random fashion but must be re-ordered according to specific principles of hierarchical organization. The existential counterpart to this biological process is the personal myth, the psychic narrative that tells a coherent story about how an individual has coped with the vicissitudes of life. We may say, therefore, that the life story is made possible because the mind seeks order.

The question then arises, from a phenomenological point of view, how do we experience re-ordering and renewal? How do we write a life story that is always essentially incomplete? This is a question concerning meaning, creativity, and the construction of a vital design. Simply stated, our task as the makers of our own meaning is to build a coherent image of our future and to make choices that will allow us to grow into this image. Ortega y Gasset expresses this idea in the following way: "Life means the inexorable necessity of realizing the *design* for an existence which each one of us is.... The sense of life...is nothing other than each one's acceptance of his inexorable circumstance and, on accepting it, converting it into his own creation." To the extent that we are able to live out this vital design, we experience a sense of gratification and achievement, a conviction that we are becoming what we were meant to become. It is an experience of authenticity.

However, we cannot construct a vital design in a social vacuum. Living means living with other people in community. Our relations with these others must be governed by principles of mutuality in which we support their designs for living even as they support ours. This mutual social regulation is not possible without the fundamental existential category of care—the glue that binds self and other. Without care the authentic reciprocity between self and others is impossible and the self-process ceases to function.

How do we recognize the relative success of self-in-process? Given the frailty of our imaginative designs for living and the brute power of environmental constraint, how do we know those moments when our desperate struggles are fulfilled? We recognize them through the emotion of joy. The experience of joy is made possible primarily through suffering. If happiness is the absence of discord, joy is the recognition that discord is necessary for psychic renewal, making available to us new possibilities to explore (May 1981). Joy, then, is a kind of release, a letting go of our old self to make way for the new. Joy is the experiential signature of the successful self-process.

In these five principles of the self-process—flexibility within constraint, mind seeking order, the construction of a vital design, care and community, and joy—we have described a horizon of meaning wherein we can understand some of the threats confronting the self-process. While continuing to hold the issue of nuclear war in abeyance, let us see how modern life threatens to unravel this marvelous tapestry.

Many social critics and psychiatrists in America have written about the problem of narcissism (May 1981; Lasch 1978; Kohut 1971; Kernberg 1975). In its most general sense, narcissism is the tendency of individuals to focus on their own feelings and problems in such a way as to exclude other people from their emotional orbit. Narcissists care mostly for themselves, while other human beings are simply means to this end. In this sense, narcissism is essentially a threat to community because the individual refuses to acknowledge his debt to the society that nurtured him. In this search for freedom from entanglement with other persons, the narcissist inevitably suffers from his failure of compassion and commitment. Narcissism is a failure to care authentically, a refusal to cooperate in the mutual construction of vital designs, and it destroys the social fabric binding the generations of mankind.

A second threat to the self-process is a psychological style Robert Lifton termed "proteanism" (Lifton 1967, 1970). The protean style is characterized by a series of experiments in living, each of which can be readily abandoned in favor of new and better quests. Protean man, then, jumps from role to role, switching masks at such a rate that he is no longer certain who he is. Protean people do not experience a center in their lives and their life story does not contain a unitary theme. Lifton argues that the Protean style is an adaptive response by the self to the flood of images and superficial messages mass-produced by the media. By constantly shifting the meaning of his life, Protean man can maintain a better adaptive equilibrium in a rapidly changing cultural environment. But there is a real danger to this psychological stance. In Lifton's analysis, the Protean style is a symbolic form of father-less-ness, a breakdown of the super-ego, a blurring of the criteria between right and wrong such that one's conscience requires only momentary and superficial justifications. Because Protean man cannot commit himself to a single lifestyle long enough to probe its depths, he experiences a nagging sense of unworthiness, like a plant that cannot find suitable ground in which to sink its roots. The Protean person moves from place to place and person to person, searching for authenticity, but never finding it. The Protean style threatens the coherence and integrity of the self-process because it denies both the center around which to organize experience and the personal responsibility such a center requires.

When the self is cast adrift in search of personal identity in a time when social, economic, and political turmoil are rampant, another threat to the self-process provides an alluring but dangerous solution, namely, the tendency to commit one's self to a narrow and exclusive ideological worldview. This tendency, referred to as "totalism" by Robert Lifton (1979) and Erik Erikson (1980), is dangerous because it surrenders the autonomy of the self to a predetermined set of beliefs. Rather than develop a set of hard-won personal beliefs that resonate with the full psycho-social historical development of the self, totalism suggests that we submit ourselves to a set of simple prescriptions for existence and salvation. The price of admission to a totalistic system is the surrendering of responsibility for one's life. The promise is that of shelter from a tumultuous world. But the price is too high and the promise is counterfeit because ideologies are too narrow to encompass and respond to the full complexity of reality. Simplifying personal choice requires limiting personal choice, and in a world of rapid change the self needs a great range of possibilities and flexibility in which to maneuver. Ideologies by definition are essentially rigid and conservative, but personal, social, and natural reality is not. The result of totalism is a dangerous split between cognitive reality (the world as we understand it) and the real (the world as it is). Furthermore, totalistic thought often fails to resonate with the personal history of each of its adherents, and as a result it provides superficial and inauthentic solutions to complex and deeply felt problems. In general, totalism is a threat to the integrity of the self, because it exchanges the autonomy of the individual for simplistic and short-range solutions.

The final threat I want to discuss is "infantilism." Infantilism refers to the basic store of unconscious, childish rage in the adult, a rage with great potential for destruction. For purposes of clarification, we may say that acting childlike is a regression in the service of the ego, but acting childishly, or with infantile rage, is a submission of the adult ego to self-indulgent feelings of dependency, hatred, and revenge. Erik Erikson (1964) argues that the rage of infantilism is evoked as a result of "adaptive impotence." When the ego experiences frustration and self-doubt in its attempts to respond to the constraints of reality, it responds like a baby. One danger of infantilism, argues Erikson, is that such rage can be exploited by political leaders for ostensibly moral purposes. Submerged feelings of rage can surface in the adult as moral indignation and condemnation of others. According to Erikson (1964):

> Irrational and pre-rational combination of goodness, doubt and rage can re-emerge in the adult in those malignant forms of righteousness and prejudice which we may call *moralism*. In the name of high moral principles all the vindictiveness of derision, of torture and of mass extinction can be employed. One surely must come to the conclusion that the Golden Rule was meant to protect man not only against his enemy's attacks, but also against his friend's righteousness. (pp. 223–24)

The function of the ego is to guard against such irrational intrusions, but when the ego is weakened it is more likely to submit to the irrational. This is especially true in times of rapid change. Stressful times require an ego strength bordering on the ascetic, but infantilism threatens the ego's ability to cope with the irrational. In so doing, infantilism manifests itself as childish behavior between adults, political groups, and nations, causing immature actions that are justified by a simplistic morality.

These four threats to the vitality of the self-process—narcissism, proteanism, totalism, and infantilism—are symptoms of our times. Our task as psychological healers is to confront and understand these threats in order to sustain the integrity of the self-process. Of course, this list of threats is by no means exhaustive and few suggestions have been offered how best to deal with them. Nevertheless, this descriptive overview of the self-process and the threats to it provides a field of understanding in which to contextualize the anxiety caused by nuclear war. Let us now lift the brackets separating our understanding of the self-process and its relation to nuclear anxiety in order to explore further the psychology of extinction.

THE PSYCHOLOGY OF EXTINCTION

There are a number of ironies that arise when human beings reflect on their own extinction. For instance, extinction is a very common occurrence. According to evolutionary theory, 99.9 percent of all the species that have ever lived on the planet Earth are now extinct. Human beings are merely a recent experiment in evolutionary design, and if they cannot adapt to the threats of the nuclear age they will cease to exist. The real irony is that in the event of an all-out nuclear war, the human species will destroy the very possibility of future species.

A second irony is that extinction is a limiting concept; it can never be experienced. Extinction does not happen to anybody because, by definition, there will be no one there to experience it. A question arises as to the appropriateness of using this category. But extinction is analogous to death, which always stands outside of life, yet which conditions it in a powerful way. Just as death affects the living more than the dead, so it is with extinction. In the words of Jonathan Schell (1982), whose writing on this topic is quite eloquent,

> Like death, extinction is felt not when it has arrived but beforehand, as a deep shadow cast back across the whole of life. The answer to the question of who experiences extinction and when, therefore, is that we the living experience it, now and in all the moments of our lives. Hence while in one sense it is true that extinction lies outside human life and never happens to anybody, in another sense extinction saturates our existence and never stops happening. If we want to find the meaning of extinction, accordingly, we should start by looking with new eyes at ourselves and the world we live in and at the lives we live. (p. 147)

Let us turn now to the specific threats to the self-process caused by the anxiety of nuclear war.

The first thing to realize about nuclear anxiety is that it makes all the other threats we have discussed more acute. People may choose to ignore the realities of nuclear conflict, but they are nevertheless burdened by the possibility. As social bonds become more tenuous and uncertain, the narcissist is even more justified in withholding authentic relations with others, while the protean style is strengthened because, when the Earth itself is threatened, there is no virtue to sustained commitment and responsibility. Likewise, totalism is encouraged as the search for simplistic answers is intensified and feelings of helplessness in a world that cannot be controlled engenders a great deal of regressive rage.

Perhaps the dimension of human existence most deeply affected by nuclear anxiety is the sense of psycho-historical embeddedness in a culture with a coherent past, a meaningful present, and a promising future. When more than 50 percent of the youth in advanced industrial societies consider the possibility of nuclear war likely, we are confronting a serious impairment to the adolescent's perceptions of the future. "Why should I invest my time and energy in a future that, in all probability, will not exist? Why should I not indulge myself in the present?" This pattern of reasoning will occur to anyone, child or adult, whose thoughts about the future contain nuclear imagery and the possibility of the destruction of all future generations.

The imaginative destruction of a viable future also affects the present. "Live for today because tomorrow you die" is a reasonable alternative to anybody living in a futureless world, providing a useful license to enjoy life in the moment with few restrictions. But this attitude eventually begins to wear thin as the pleasures of the moment fail to disguise an underlying sense of loneliness and emptiness. In Jonathan Schell's (1982) words:

> The moment itself, unable to withstand the abnormal pressure of expectation, becomes distorted and corrupted. People turn to it for rewards that it cannot offer—certainly not when it is ordered to do so. Plucked out of life's stream, the moment—whether a moment of love or spiritual peace, or even of simple pleasure in a meal—is no longer permitted to quietly unfold and be itself but is strenuously tracked down, manipulated, harried by instruction and advice, bought and sold, and, in general, so roughly manhandled that the freshness and joy that it can yield up when it is left alone are corrupted or destroyed. (p. 159)

Just as perceptions of a nonviable future lead to a bloated present, so do they also lead to a trivializing of the past. Without the assurance that there will be a future, it is difficult to muster the motivation for mastering the past works of mankind, the very cultural matrix in which meaning is made possible. What is being threatened here is the basis by which we construct an intergenerational common world. The ties that bind us as a particular people located in a certain space-time have been unraveling for some time, but the threat of nuclear war exacerbates the process.

Let us turn now to the way in which nuclear anxiety participates in and affects certain cognitive processes. Gregory Bateson (1972) coined the term "double-bind thinking" to describe the etiology of certain schizophrenic behavior disorders. In Bateson's view, the victim of a double-bind situation has been given two mutually contradictory messages such that responding to either message constitutes "wrong" behavior. The result is a cognitive confusion that can eventually lead to schizophrenia. There is no doubt that the current negotiating strategy between the United States and the Soviet Union contains patterns of double-bind thinking. MAD strategy is based on a theory of nuclear deterrence which reasons that only by threatening to use our nuclear capability can we prevent the other side from attacking us. In other words, we avoid self-extinction by threatening to perform the act. The double-bind irony of this negotiating strategy becomes particularly obvious when we realize that our only protection from nuclear war is to place our trust in terror. Unfortunately, the very people whose lives depend on this strategy have no experiential context in which to understand this ironic juxtaposition of trust and terror. No mother has taught her child to trust terror.

Another way of reasoning that contains patterns of double-bind thinking concerns the role of self-criticism in the setting of the nuclear policy of democratic countries. Because both sides of a nuclear confrontation must show their willingness to strike at a moment's notice, neither side can afford to display any kind of internal weakness. What happens, then, when a particular policy needs revision or change? It must be done in secrecy or not at all, thereby nullifying the very checks and balances that make for a strong democracy. In other words, deterrence deters debate about itself and in so doing chokes off the very democratic values it is designed to protect.

The deleterious effects of double-bind thinking are not limited to the rarefied atmosphere of international nuclear negotiating strategy. Consider the plight of school children, many of whom have been exposed to images of nuclear destruction by the age of five. If parents refuse to discuss with children the fears engendered by this imagery, then the active imaginations of school-age children are free to assume the worst possible scenarios. But even if the most reasonable parents discuss the nuclear issue in a realistic way, they must still insist that the children live in full knowledge that a series of bombs capable of great destruction can fall on them at any time and yet they should continue to live their lives in a normal way. It is not surprising that children are confused by the problem of nuclear war.

What is the effect of this kind of thinking on individual psychology? Double-bind logic leads to a dissociation between thought and feeling, a psychic gap caused by the fact that in order to go about "business as usual" we must deaden our feelings about what we know. When feeling is inhibited or repressed, the people and things of the outer world diminish in value. Their apparent loss of importance renders them vague and unconvincing. We lose interest in the outer world; it becomes dull and flat, incapable of arousing our passions concerning its present plight. We drift toward the end of our world in a profound and lethargic state of apathy. This response to the effects of double-bind thinking has been called "psychic numbing" by Lifton and others. It is perhaps the most prevalent and dangerous response we can have to the anxiety of nuclear extinction. It is especially dangerous when political leaders become numb to the consequences of nuclear war. At this point they begin to use a rhetoric of "limited nuclear war" in the belief that such a war can actually be won. They become victims of a distortion of human experience, the glorification of knowledge to the detriment of feeling. The psychic costs of this split between thinking and feeling are seen in the huge gap between our technological skill in manufacturing and deploying weapons of great violence on the one hand and limited capacity for moral and spiritual imagination on the other. In fact the psychic split between thought and feeling is the heart of the psychological dilemma posed by the threat of nuclear extinction. The size of this gap is an indicator of our lack of progress, and the gap itself is the oozing wound that the psychic healer must stanch, both in himself and in others.

Are we then caught in a double bind, strung between a position of psychic numbing and helplessness? How do we counsel individuals who are willing to confront the problem but do not know how? The situation seems to breed despair; indeed despair seems to be the only valid response. Yet, as we shall see, it is despair that provides the seeds of our renewal.

The origin of despair can be elusive. It may be experienced as a conscious response to the possibility that the human species may destroy itself in a nuclear war; but more likely it will be experienced as a vague feeling that, for some unknown reason, the future holds no hope. In either case, despair is an admission that we are powerless to do anything about what will happen to us.

The experience of many psychotherapists has been that by getting their clients to admit and own their despair, rather than repressing it, a feeling of relief is experienced. Rollo May (1978) describes the psychotherapeutic function of despair in the following way:

> We know in psychotherapy that often despair is essential to the discovery on the part of the client of his or her hidden capacities and basic assets. The function of despair is to wipe away our superficial ideas, our delusionary hopes, our simplistic morality. There are some misguided therapists who feel that they must reassure the patient at every point of despair. But if the client never feels despair, it is doubtful whether he ever will feel any profound emotion. (pp. 236–37)

Just as suffering is often a prerequisite to joy in the self-process, so those who can confront despair and survive are those who can experience the most intense elation. In mythical terms, the celebration of death is a precursor to any rising from the dead; to win the Holy Grail we must be willing to endure the dark night of the soul.

So what happens when we are willing to admit our despair? In her work with despair groups whose specific concern was nuclear war, Joanna Macy (1983) discovered that by owning one's own despair, individuals release a great deal of emotional energy that was previously blocked. The result is a resurgence of hope as the individual recognizes that the anguish is rooted in a deep caring for the Earth and its inhabitants. In Macy's experience, breaking taboos against despair and permitting it to be openly expressed results in a release of emotional energy and a stronger commitment to resuming the task of human survival. Through this psychotherapeutic ordeal, an even deeper discovery is made, one which validates the latent healing power in the threat of extinction. In Macy's words:

> Through our despair something more profound and pervasive than our despair comes to light. It is our interconnectedness, our interexistence. Beyond our pain and because of our pain we awaken into that. For our feelings of despair for the planet and its beings are concerns that extend beyond our separate egos. Therefore they testify to our essential unity—and by owning them we re-experience that unity, emerge into it afresh. In that dawning we recognize that the very crises of our time can open us to new dimensions of awareness, a sense of mutual belonging so real that the response is one of wonder, even joy. That is why the workshops are often called "Despair and Empowerment." (p. 241)

Thus the despair generated by the threat of extinction can become a kind of virtue in that it provides us with a source of emotional energy that can be used for purposes of social responsibility. Despair can also awaken us to the fact that we are truly interconnected with other human beings on the planet. The value of reaching this conclusion through despair rather than intellectual insight is that through despair an emotional component accompanies the understanding, thereby intensifying the authenticity of the experience. The idea of the interconnectedness of human beings is further enhanced when we realize that, because the threat of extinction is a problem shared by all, it can serve as a focal force by which to define a common humanity. As Schell (1982) puts it, "nothing underscores our common humanity as strongly as the peril of extinction does: in fact, on a practical and political plane, it establishes that common humanity" (p. 227).

Whether despair is induced specifically by the nuclear threat or generally by an inability to cope, individuals invariably gain valuable self-knowledge as a result of their successful confrontation. Being more psychologically aware, they begin to discover an inner world that contains the same potential for good and evil that the outer world contains. They begin to discover that they are not merely victims of social circumstances but that they have allowed themselves to become victims. Recognizing one's own capacity for evil is a first step to controlling it. Thus, the virtue of despair is that it enhances our self-knowledge while liberating our motivational power. In so doing, despair provides the seeds of our renewal.

EXPERIMENTS IN SOCIAL RESPONSIBILITY

Given the fact that despair, when overcome, is a vital reminder of our social interconnectedness and leads to a heightened self-awareness, what principles can individuals use to direct their newly liberated energies toward a resolution of the nuclear threat? How can we cease to feel helpless? Recall the basic virtues of the self-process—flexibility within constraint, mind seeking order, the construction of a vital design, care and community, and joy. Despair revitalizes the latter two virtues, but it is the first three that inform our response. The decision to act on behalf of social responsibility after a confrontation with despair requires the development of a coherent plan or design. But the key to the construction of this plan is to remain open and flexible to the constraints of the environment while remaining true to the thematic motifs of the life story. The search for such an authentic design is a search for existential truth, the living truth that one "is." In this view, truth is not an absolute toward which one gropes; rather truth is a process of lived experience and is constructed through experimenting with one's life.

Consider the example of Mohandas Gandhi, who titled his autobiography *The Story of My Experiments with Truth.* Gandhi's life was a series of experiments concerning nonviolence, truthfulness in thought and word, celibacy, and God. Gandhi showed that truth is a product of action, that we construct our own truth through deeds. Gandhi's message was a call to strengthen the self's will in the context of an expanded morality. His saintliness lies in the fact that his life was a paradigm of this search for truth. It is important to understand that this does not imply that we should simply appropriate Gandhi's truth as our own. This is the path that leads to totalism. Rather, we should appropriate Gandhi's *method* for achieving the truth, realizing that the truth we seek is a unique product of our own historical struggle to become an authentic self.

Applying this insight in the context of the peril of extinction, we can see that our own personal vital design for social responsibility should be constructed as an experiment, the efficacy of which is dependent on the results. Of course, good experimentalists design their experiments so that the probability of success is high; but it is more important to realize that knowledge is gained even when the experiment fails. As long as a principle of coherence is maintained throughout these life experiments, we are presented with a reverse double bind—instead of being unable to win, it seems we cannot lose.

But calling for a new asceticism of the will is not adequate in itself. We must learn to exercise our will in the context of an enlarged concept of love. Instead of thinking only in terms of caring for our immediate family and friends, city or nation, we must begin to define ourselves in the context of our love for the planet. In other words, the moral imperative for social responsibility in the nuclear age must be a genuine caring for the Earth, the ecos in which we and all other things live. An important dimension of this ecological care and concern is the idea of universal parenthood, the realization that, whether we have children or not, we are all parents of the future generations of mankind. Such a love must be like parental love, which begins before the child is born and which is unconditional. Parental love does not attach to any particular quality of the beloved; it only wants the child to be and it is quick to forgive any shortcomings. Forgiveness, then, is an essential element of planetary care and an important antidote to the rage we feel toward the various forces that put us into this nuclear predicament.

As examples of experimenting with social responsibility, I would like to briefly describe two projects I am currently conducting in the city of Hiroshima, Japan. These experiments are proceeding in the belief that peace education must address itself to both the social dynamics of the outer world as well as the psychological dynamics of the inner self. Because these projects are "in process," I am not in a position to judge their efficacy; they are worthy of mention only insofar as they stimulate other experiments by other concerned citizens of the planet Earth.

As a teacher of a single classroom of 12- to 15-year-olds at the Hiroshima International School, I have been experimenting with the idea of global education. I began with the assumption that the task of global education is to inculcate values of global unity in my students. But the problems began to arise when I pondered the question of how best to teach these values. Clearly, a broad knowledge of the social and political structure of the world had to be an essential part of the curriculum. Equally important was the focus on specific problems that illustrate the interconnectedness of human beings, problems such as pollution, war, hunger, poverty, and so on. Valuable as this information was, I began to realize that there was a missing element to my instruction. I was asking my students to learn human values by talking about those values. As long as my instruction remained at this purely cognitive level, I was unable to change the underlying attitudes of my students. I had to find a way to penetrate the affective web of understanding, to educate the very roots of motivation. But how?

One answer, I have come to realize, lies in the everyday interpersonal conflicts that occur with dismaying regularity in any classroom or playground of incipient adolescents. What better laboratory to learn the skills of conflict resolution than in the heat and rage of an argument over some trifling matter like a neighbor tapping his pencil too loudly or a student accidentally (or purposefully) bumping his classmate? It is precisely when the emotions are aroused that the most valuable affective education takes place. In those volatile moments I try to shape the act of empathy whereby one person experiences the thoughts and feelings of the other. "Forget who is right or wrong," I say to my students, "and focus on what your adversary *must be thinking* in order for him to feel the way he does. How is it *possible* for both of you to observe the same incident yet interpret it so radically differently? Given your opponent's perspective, would you have behaved in the same way?" Of course the dynamics of the classroom do not allow every interpersonal conflict to be an exercise in global conflict resolution, but the lesson to me has been clear: social perspective-taking is the key to inculcating the values of global utility in children. To emphasize the point, I have prominently displayed in my classroom a large photograph of the entire Earth, above which are written the words "Home Sweet Home."

My second experiment in social responsibility is called "The Dream Peace Project." Confronted with the problem of intellectual knowledge devoid of emotional understanding, I began many years ago to study the psychology of dreams. Experimenting with the interpretation of dreams, first my own and then those of children of various ages, I began to realize the motivational power of the dream image and its ability to anticipate and accompany psychological growth. I also began to realize that one's dream life is a training ground for the development of the inner self.

When I came to Hiroshima I established a small study group of dreamers, with several questions in mind. First I was interested in collecting dream images of war, especially nuclear war, in the hopes that a typology of the imagery could yield some insight into the psychological dynamics of conflict and fear. Furthermore, the various ways in which the dream contextualized and resolved the imagery might lead to some new insights into how the ego could attenuate or resolve conflict situations in waking life. Second, I was interested to see if the powerful symbolism of Hiroshima itself might induce or "incubate" particularly powerful images of war and peace. I knew that my own dream life was being altered by the fact that I was living in the shadow of the bomb. But was the same thing happening to foreign visitors? And more important, in what way was it happening? And what about longtime residents of Hiroshima, including the hibakusha, the survivors of the A-bomb? How were their dreams affected by this experience? Having suffered more than my share of nuclear nightmares, I became convinced that anyone who experiences the terror of annihilation, whether in a vivid dream or in real life, is hibakusha and as such has both the right and the responsibility to speak out concerning the horrors of nuclear war. Furthermore, I believe that more and more people are experiencing the terror of nuclear nightmares as a collective response to the present possibility of nuclear conflict. Can these dreams be a biological reaction on the part of the psyche designed to cut through the numbing defenses of the ego in order to make us really *feel* the terror so as to prevent it?

A third idea that motivates my experiments with dreams is the construction of a collective myth written by all members of the dream group. Was it possible, I asked myself, to write a story based on the images of our collective dreams that not only symbolized our struggles with the nuclear issue but that also suggested a solution? The experiment has been divided into three parts. The first is a long nuclear nightmare dreamed by one of our members that ends with an unexploded nuclear bomb leaking radioactivity. A group of concerned citizens, suffering from radioactive contamination, meets in a restaurant. At this point, I wrote a short transition section in which a disembodied voice speaks to those assembled:

> *"You question deeply for difficult answers. It is a beginning, but it is not enough. The balance of the world sways in the wind, yet it bends toward truth. Seek out this truth. You will find it first beyond the darkness of your own heart and then in the collective spirit of your group endeavors. The path is long and difficult, but your hope shall make you strong."*

In mythological terms, this voice is the "call to adventure" that beckons the hero to assume the quest. Notice that the task of the hero is first to confront the shadow, the evil within one's self, before attempting to participate in responsible social action. In real life, understanding the shadow and social action proceed in dialectical fashion, with each new insight from one dimension informing the other. However, the sequence of the narrative allows us to place our emphasis first upon understanding the darkness of one's own heart.

The second task of our myth writing is to confront doubts and fears we have concerning the possibility of war and peace by forcing our alter ego in the story to ask our questions for us. The answers are provided by a wise person encountered in the narrative. Note that the author both asks the questions and provides the answers, albeit through the mouth of a wise one. A gift is extracted from this wise person, but its power is not known. As the hero returns to the restaurant, he or she is assaulted by dark forces drawn from the author's imagination. The battle that follows is eventually won through the grace of the gift, the full power of which is now revealed. The third part of the myth takes place when we all meet again at the restaurant, wiser now for having confronted the dark side of ourselves, ready to pool the resources and talents of those present for purposes of social action. Throughout the myth, dream images are woven into the narrative. In this sense, the writing process is a form of active imagination as described by C. G. Jung. The hypothesis of this dream experiment is that by utilizing techniques of active imagination and guided imagery we can become more fully aware of our inner lives, revealing both the source of evil and the shape of the healing power that resides within the psyche of us all.

This essay has been an attempt to understand anxiety in the nuclear age by naming the patterns of experience working for and against the processes of self-realization and fulfillment. But, as Wittgenstein reminds us, the thing named is not the thing itself. For us this means that while the professional task of the helping professional may be to name the phenomenon, the personal task of the helping professional is to live it. Likewise, the task of any hero in the nuclear age is to actively seek the evil within in order to better recognize its insidious encroachment on the quality of life in the outer world. Battle lines are symmetrical within the psyche, one facing inward and the other facing outward. We must proceed on both fronts. But only the hero can come to know the true meaning of what he or she does and why. The task of the helping professional, then, is to assist individuals in their quest for authentic meaning by providing support, clarifying choices, and serving as an object of transference. But given the moral imperative suggested in this essay, any assistance rendered by the helper must be given in the knowledge of the possibility of extinction. Used judiciously, this knowledge can be a sorely needed voice for the cause of life itself.

5

Reveries on Martin Luther King's Birthday

1989

FOR ME, MARTIN LUTHER KING JR.'S BIRTHDAY is the occasion to reflect on the nature of Satyagraha, the "holding to truth" that is the force behind nonviolent resistance. The memory theater in my heart returns to some significant stops along the way of my understanding. Recall 1968. I am a senior in high school studying in a boarding school dormitory room. The deejay on the soul station to which I am listening cuts into the music with an anguished voice. Radio drops its propriety and the weeping announcer shouts it out, "Martin Luther King has been shot dead!" In an instant: happy soul to funeral dirge. That night I watch from the roof of my dormitory overlooking the city of Washington, D.C. Flames lick halfway up the Washington monument. Smoke rises ominously. The city appears to have been bombed. That memory image, and my subsequent walk a few weeks later through the charred remnants of a D.C. ghetto, are sources for my wonder about collective power, frustrated desire, and psychological evil. What force is powerful enough to burn a capital city, the head of the ruling power, from *within*? Where does it come from? Why does it arise? Where is it going?

I continue to wonder about Satyagraha and the legacy of Martin Luther King Jr. I know that *Sat* means "Truth" and *agraha* means "force." I know Gandhi felt that Satyagraha was a spiritual power inside each person that, when incarnated, could move mountains or the British Empire, whichever was more difficult—or more important. Satyagraha is indeed a force, but unlike Wilhelm Reich's orgone energy, it cannot be bottled separately from its enactment in a human being. The Satyagrahi embodies a way of life, not a mere technique.

The frames of my memory theater begin to move again. It is 1973. I am a crab fisherman, a poor one at that, outside of Frogmore, South Carolina. It is Sunday, too hot to work. Hadn't I just seen Marine recruits at Parris Island dropping like flies on the sizzling parade ground? A friend and I drive into Frogmore, population 120. We know it is the place Martin Luther King Jr. used as a spiritual retreat when times were bad. It is far away from the rest of the world. The town is motionless as we enter. From a distance a groundswell of singing rolls and reverberates through the air. Like white beggars, we stand outside the small Baptist church, wanting to hear more. A wizened black man with deep eyes motions us up the stairs and welcomes us into the church. Heads turn, a sea of black faces. I am afraid. The man smiles at us and in that smile I see...redemption? The singing becomes divine.

And in this image I am reminded of the healing power of love, the essence of Satyagraha. That man really loved me, and in the presence of that love I was liberated from the oppression of my own white, middle-class background. Satyagraha, Truth, knows that, in Thomas Merton's words, "The only real liberation is that which liberates both the oppressor and the oppressed...the only way truly to overcome an enemy is to make him or her other than an enemy" (Merton, pp. 14–15). As M. L. King said in a live interview during a demonstration in the suburbs of Chicago, shouts and gunfire in the distance, "We must bring the evil out into the open so people can see it." Yes, because once we *see* it, the truth of our own being, the moral Self, the inner eye of God, will recognize and transform it.

The image of the old black man at the top of the church steps says more: the spirit of nonviolence emanates from a vital inner unity of human experience. The man's eyes communicated that he was *already there*, immersed in the integrity of a vital process well lived. I was not his experiment in achieving Satyagraha. The ability to exercise Satyagraha is the fruit of inner work already achieved; it is not the means to attain that unity. To use Satyagraha as an isolated technique to achieve a pragmatic end is schizoid, distorting truth from being something I *am* to something I *have*. As soon as the short-term end is achieved, the method can be discarded. No inner peace is achieved, no inner unity, only the same divisions gnawing away at the fabric of intergenerational care, which thus become merely another contribution to the epidemic of ego-/adulto-/ethnocentrism. Contrast this technical approach to Gandhi's method of awakening Satyagraha through experimenting with the truth of one's own life, a task that requires a total commitment to ends that transcend political expediency (Gandhi 1968).

I hear the whirr of shifting images. It is 1984 and I am standing at the memorial cenotaph in Hiroshima's Peace Park. I am leading a small tour of Europeans through the park. The distinguished guest is Credo Mutwa, an aging South African witch doctor from Soweto, amulets hanging from his arms, a stone the exact shape of a human heart heavy on his chest. I explain to the group that the cenotaph is the most sacred space in the park. We stand back as an electrical field seems to constellate around Credo. In silence and awe we watch him step determinedly to the altar and kneel in prayer. He removes his sacred headband, given to him by his grandfather who had worked with Gandhi in South Africa. He lays the colorful piece of African cloth into the gray ashes of incense. When he gets up we hear his voice, clear and distinct. To no one in particular, to us all, he announces, "I *must* accept responsibility for what has happened here." It is a statement that haunts me still. How can a black South African accept responsibility for a bomb dropped by Americans on Japanese? And yet cognitively I recognize that I am in the presence of a true Satyagrahi, one who knows in his heart that true freedom requires an inner strength capable of first seeing, then of assuming, the common burden of evil that tyrannizes us all. Contrast this approach to false freedom, which cannot bear one's own evil and so projects it onto the other—no insight, no burden (Keen 1986).

Credo reminds me, after too many forgettings, that the interior life is not an exclusively private affair. True, a person deepens his or her own thought in silence, but deep solitude eventually and inevitably leads to an awareness of belonging. As Sam Keen says, "At the heart of my privacy I discover how public I am" (p. 167). Somewhere along the path of solitude, one realizes that, as Thomas Merton puts it, "The spiritual life of one person is simply the life of all manifesting in [her]...as [she] becomes engaged in the crucial struggles of [her] people, in seeking justice and truth together with [her] brother [and sister], [she] tends to liberate the truth in [her]self by seeking true liberty for all" (p. 6). The tyranny of the Cartesian imagination would have me believe that the inner world and the outer world are separate and distinct. Credo's example brings to mind the image of a mobius strip, where the cures of the introverted imagination *are* the cures of extroverted action, where the thick smog of my twisted instinctual life and the billowing smoke of the Amazon rain forests emanate from one and the same torch.

Credo, I believe. I believe too that you have given me a ruby of great price, the hope of Satyagraha that evil is not irreversible, that I do not need to despair of living in a society of persistent disorder, stunted desire, moral confusion, and organized greed, because that society *is* capable of change. Furthermore, you have shown me that it is my vocation to assist in this transformation. Just as Satyagraha was refracted through the prism of Indian spirituality in Gandhi, so it begins to shine through the emerging spirituality of Gaia in me, in us all. It reminds me that the spiritual task of our times is to "pass over" through sympathetic understanding from our standpoint to those of other religions, cultures, and peoples in order to return to our own with renewed insight (Dunne 1972). It is the grand experiment of de-centering ourselves, our egos; of shifting our orbit to the greater Self. I began in anger and frustration. What a gift to be shown how to accomplish this task in love, without losing anger's indignation or impetus.

I am a neophyte in these matters. I still find it an overwhelming task to cease cooperating with the disorder, injustice, and perversions of the society that informs me. I continue to grope toward the enactment of my heart's desire. But hope and courage quicken in the presence of human beings who incarnate Satyagraha. Happy birthday, Martin. I am so grateful for your presence. The ark of the universe *is* long, but as you said, it bends toward Truth.

6

Reveries on Hiroshima and Education

(with Walter Enloe)

1990

WE ARE TWO EDUCATORS WHO HAVE HAD the unusual experience of practicing our profession for many years in Hiroshima, Japan, working at an international school with children from all regions of the world. Since returning to the United States, we have been struck by the intense interest so many people have about Hiroshima: "What is it like there?" "Is it still radioactive?" "Do things grow there?" "Do the Japanese A-bomb victims hate us?" These questions, and more, indicate the deep fascination of Americans with the first dropping of an atomic bomb on a civilian population. Hiroshima has become a living symbol in American consciousness. But of what is it a symbol? Self-righteous retribution? Man's inhumanity toward man? A future nuclear wasteland? In this essay we would like to return to the root of apocalypse, which means to reveal, to see how Hiroshima can instruct us. What does Hiroshima reveal to us about the state of the world and of humanity's place in it? What does Hiroshima reveal to us about how to prepare students to live in the twenty-first century? What does Hiroshima reveal to us about our vocation as educators?

A primary function of any culture's education is to help students comprehend their own image in the context of self, other, and world, and from that perspective to act accordingly. But a fundamental crisis confronting educators is our refusal or inability to accommodate a new paradigm of human being and meaning developing in the human psyche. As if in direct compensation to the horror of Hiroshima, this new image of humankind was inaugurated in the psyche when human beings first glimpsed a holistic image of the Earth as seen from the moon. The sheer beauty of the living reality of Gaia herself, devoid of political boundaries, has conjured a new sense of hope and urgency that transcends cultural differences. It is an image of humanity in relationship with nature, as an interconnected whole. It is a view of the world that radiates the interconnectedness of life. In this context, the Hiroshima experience reminds us of the fragility of human and natural ecosystems and the fact that the problems our planet faces are specifically human problems. They are problems of human values. Hiroshima reminds us that, for the first time in the history of the universe, a power other than God has the ability to terminate the consciousness through which creation can apprehend itself. Who is going to bear the responsibility for this power. If not you, then who? Clearly, if education is to be both relevant and meaningful, it must respond to the basic question of how we are to improve the quality of human life in the face of diminishing resources, global pollution, and the threat of nuclear annihilation. But Hiroshima pulls us deeper. It forces us to realize that social education must address critical questions about how human groups tend to perceive themselves as "other than and superior to" their fellow human beings. This tendency has been called "pseudo-speciation" by Erik Erikson, and its dynamics lie at the root of all state, cultural, and racial conflict. Are we teaching our students about the nature of the hostile human imagination, how we tend to project our own fears and frustrations onto the "enemy"? Are we giving them the skills to manage their own aggressive impulses? How can we build upon students' intimate personal and social experience at the microcosmic level in order to facilitate their understanding that, at the level of macrocosmic human interaction, the behavior of one person affects that of others in an intricate web of mutual interdependence? We believe that the task of education is to facilitate what Jean Piaget called "de-centering," a gradual cognitive and affective process by which we liberate ourselves from the ties that bind us to our own egocentrism in order to include the perspective of the other. Empathy, cooperation, and responsibility are all threads of one weaving.

So what are the basics our children need to live productively in the twenty-first century? What basic attitudes, knowledge, and skills do they need to possess for American citizenship in such a globalized world? The resolution of these questions is imperative for our schools. If we are unable to develop appropriate teaching methods and curricula; if we are unable to foster a school community ambiance of cooperation, empathy, and tolerance for others; and if we fail to foster a global commitment to the world and our fellow humans, we can have little hope of resolving our present predicaments. From our experience with children from all over the world, we believe that students must learn through active, cooperative, lived experience that a person is foremost, not a particular gender, nationality, or race, but a member of the human species, sharing common organizational structures of mind and adaptive capacities in a given bio-social world.

And what of our own personal situation as educators? How can we expect our students to imbibe global values if we have not allowed ourselves to be moved by the moral tension generated by the threat of extinction that is at the heart of the Hiroshima image? Do we have the courage to move through the psychic numbing that the Hiroshima experience presents? Can we begin to understand that holistic education is not a series of optimistic platitudes that can be poured into students' heads as though they were facts to be memorized? Values are taught only through human beings who incarnate them, so holistic education must be a way of life that emerges from a confrontation with and integration of the dark side of our own souls. In a sense, every educator must be a spiritual warrior, advancing both inwardly and outwardly. Nothing less will do.

Having brought consciousness to our own culpability in the Hiroshima experience, can we still teach from a position of compassion and vision? In response to this challenging question, we would like to invoke a healing image that becomes possible only in a post-Hiroshima age. It is an image that is fallout from the apocalypse, gold to be mined from the mushroom cloud. Jonathan Schell, in his brilliant book *The Fate of the Earth,* conjures the image of "universal parenthood." Schell writes that the very idea of human extinction makes all of us, whether we have children or not, the parents of future generations. This is so because any given generation that holds power in the post-Hiroshima age has the power of choice about nuclear annihilation. Each subsequent generation that lives on is thereby indebted to past generations for having allowed them to exist. Thus the living can look at the gift of life as a temporary trust to be used for the common good.

This image points to the need to forge a new "partnership of generation" wherein the ties that bind us as a species, the very ties that are both elucidated and threatened by nuclear extinction, are seen to be in service to the stewardship of the Earth. It is binding imagery like this that can motivate our best efforts as educators and advocates of global peace and justice. We worry that recent positive developments in Eastern Europe may blunt the urgency of acting on behalf of the new image that is aborning in the human psyche. But Hiroshima lives in the hearts and minds of us who have been touched by the courage, pathos, and grandeur of Hiroshima's experience. We have finally come to understand that we are all hibakusha survivors of a nuclear nightmare, working on behalf of generations both present and future, firm in our conviction that there must be "No More Hiroshimas."

As always, the question in the end returns to us, the educators who are reading and writing this essay. Given the tension between a heightened anxiety about our global peril and the growing vision of a new image of human beings, are we inculcating values of global utility in the context of American citizenship? Are we facilitating thoughtfulness and forms of social commitment to be acted upon? Are we fostering values that go beyond mere survival techniques and strategies for coping, to include a revitalizing of our own and others' worth, a revitalization that can lead to mature commitment and reasonable participation in our democracy as well as resacralization of our planet?

We invite you to imagine the Earth as seen from the moon. Draw closer to the brilliant blues and greens, the swirling white clouds. Enter the atmosphere above the Japanese archipelago. See yourself in Hiroshima City. Enter Peace Park and face the children's monument dedicated to the thousands of children who have died from the atomic bombing. Read the inscription at the monument's base: "This is our cry. This is our prayer. To build peace in this world." Now enter the Peace Museum and stand before stone steps on which is permanently etched the shadow of an unknown, vaporized human being. And wonder with us: Is not the fundamental crisis in education our refusal to take these images seriously?

7

Education for Apocalypse

A Depth Psychological Approach

1997

> *God wants to be born in the flame of man's consciousness, leaping ever higher. And what if this has no roots in the Earth? If it is not a house of stone where the fire of God can dwell, but a wretched straw hut that flares up and vanishes? Could God then be born? One must be able to suffer God. That is the supreme task for the carrier of ideas. He must be the advocate of the Earth. God will take care of himself. My inner principle is:* Deus et homo. *God needs man in order to become conscious, just as he needs limitation in time and space. Let us therefore be for him limitation in time and space, an earthly tabernacle.*
>
> C. G. Jung
Letters

MEDITATION ON HIROSHIMA

> *We waited until the blast had passed, walked out of the shelter and then it was extremely solemn. We knew the world would not be the same. A few people cried. Most people were silent. I remembered the line from the Hindu scripture, the* Bhagavad-Gita: *Vishnu is trying to persuade the Prince that he should do his duty and to impress him he takes on his multi-armed form and says, "Now I am become Death, the destroyer of worlds." I suppose we all thought that, one way or another.*
>
> Robert J. Oppenheimer
after the detonation of the first atomic bomb

MEDITATIONS ON THE BOMB

Imagine, if you will, a meditation dedicated to that moment (8:15 a.m., August 6, 1945) when an atomic bomb was first detonated over a densely populated city. Imagine preparing for this meditation by reading about the history of World War II, the war in the Pacific, the evolution of the Manhattan project, the accounts of the devastation visited upon the city of Hiroshima as the bomb released its power and the city was flattened. To make the images of your meditation more accurate, it would be important to study the pictures taken from the point of view of the delivery plane, the *Enola Gay*, as well as the few photographs taken from the ground that day, and especially the color drawings rendered by survivors as they trod through the burning remnants of their city.

Having prepared yourself with this study, imagine clearing a space for yourself in a special place where you will not be disturbed and you can be assured of solitude. Research the exact moment in your time zone that corresponds to 8:15 a.m. Hiroshima time and begin to settle your mind and breathing for some time in advance of this moment. More than likely, your imagination will begin to participate in the events as they unfolded in 1945—the long, monotonous plane ride, the children on their way to school, the young people clearing fire lanes, the complaints about the false air raids during the previous night. Then events will quicken—the excitement as the bomb is armed and dropped, the precise movements of the people on the ground as they prepare to meet their fate, the instant of the detonation.

If you have taken the trouble to enact this meditation, to witness Hiroshima through the deep imagination, you will have an imaginal experience unique to your own psyche. Nevertheless, certain patterns of experience are likely to occur. The tremendous flash-boom of the atom bomb will probably carry you into a region of your own soul rarely, if ever, visited. First there is the encounter with the *mysterium tremendum* of the detonation, then a set of visceral experiences often beginning in the lower abdomen and coursing up though the gut and into the chest region, the area of the heart *chakra*. An identification with the souls of those who were instantaneously incinerated often triggers sharp pains that manifest in various body locations. Then there is the identification with the suffering of those left behind—the peeling skin, the embedded shards of glass, the helplessness of witnessing a loved one burn to death in a collapsed home. At this point, one can only cry.

The experience will then become even more intense as the witnessing imagination becomes aware that at that very moment there are 50,000 people in Hiroshima's Peace Park who are observing a minute of silence in relation to the same set of images. Indeed, there are people all around the world who are pausing in that moment to witness the immensity of that event. It is difficult to predict the direction that the meditating ego will take at this point. The key is to stay with the experience, not to flinch in the gaze of Hiroshima's terror. This much can be said: having dropped into the dark maw of Hiroshima's suffering, the ego is stripped of its moorings and an imaginal landscape common to humanity is entered. One rarely encounters this place without some sort of revelation taking place. If you visit this place, stay there as long as you can—waiting, watching, listening. Then slowly observe the natural movement in the psyche that signals the completion of the experience. Something says, "It is enough!" The meditating ego begins to reconstitute itself and to pull back from this other world into more familiar terrain. Time begins to make sense again and one recognizes the signposts of ego's familiar reality. An apocalypse has been encountered and survived. Time to dry the tears, review what has been seen and learned, and rededicate one's life to being a peacemaker.

This essay is an attempt to understand such an experience. As a resident of the city of Hiroshima for several years, I feel compelled to make sense of what happened there. After fifteen years of wondering about it, I am just beginning to penetrate the mysteries of that event. My thesis is this: what lifts the Hiroshima event out of the ordinary course of historical events is that it forces an encounter between the human psyche and the divine imagery of apocalypse.

I begin with an explication of the dynamics of the human psyche in relation to images of apocalypse and the role that these images play in our current historical situation. After I establish the idea that images of apocalypse are a doorway to personal and cultural transformation, I meditate on the kind of education necessary to prepare individuals to become vessels for the sacred aims and intentions of the deep psyche. The language I use comes from depth psychology in the tradition of C. G. Jung. The object of study in this psychology is the human psyche, which is understood to have at least two levels of depth—personal and collective. It is understood in Jungian psychology that since both personal and collective images are experienced within the psyche itself, they are separable only in theory. However, as we shall see, their differentiation is essential to understanding the psychic dynamics of apocalypse. For our purposes we may say that the personal psyche is circumscribed by images that are grounded in personal experience while the collective psyche is grounded in images that come from outside of our own experience and therefore from what may be called the "objective" or "impersonal" psyche. It is not essential that the reader be familiar with the language of depth psychology; I include references for those who wish to know more about certain ideas.

THE FUNCTION AND DYNAMICS OF APOCALYPTIC IMAGERY

> *In my dream, a friend tells me that a nuclear exchange is imminent between the United States and the Soviet Union. I am shaken with disbelief, but looking up in the sky, I see two missiles collide in midair and a mushroom cloud rising up in the heavens. When the cloud disperses, I see the Pleiades. It's as if somehow the nuclear explosion itself created the stars.* (Hill, p. 118)

The word *apocalypse* comes from the Greek *apocalypses* meaning "to reveal" or "a tearing away of the veil of that which conceals" (*kalyptein*). Embedded in the history of this word is the image of two realities between which exists a partition, a thin veil that conceals something of great value on the other side. Most often, this sense of "passing over" from one reality to the other is understood to be a function of the religious imagination in humans. One lifts the veil that separates the everyday, material, profane world and communes with the extraordinary, spiritual, and sacred world that is revealed on the other side. It is also imagined as a two-way street—something from the spiritual world can tear away the veil and insinuate itself into the mundane world. When the imagining ego beholds a visitation from "beyond the veil," it is experienced as a revelation. Let us call a revelation that is experienced in a waking state a "vision" and one that is experienced in a sleeping state a "dream." A hundred years of depth psychology has taught us something about how revelation is experienced within the psyche, and I would like to review some of the more salient features here.

A first principle of depth psychology is that the images that appear within the psyche as revelation use a symbolic language that is fundamentally different from the linear language of the everyday waking ego. Because they are mediated by the waking ego, however, the images of revelation are translated into the literalisms and concreteness that are the ego's normal mode of comprehension. The psychological task, then, is to de-literalize the image. For example, if you have a dream in which a voice tells you to kill your neighbor, it is important not to take this image literally. A more generative approach would be to explore the symbolic meaning of the image by considering your relationship with your outer neighbor in all its dimensions, as well as your relationship with the neighbors of your own psyche. What are neighbors, anyway, and how does "killing" affect your consideration of them? The waking ego must then take a moral stand with respect to the revelation. Why this image right now? What is being asked of me? If the ego blindly follows the injunction of the image and commits the murder, we could say that it has become possessed. The ego has lost its own choice-making power, a dangerous state indeed.

The stakes get higher when we consider a revelation taking place not at the level of an individual psyche, but in the psyche of humankind as a whole—the collective psyche. Consider, for example, the oldest collective revelation of the Western psyche and the origin of most people's images of apocalypse, the Book of Revelation. Over the centuries, this book has had a special appeal for literalists who see within the dark and destructive imagery a divine plan for the destruction of this sinful world and the coming of a new age of Light brought by the Messiah. While this imagery clearly has redemptive power, there are two main problems with literalizing it. First, it infantilizes the moral ego by taking away its choice-making powers with respect to the revelation. Without a discerning ego, it is quite possible to enact the will of false or evil gods. Second, it can hasten the actual destruction of the world through a process of "immanentizing the eschaton," that is, by making choices that accelerate the process of the world's destruction in order to fulfill the prophecy.

If we de-literalize the images, however, the story is more credible and has much more to say. From the point of view of the psyche, the mythology of the Book of Revelation provides imagery that speaks to the soul's yearning for a new way of being, a transformation of values, a new beginning. This call works at two levels. At the personal level the apocalyptic images of the Book of Revelation call for the death of habitual ego attitudes and a new life in relation to transpersonal values. At a collective level, these images call for the death of habitual cultural attitudes and a new cultural renaissance in relation to a new image of the divine. In Jung's view, apocalyptic imagery is a call from the collective unconscious for a new mythology taking shape in the objective psyche. He even goes so far as to assert that what is coming to meet us is an entirely new image of the divine that is being constellated in the objective psyche. From this point of view we may say that the purpose of any revelation is to bring about transformation, whether at the personal level or the collective level. Thus, when apocalyptic imagery arises spontaneously within the psyche it is acting as an initiation into a new mythology.

To understand the dynamics of this process more thoroughly we need to draw on a second principle of depth psychology, namely, that the psyche is a self-regulating process that is intentional. This means that the psyche is teleological; it pursues aims and intentions that are beyond the comprehension of the ego. This assertion is amply documented at the personal level by a century of clinical experience in which dreams and other manifestations of the personal unconscious are seen to have an uncanny knack for pinpointing the precise needs of a one-sided ego attitude. It is as if there is an "other" within our own psyche that knows just what we need to achieve optimum health and well-being. This "other" reveals itself in and through unconscious processes such as dreams, visions, body symptoms, illnesses, and so on. It is the responsibility of the moral ego to convert these messages into an ethical obligation by acting upon the hints given by the "other." This is not an easy thing to do since the compensatory hints given by the intentional psyche often run counter to the aims of the waking ego. It is for this reason that Jung states that an experience with this larger sense of the psyche is "always a defeat for the ego" (Coll. Wks. 14, para. 778). Moving beyond our habitual ego attitudes usually involves a painful crisis of letting go, but it always opens up a wider, non-ego perspective that represents a major advancement in personal growth and a new relationship with the divine.

The corresponding dynamic at the collective level is even more profound. Perhaps Jung states it best when he says:

> Our personal psychology is just a thin skin, a ripple on the ocean of collective psychology. The powerful factor, the factor which changes our whole life, which changes the surface of our known world,

which makes history, is collective psychology, and collective psychology moves according to laws entirely different from those of our consciousness. The archetypes are the great decisive forces, they bring about the real events, and not our personal reasoning and practical intellect....The archetypal images decide the fate of man. (Coll. Wks. 18, para. 371)

What Jung is saying here is that from the point of view of the psyche, the transpersonal patterns of images that he calls archetypes are not located within human beings. Rather, human beings are located in and subject to the intentions of the archetypes. Hence, when the archetypal images that have governed the collective body of a culture begin to shift and transform, so moves the fate of mankind. It is my contention that at the end of the twentieth century, a lethal century that has left 80 million people dead in massive epidemics of violence, we are witnessing in the imagery of apocalypse the transformation of archetypal dominants in our culture. If we literalize these images, which are often received as divine injunctions, we are in great peril. If, on the other hand, we receive these symbolic images in great humility and marshal the will to enact their symbolic hints as though they were opening our culture to new opportunities for healthy growth, we are in a position to receive the lineaments of a new mythology that is asserting itself in compensation to the one-sided attitudes of a myopic, murderous, and dysfunctional culture. Jung personified the new myth that is coming into being by calling it "the coming guest." In a letter near the end of his life he writes:

> Who is the awe inspiring guest who knocks at our door so portentously? Fear precedes him, showing that ultimate values already flow towards him. Our hitherto believed values decay accordingly, and our only certainty is that the new world will be something different from what we were used to....
>
> We have simply got to listen to what the psyche spontaneously says to us. What the dream, which is not manufactured by us, says, is just so....It is the Great Dream which has always spoken through the artist as a mouthpiece. All his love and passion (his "values") flow towards the coming guest to proclaim his arrival....
>
> What is the great Dream? It consists of the many small dreams and

the many acts of humility and submission to their hints. It is the future and the picture of the new world, which we do not understand yet. We cannot know better than the unconscious and its intimations. There is a fair chance of finding what we seek in vain in our conscious world. Where else could it be? (Adler, pp. 196–97)

If it is true that we are living within the intimations and intentions of transpersonal factors seeking to heal a culture that is dangerously out of balance and that an encounter with an archetypal image involves a "defeat for the ego," a painful process of letting go in order to grow, then we need to draw upon a third insight of depth psychology—how to die well. This dying of which we speak is not a literal death, but a symbolic death; however, the death imagery appears real enough when it enters the psyche and is virtually indistinguishable from a literal death. The fear generated by this process is intense, which is why many people refuse to engage the process. In the language of depth psychology, we learn to die well when we undergo an initiatory rite of passage, and it is in the psychology of initiatory process that we will find the true purpose and promise of apocalyptic imagery.

In his brilliant and inspiring study of apocalypse as a rite of passage, Michael Ortiz Hill begins by saying:

> Initiation into the apocalyptic mysteries seems to be a requisite for living a full and awake life during these exceedingly troubled times. This is not to say that the way of myth and dream is the only way of initiation—indeed I suspect one enters into the apocalyptic mysteries whenever one seriously and with concentration looks hard into the realities of who one is and into the times in which one is living. These dreams do, however, give a very vivid and raw picture of the psyche's perception of its situation. (Hill, p. 50)

The dreams to which Hill is referring are a collection of nuclear nightmares that he has arranged in the traditional three stages of initiatory process—separation, initiation, and return. These dreams are remarkable in their intensity and intelligence. They confirm many of the experiences I have had in my own nuclear dreams as well as those of others who have shared their nuclear dreams with me. Briefly summarized, the initiatory process of separation is often imaged by the psyche through apocalyptic imagery involving the suffering of children—children who are abandoned, seeking refuge, or in other ways suffering great pain. It is through witnessing the suffering of children, or any suffering, for that matter, that we can begin to separate from our own egoistic needs and move beyond them into the depths of our souls.

The second stage of initiation proper takes us into the landscape of the archetypal forces themselves. Here is encountered the beauty-terror of divine chaos, which dismembers the ego's attitudes and reconstitutes them into new forms, transforming the values by which the ego lives and imparting a gift of new knowledge that is meant to serve both the individual and the community as a healing elixir. The third stage of initiation, then, involves the return of the initiate to the embrace of the community bearing the gift that one has become, a healer and harbinger of a piece of the new myth.

The initiatory process of death and rebirth provides the most generative way of understanding apocalyptic nuclear images as they appear in dreams and cultural artifacts. By de-literalizing the images and understanding them as psychic messages that are trying to teach us something about how to transcend the destructive trajectory of modern culture, we are more likely to avert the literal and unconscious enactment of apocalypse in the world. As Hill (p. 53) puts it, "Rather than enacting apocalypse in the world unconsciously, we deliberately enter the apocalypse of the psyche for the sake of the world.... Such initiation is essential to living responsibly and with heart in an apocalyptic era." From a psychological point of view, this is what it means to "die well."

Before we turn our attention to the implications of these ideas for adult education, let me say that while we have entered into the psychic landscape of apocalypse via the imagery of Hiroshima and nuclear annihilation, there are other modes of access. With the breakdown of the Soviet Union, the disappearance of our "evil" twin brother, and the reduction of nuclear stockpiles, the images of apocalypse used by the collective unconscious have shifted somewhat to include other sources of apocalyptic destruction. Images of environmental catastrophe, invasion by aliens, annihilation by meteor strikes, genocidal viral epidemics, and so on, are increasingly populating our imaginal lives. However, the essential psychic dynamics remain the same—archetypal realities are shifting, a new mythology is being born, and we are being called in particular ways to undergo an initiatory rite of passage by entering into the most difficult psychic realities of the twentieth century for purposes of healing and transforming our culture and the world. The question that remains is to ask what forms of adult education can best prepare individuals to serve the aims of this process.

TOWARD A LIBERAL ARTS EDUCATION FOR APOCALYPSE

I am approached by a bright light. It has definite form. I recall feeling very excited and knowing that "it" was a messenger from God. It hands me a letter. I take the letter and feel thrilled that I am personally being sent a letter from God. I feel chosen! I keep saying to myself, "I knew it. I am special!" With a feeling of great elation and anticipation, I open the envelope. I read the greeting: "Dear Humanity," and feel a sense of disappointment because the letter is not addressing me personally. I feel as though I have just received some form of cosmic junk mail from God…like the "Dear Occupant" junk mail we all get from time to time. I experience a tremendous sense of deflation. I am disappointed to realize that I am not special after all. Suddenly I have a realization: I am humanity! A sense of joy and elation washes over me…a sense of "Oh, now I get it!" (Dream Network Bulletin)

Depth psychology has long asserted that the task of the second half of life is to undergo a relativization of the ego in which conscious life discovers that it is a part of a much larger psychic structure. Through undergoing a series of numinous or "divine" experiences that are initiatory in nature, the ego comes to realize that it is living in relation to an "other," which is variously represented as either "God" or "Spirit" in religious language or "the greater Self" in psychological language. The process by which the ego hears the call of the Self and navigates the required transformation is called "individuation."

We have seen how this process is affected by the presence of apocalyptic imagery. We do not enter the landscape of apocalypse for ourselves alone, but so that our people might live. The educational question is this: How can we as adult educators create the conditions for the possibility of grace, for the possibility that the divine archetypal realities will enter, teach, and transform the ego on behalf of personal and cultural healing? If the preceding analysis holds any truth, as I believe it does, then the fate of the Earth (or at least of the human species) hangs on the answer to this question. As Jung put it so succinctly, *"The fate of the earth rests on a single thread, and that thread is the individual human psyche."*

To answer this question I would like to share with you some of the teaching principles and techniques I have used over the years. As a professor of liberal studies in a bachelor of arts completion program for adults, I have had ample opportunities to teach directly out of what I think is most important. However, like any teacher, I am constrained in various ways by the aims of the institution in which I work. While I have been given a relatively free hand in choosing and shaping my courses, the constraints of designing classes that meet once a week for two and a half to three hours for ten weeks is often a drawback to the kind of intense encounters required to work in the shadow of apocalyptic imagery. With these disclaimers in mind, I would like to begin by making some general comments about curriculum before describing several of my classes in more detail.

It is not possible within the scope of this article to spell out a consistent and coherent curriculum for apocalypse. All I want to do is submit some of my own thinking for your consideration. For the purposes of exposition I will divide my comments on curriculum into two parts: traditional and nontraditional.

I have always been a firm believer in the idea that the proper study of mankind is mankind. To know anything of value, one must know who one is as a human being. I tend to follow the reasoning of Ernst Cassirer, who divides knowledge into two parts—philosophical anthropology and philosophical cosmology. While both are crucial, the anthropology takes priority since considerations of cosmology alone tend to be conditioned by human projections. Philosophical anthropology is always looking for the presuppositions of conscious activity and as such is the bedrock of all forms of inquiry. This is why every liberally educated person should have a strong background in life-span human development. To know who we are, we have to know from whence we came and to what we aspire. We also need to differentiate images and ideas about the feeling systems of the human soul so we understand the beauty and complexity of what it means to be human.

The same is true at the level of the collective—to know who we are as a culture we have to know from whence this culture came and to what it aspires. This is why every liberally educated person should have a richly elaborated set of images for cultural, biological, and geological time frames. When I taught middle-school-aged children I would always begin with a lesson in which we used yarn of different colors to make three time lines around the classroom. One color represented geological time, and its scale was billions of years. Another color represented biological time, and its scale was hundreds of millions of years. A third color represented cultural time from a global perspective, which was measured in terms of thousands of years. We then cut out images of different places, animals, and human events and placed them at the appropriate intervals with small cards that told the story of that image. We also left some room at the end of each line for imaginative constructions of possible futures. To me, being liberally educated means that you are continually adding knowledge to these time lines.

Further elaboration of these images can take place through literature, a medium that allows one to participate with other beings in their subjective states. This is particularly valuable with respect to the creation of a global culture in which we need to appreciate each other's cultural assumptions. As Jung once said, "Absolute truth, if there is such a thing, will only be heard in the concert of many voices." Reading literature by and about people from cultures other than our own opens our heart to a compassionate acceptance of diversity.

A third crucial element of a liberal education for apocalypse is a corollary of the first—a thorough understanding of the rise of Western culture and especially Western science and technology since the Renaissance, with a special emphasis on the triumphs and tragedies of the twentieth century. I often tell my adult students who see in the Western tradition the source of apocalyptic self-destruction, that to find a new way one must know how we got here. Since Western culture holds hegemony over much of the developed world, it is essential to understand the history of ideas that have supported it. I caution that it is important not to pre-judge Western culture. The danger of throwing the baby out with the bath water is too great.

The last area of traditional liberal learning that I would like to mention is in the area of service learning. It goes without saying that a major goal of liberal education is to create reflective human beings who are prepared for acting on behalf of social justice. We cannot be said to "know" something unless we are able to act upon it. The idea of using the classroom to facilitate group dynamics that explore the relationship between reflection and social action is an integral aspect of an education for apocalypse. It is the only way in which ideas can make a difference.

It is possible to obtain most of what I mention here in traditional centers of education, although the mode of delivery is crucial to the assimilation of the knowledge and this will vary considerably. Let us turn our attention now to the nontraditional learning and teaching that is crucial to a liberal education informed by apocalyptic imagery. Again, I can only hope to sketch the broad outline of these points.

The first and most important learning has to do with ritual process. To be liberally educated, each individual should know the elements of ritual practice and how to create ceremony both for one's self and for groups. It is important that the learner be able to tailor the ritual to the needs of the participants, and therefore a good knowledge of the world's religions and spiritualities is essential, as is the openness of heart required to practice in the spirit of what Matthew Fox calls "deep ecumenism" (see Fox 1988 and Madhi et al. 1987).

A second crucial area for this kind of learning is dream work. Every liberally educated person should know something about the biology and psychology of the dreaming process and how to extract meaning from their own dreams. (see, e.g., O'Conner 1986). A consideration of dreams quickly evolves into a consideration of visions, hallucinations, psychotic episodes, and other manifestations of "daimonic" reality. It also requires that one have a philosophy of human-divine interactions capable of accounting for the revelatory power of these psychic phenomena. But perhaps the most important aspect of doing dreamwork is that paying attention to dreams stimulates a corresponding response from the psyche itself. The result is an increase in consciousness. As the alchemists once knew, when an adept takes an interest in alchemy, alchemy takes an interest in the adept (Edinger 1985). So it is with dreams. If you take an interest in them, they will take an interest in you. In short, working with dreams is a sure way to directly experience the larger dimensions of the psyche.

A third important area of nontraditional learning is somatics, the understanding of the anatomy, physiology, and energetics of the human body (see Raheem 1987). Anatomy and physiology can be studied in traditional ways, but the integration of this knowledge into an awareness of the energetic pathways of the body is crucial. I tend to recommend that students begin with the study of a martial art or yoga for some period of time before turning their attention to a study of the chakra system. Further study requires experience with a variety of bodywork modalities and should include familiarity with the principles of acupuncture and the body meridians. A philosophical understanding of how trauma is held in body tissue and how this has manifested in the student is essential to this kind of inquiry.

Fourth, I think that a deeper nontraditional understanding and appreciation of natural phenomena is required (see Roszak et al. 1995). What I am saying is that in addition to traditional modes for understanding nature such as one acquires in botany, zoology, oceanography, astronomy, and geology classes, it is important to learn wilderness awareness skills that would allow us to bring more imagination to our perception of nature. A thorough grounding in natural history is important, as is knowing the names and characteristics of the flora and fauna that populate a particular region that is familiar to the student. Sitting in one spot for twenty-four hours, for example, allows one to enter into the subjectivity of the land in a unique way. Studying non-Western ideas about nature helps to liberate us from the hegemony of Western dualistic thinking. Developing a philosophy that can account for the subjectivity of natural phenomena, of the soul that inhabits nature (the *anima mundi*) is essential for cultivating this perspective.

And finally, I would say that a renewed valuation of the importance of personal expression is essential. Genuine revelation cannot do its work unless it is transformed into a form of communication. Whether through storytelling, poetry, creative writing, drawing, painting, or the plastic arts, the images that are welling up from the collective unconscious need to be enacted for the purposes of communication. The notion that artistic communication is reserved for specially trained individuals called "performers" does a great disservice to the numerous revelations occurring to less accomplished individuals. I advocate the creation of small ad hoc communities for the express purpose of telling dreams, reading personal poems, showing amateur art inspired by revelation, and telling stories of initiation. In the end, expression that is inspired by apocalyptic imagery has the power to transmit meaning and inspire transformation in the individuals who are its recipients. The insight provided by such images must be converted into a moral obligation, must be "enacted" for the purpose of incarnating the "coming guest."

Having reviewed some of the important educational principles that are foregrounded by a consideration of apocalyptic imagery, I would like to illustrate how I have incorporated some of these elements into my classes. My discussion will be necessarily brief, but perhaps it will be enough to stimulate your own imagination.

For several years now I have taught a sequence of three classes throughout the academic year. I begin the academic year in the fall with a class called "Alchemy and Science: Toward the Re-Imagination of Nature." It is the most intellectually rigorous of my classes since it is a consideration of the history of ideas in the West, beginning with the Pre-Socratics, that have led to the development of modern science, the way in which our imagination of nature changed with the advent of the positivistic sciences and the task of re-imagining nature that is now confronting us at the end of the second millennium. I lay the foundation for these ideas through the use of an excellent book by Richard Tarnas titled *The Passion of the Western Mind* that skillfully navigates the stream of ideas that have been privileged by the power elite of Western culture. These are the ideas that have shaped the cultural unconscious of the West, which has in turn shaped our own forms of thought.

When we get to the European Renaissance, I turn to follow the thesis in the first half of a book by Morris Berman, *The Re-Enchantment of the World*, in which he employs a dialectic that begins with the alchemical, hermetic worldview of the fourteenth to sixteenth centuries. He describes how this view was able to perceive the subjectivity of nature through its appreciation of the *anima mundi*, the soul of nature. He then shows how the antithesis of this worldview, often referred to as the mechanical or Cartesian-Newtonian worldview, de-animated nature through its assumptions about the nature of mind and reality. The social, economic, and political climate of the times were conducive to this shift away from the irrationalism of hermeticism and into a sober rationalism capable of wresting nature's secrets from her for the purposes of domination and control.

At this point in the course, we turn to a consideration of the myth of Frankenstein by watching the film *Mary Shelley's Frankenstein* and reading Theodore Roszak's incredible retelling of the Frankenstein myth, *The Memoirs of Elizabeth Frankenstein*. Special consideration is given to the tensions between the competing images of nature and how it affected the treatment of women. It is no coincidence that while the battle between hermetic and mechanical philosophy was being waged, millions of women were being burned at the stake as witches. Epidemics of violence are always a hallmark of worldview transitions. We then return to the exposition given by Tarnas as to the triumphs and failures of mechanical science, the revolution of thought initiated by Einstein, and the possibility of a new synthesis of the hermetic and mechanical worldviews, a vision of nature that restores her soul through a process of re-animation and that relativizes the role of the human to one amongst many in a "council of all beings."

In addition to writing a formal essay that tells the story of the transition between worldviews and speculates on the newly emerging view of nature that is coming out of the new sciences, students are also expected to engage with the point of view of various characters in Roszak's novel. They are then asked to complete an "*anima mundi* project" that involves some kind of experience in a natural setting. Using whatever medium they choose, students are asked to illustrate their engagement with the ideas and feelings generated by the class material. I believe the themes that are covered by this course are one way of helping students understand the cultural thought forms that constrain and limit their habitual thoughts about the environment and prepare them to be receptive to new possibilities about the relationship between humans and nature. The class is an attempt to create the conditions for the possibility of new insights that will transform the student's relationship to nature. To my way of thinking, this is education for apocalypse.

A second course that I teach in the winter quarter is called "Interdisciplinary Perspectives on Childhood and Adolescence." Just as the Alchemy and Science class attempts to trace the dynamics of Western culture that forms the cultural context in which we live, so this class on childhood and adolescence traces the dynamics of individual development that form the psychological and spiritual context in which we find ourselves as reflective adults. We begin with the thesis that as adults we never see children as they really are but only as we imagine them to be, so we must imagine deeply. To deepen our imagination we must engage the stories we tell ourselves about our own childhood since we have an unconscious tendency to project our feelings about our own childhood onto the children with whom we have contact.

What are these stories that so secretly inform our perceptions? To inquire into them, students create a portfolio of childhood memories called *Reveries on Childhood*. Using the idea of reveries as explicated by Gaston Bachelard in *The Poetics of Reverie*, we write one story a week, revise it, and enter it into the portfolio with accompanying pictures or art work. For many people, the prospect of dredging up old memories is a daunting task and for this reason each person is paired with a "chum" for the duration of the quarter who can serve as a sounding board and emotional companion. The affect generated by this opportunity to enter the doorway of childhood is often quite intense. After ten years of teaching this class, I am no longer stunned by the number of adult students who self-identify as being either physically, sexually, or emotionally abused. Paralleling this internal work, each student is required to observe a child in a natural setting on three separate occasions and to write about what they have experienced by applying the ideas discussed in class and the feelings that have been constellated through their encounter with the child.

The intellectual work is also intense, beginning with an article on the history of childhood by Lloyd DeMause (1974) that begins with the statement, "The history of childhood is a nightmare from which we have just begun to awaken." Many students are brought to tears by reading about the treatment of children as it has evolved in the Western world. We then consider the vicissitudes of the human sciences as we try to understand the various psychological maps that have been laid on children in order to understand them. We study one of them in more depth, namely, Erikson's stages of ego development. Early in the course we try to notice how our imagination of children is conditioned by our own race, class, and gender. What kind of kids show up in our minds when we think about child development? By including readings from diverse cultures, we expand our imaginations to include children of all kinds.

Issues of gender bias are engaged through Gilligan's (1982) critique of Erikson's stage theory. The secular bias of most developmental theory is engaged through readings on transpersonal developmental psychology (see Whitmont 1982 and Rudolf Steiner). The ego bias of most developmental theory is engaged by reading about the essentialist "acorn" theory of James Hillman (1996). Then we study the issue of discipline and punishment as it affects the development of conscience in the child and hence in the adult students who are studying it. This subject is particularly engaging since it is relevant to adult students as both grown children and as current or prospective parents. We are then in a position to take on the subject that makes many students anxious—the wounded child. While various readings are used to display a variety of perspectives on wounding and healing (see Jeremiah 1990), the key to this class is to let each person do his or her own emotional work through the use of artistic drawings. Using a meditation, silence, and large pieces of newsprint, each student is asked to make four drawings: the idealized archetypal child, the child in the family, the abandoned child, and the child as carried by the adult. No more that five minutes is given to the completion of each picture in order to allow the psyche to address each theme unmediated by the critical ego. Quite often, healing is received simply through the creation of the images.

Finally we are in a position to take on the question of adolescence. Time constraints make it impossible to do justice to this rich topic, so I do what I think is most important—rites of passage. We consider the archetype of initiation that constellates in adolescence and talk about our own experiences with it and how it is currently being tended by the culture. The next week we have a guest speaker who works with at-risk adolescents using ritual process and initiation techniques. The class concludes with a consideration of the future of children in our culture and encouragement to follow up on the themes of the class by taking another class taught by a different teacher the following quarter titled "Children and Social Policy." We end with a ritual circle into which we invite our own inner child, the child we observed, our own children, the children we have read about, the suffering children of the world, and the spirit of those children yet to be born. We bless them, honor them, and vow to work on their behalf. Then we let them go. A meditation on children and childhood is an essential aspect of an education for apocalypse.

Each spring quarter I try to teach a class that has something to do with dreams and/or mythological studies. Over the years this has included courses with such titles as "The History of Dream Interpretation," "Dreams and the Earth," "Cross-Cultural Perspectives on the Spiritual Quest," "The Legacy of Joseph Campbell," and "An Inquiry into the Myth of the Holy Grail." All of these classes are designed to teach students how to relate to the products of the personal and collective imagination. I would like to share with you short descriptions of two of these classes, beginning with "An Inquiry into the Holy Grail," since I believe that this myth has much to teach us about apocalyptic revelation.

Understanding the grail myth is a valuable tool for clarifying the nature of divine-human interaction. We begin our inquiry by reading von Eschenbach's *Parzifal* before the first class. To me, this is the most psychologically rewarding version of the myth because it was written prior to the Albigensian crusade, which severely curtailed the ability of writers to include the earlier pagan elements of the myth. Later versions of the grail myth lose their psychological power as they attempt to Christianize the original story. Our first class sessions are spent setting the historical context of the myth beginning with Celtic Europe and Ireland, Roman Britain, the historical King Arthur, and the events of ninth-century Europe, which many believe is the historical period that is mirrored in Eschenbach's tale. We then turn from this exoteric history to a consideration of the esoteric (or hidden) history of the myth, since it is in these stories that the deeper symbolic levels of the grail legends are accessed. We pause at this point in the class to develop a critical assessment of the respective truth claims of exoteric and esoteric histories. We then dive in to the esoteric material because it is through reading these stories, whether historically accurate or not, that the psyche of the student is most activated. We pay special attention in our historical considerations to the evolution of the church's attitude toward individual religious experience, noting how the church has a vested interest in controlling revelatory images of the divine.

Every class session begins with either a meditation or a visualization relevant to the assigned readings for that week. Students are asked to keep a journal of images as they come up in these class meditations and visualizations, including any relevant dream images that arise during the week. Once the historical context of the myth is set, the class then turns to consider three symbolic dimensions of the myth: the role of women and the figure of Sophia; the development of the ego as represented by Parzifal, Gawain, and Firefiz; and the problem of evil at the Castle of Wonders.

Discussion of these topics invariably leads to questions about the role of the feminine in the human psyche and the historical eclipse of the Goddess in Western religion; the need for the questing ego to learn holistically through head (intellect), heart (feeling), and hands (will); and the psychodynamics of evil understood as "passion without constraint." The relationship between the rise of romantic love in the Western psyche and its relationship to experiences of divine love is an integral aspect of this learning. A key text we use to understand the development of the story is *The Speech of the Grail* by Linda Sussman. The author's thesis is that the grail myth is itself an initiation into the power of speech, the ability of the ego to mediate and express the inspiration that comes from the divine through the imagination.

To understand more deeply what the author means by an initiation into speech, each student is asked to construct a mask of a character from the grail myth. Made out of plaster of paris, these masks are contoured to the faces of the students so that they can be worn. At our closing ceremony, each student is invited to put on the mask, become the character of the mask, step behind a podium that is alight with candles, and give a speech using the voice of that character. Many students report a kind of transit made by their consciousness wherein their waking ego fades and they are animated by the spirit of the mask. Having witnessed many of these mask speeches, I can report that there is considerable variation in students' abilities to surrender ego control to the spirit of the mask. Voice inflections, accents, figures of speech, and so on are all indicators of the relative presence or absence of ego dynamics. But regardless of how deep they go, every student is given a lesson in the nature and dynamics of spiritual experience. The Grail class ends with a consideration of how this myth may be the harbinger of a new form of spirituality taking shape in the human psyche, a spirituality in which the human has become a vessel for numinous experience and therefore a carrier of divine meaning. We consider the possibility that each one of us *is* the grail and our life purpose is embodied in the acts of speech we make on behalf of the divine.

The last class I will discuss here is titled "Dreams and the Earth." This class has several goals: to learn how to tend dreams, to learn how to listen to the voice of nature as it manifests in dreams, and to create a supportive community of dream workers. Most often, I teach this class outside of the university setting so that I have more freedom to engage ritual practice and ceremony. However I make a strong point that this class is not intended to be psychotherapy, that I do not "interpret" dreams, nor do I prescribe "treatment." Instead, I take an educational approach to dreams, teaching various techniques for cultivating or "tending" dream images. While there is obviously a great deal of social interaction and individual revelation that occurs in class, I work primarily as a facilitator and instructor rather than a psychotherapist.

The class begins with an overview of both the safety and discovery factors that contribute to successful work with dream groups. We then turn our attention to the history of dreams as they have been understood around the world, as well as more recent information on the biology of the dreaming state. Then, using a model developed by Stephen Aizenstat, we carefully examine the assumptions of what he calls "the multidimensional psyche." We devote a week to the study of each of the three dimensions of the psyche—the personal unconscious as explored by Freud, the collective unconscious as explored by Jung, and the world unconscious as explored by post-Jungian, archetypal psychologies. Each dimension of the psyche has various techniques that are used to explore the meaning of dream images. While most dreams do refer to personal material that is couched in cultural imagery, the goal of this class is to move toward those dreams that come from the world unconscious, because they seem to carry something of the intentionality of nature herself. Most often, these kinds of dreams contain elaborate natural landscapes as well as a variety of animals that have varying abilities to "speak" in the dream. The possibility is entertained that these images exist independently of our observation of them and that this dimension in which they exist corresponds to shamanic realities as described by most indigenous cultures (see Noel 1997). We then learn what we can about how to navigate these realities using the dream images as guides.

To learn more about the nature of these imaginal landscapes, the class is invited to participate in a sweat lodge experience. While the sweat is done in a traditional way by a traditional ceremonial leader, the psychic images that are encountered while in the lodge bear a striking resemblance to the images that appear in dreams. In this way, an understanding of the dynamics of the deep imagination forms. Meanwhile, the class begins to develop a field of trust through the rituals of dreamwork and the sweat ceremony that serves to encourage the psyche to show herself in more revealing ways.

Near the end of the class we conduct a two-day dream incubation in nature as a way of learning more about the dynamics of the world unconscious and the voice of the Earth. Of course, dream incubations are about healing, and so each person must find a relationship to a wound that needs the healing grace of divine intervention. We begin by setting up camp in a wilderness setting. Whenever possible, I ask a person skilled in wilderness awareness skills to spend several hours with us to teach us about the animals and landscape in which we will be dreaming. Students then form dyads and begin work on a particular dream that seems relevant to their request for healing. We then spend several hours sitting in solitude as we invoke the spirits of the land to help us in our work.

After a light supper and a period of solitude in which we witness the transition from daylight to dusk to night, we prepare for the incubation ritual by sitting in a circle around an altar that consists of candles, sacred objects, natural forms from the land we are inhabiting, and masks of dream figures that have been created by each person. When the drumming begins, participants go one by one to a seat that faces a mirror, watch themselves place the mask on their face, and experience themselves transit into the spirit of the mask. They then turn to the assembled group, the drumming stops, and the mask speaks spontaneously. What is said is always profound and unpredictable. I have found that the deeper and longer the preparation time for the mask ceremony, the more likely the ego is transcended and a genuine transit into the spirit of the mask is made.

When everyone is done, we ritually enter into a period of silence that is not broken until late in the morning on the following day. During this silence the dreamers are encouraged to pay careful attention to their experience, since revelation is not limited to the dream state. Usually, the morning silence is spent journaling or using art materials to capture the essence of the revelatory images. We then ritually break the silence and begin a series of talking circles through which we process the experience of the incubation. We close by giving thanks to the land. Most of the rest of the class is spent trying to make sense of what we experienced during the dream incubation. Students usually leave with a sense that nature does indeed have a subjective interiority that is accessible to the human psyche as the "voice of the Earth."

BEST WISHES

This essay began with a meditation on Hiroshima as an invocation to apocalypse. The nature and dynamics of apocalyptic imagery were discussed from the point of view of depth psychology, which sees in such images examples of the presence of divine revelation. Given the ubiquitous presence of apocalyptic imagery in our culture—from nuclear threats to genocidal wars to movies and music about Armageddon, not to mention dreams and religious mythology—it seems imperative that we de-literalize the images in order to minimize the risk of making them real. Instead, I suggested an alternative way of understanding apocalyptic imagery as potent symbolic forms, a way that preserves their symbolic power but de-potentiates their destructive power. This alternative way suggests that apocalyptic images are indicators that transpersonal archetypal realities are shifting and that the fate of the human species hangs upon a conscious interaction with these archetypal realities.

We then turned to the question of what kind of education would prepare individuals for apocalyptic encounters. I foregrounded several educational principles that I think are essential for preparing the individual to be a vessel for divine imagery and gave examples from my own teaching practice for the purposes of illustration. I sincerely hope that you have been stimulated by these words. Perhaps you recognize a kindred spirit in my own experience or perhaps you want to know more about how to pursue your learning in similar areas. In any case, I wish you well on your terribly magnificent journey. I leave you with this dream upon which to meditate:

> *I dreamt the world came to an end. There are tidal waves, earthquakes, war, hurricanes, volcanic eruptions, tornadoes, storms, pestilence, floods. The trees are torn up by their very roots. People are scattered around, dead, or like zombies, walking dead, soon to be dead. I see all my past friends, relatives, family, visions before my eyes; my life flashes before me and disappears. There are these large cracks in the earth and suddenly, from out of these cracks, come children, like seeds from the earth. But they are hurt, and burnt terribly, suffering, tired and frightened, I only know that I must get them out of the wreckage.*
>
> *I am tying leaves around their feet because their little feet are so battered, and we have to go a long distance to get to the new ground. I am carrying the smallest ones that can't even walk yet, I am not sure where we are going. It is a place that is warmer, I tell them. I must keep their spirits up. The children must be saved so that they can start a new world.*

But they are so weak, so tired, so little. I keep telling them this new place is just a little farther. Once there, they can rest and sleep and heal and play. They are crying and saying, "But we are tired. We hurt all over. We're burnt and bleeding. We can't walk any more." And I am desperate, because I know we must get out of the forest, out of the devastation that surrounds us, or I will lose them all.

I, too, am dying and must stay alive enough to lead the children to the new place, then to teach them how to take care of themselves and the world so they can begin anew. I am not afraid of dying in this dream, only afraid of dying before I can impart enough information to the children. My life has become unimportant to me beyond this. I am profoundly aware that when I die, I will continue to be there in the children, but first I must get them to a green place where they can learn to play again. I tell them stories, always, so that they will envision a greener land. (Hill, p. 130)

8

Liberating Psyche in the Aftermath of 9/11

A talk given at Antioch University/Seattle, December 11, 2001

> *As our case is new, so we must think anew, and act anew. We must disenthrall ourselves, and then we shall save our country.*
> —Abraham Lincoln

PSYCHE LOVES STORY. If, as my title implies, Psyche is in chains and awaits her liberation, then perhaps we can ameliorate her suffering in the meantime with a short story. And this is it: One day Roger Tory Peterson, the famous ornithologist and author of numerous field guides on birds, was walking on a busy city sidewalk in New York with a friend on a fine spring day. Suddenly he stopped and was quite still for a moment. He turned to his friend and said, "Did you hear that yellow-bellied sapsucker?" And proceeded to perfectly mimic the bird's lilting voice. His friend was astounded, saying that he had not heard a peep and how could Roger hear such a subtle sound in the backdrop of the sounds of the city anyway? Peterson looked at his friend and pulled out a quarter from his pants pocket. He said, "Watch this!" and flipped the coin into the air and onto the sidewalk, where it made a tinkling sound. Immediately the people on the crowded sidewalk turned to stare at the shiny coin. Peterson turned to his friend and said simply, "We hear what we are listening for."

So while I cannot predict what brought you to a lecture such as this with its quirky title and odd description, I can tell you what I hope you are *not* listening for. I hope you are not listening for a political analysis of the situation in Afghanistan or an economic explanation of third-world resentment toward the United States. I hope you are not looking for me to assist you in excoriating our president's foreign policy, nor do I want to comment on what to do about the starving millions in Afghanistan or anywhere else. These are important, pressing issues, but I leave them for someone else. Nor do I hope you have come for some clarity regarding the suspension of civil rights or an analysis of what Bush was thinking when he said that we are "drawing a line in the sand against the evil ones." Important issues all, but not what I am hoping to serve you tonight. Instead, I hope you are listening for some image, some fragment of a story, a single line of poetry, a felt inner experience, that might touch your soul at the same depth that your soul was touched as you watched the planes eviscerate the World Trade Center, as you witnessed human beings jumping into thin air to certain death, of bodies crushed by rubble, of heroes running into collapsing buildings. I am hoping that some random image in my speech will touch you in the same place you are touched when you picture in your mind someone you knew, or a friend of a friend, who died in the attack. Or the many strong and conflicted feelings you have upon witnessing the carnage being visited upon the citizens of Afghanistan, of families starving to death in each other's presence, of frozen bodies and crying children. For tonight we are leaving the daylight of the political world and its objectivating statistics, blaming tactics, ideas about collateral damage and acceptable risk. Instead, we are taking a different turn and embarking in a different direction, a direction inward and down, a movement into the realm of the soul.

One more disclaimer: I am speaking to you today as a citizen of the city of Seattle. The planes on September 11 did not wipe out the Columbia Tower in downtown Seattle, nor did they take out the capitol building in Olympia. If they had, many people I know would be dead or injured and I would be assuming a different stance in both my audience and myself. My heart goes out to the survivors in New York, but perhaps our distance from ground zero will assist us in probing for the deeper significance of this tragedy.

This underworld journey we are about to undertake may seem strange to you at first. It's like entering the twilight zone. So let us cross this threshold gently by invoking the name of one of the great gentlemen of our nation, Abraham Lincoln. In the darkness of a terrible and divisive war, he said these words, "As our case is new, so we must think anew, and act anew. We must disenthrall ourselves, and then we shall save our country." What I would give for a national leader who could speak such words today and know what they mean! The value of these words for us tonight is that in one economical move, Lincoln links the political future of our democracy to the state of the human psyche. He tells us that there is some part of us that is enthralled, held in bondage, tied in chains, and that only by waking up to that condition, and liberating ourselves from it, can our country be saved. It is this image that forms the basis of my talk tonight because I believe that the events of September 11 are revelatory. They carry the radical power of waking us up to the situation in which we find ourselves. The fireballs of the World Trade Center can shatter the illusions under which we live. It is time to break the trance so that we may assist our country to become a mature leader for the free world. This would be a country worth saving, one in which we could take great pride.

DEPTH PSYCHOLOGY AND THE TRANCE

But how does one recognize that one is in a trance? Just as in the dream state there is no way to know with certainty that you are dreaming, so too it is extremely difficult to know anything about our unconscious states. So how do we break out of our thralldom? How can we liberate psyche? To answer this question we need to work with a method that has the power to objectivate unconscious states so that they can be revealed. In the postmodern universe in which we live, method is all, for it is now a commonplace assumption that the methods we use to analyze anything determine what can become an answer. In other words, the truths that are revealed are determined by the questions we ask. So let us ask good questions! My own method of choice for asking good questions is depth psychology, that lineage of ideas that emerged from the Romantic movement, gave birth to psychoanalysis and flourished in the work of C. G. Jung, Marie Louise von Franz, James Hillman, Thomas Moore, and Robert Sardello, to name a few. Before we make a more radical move toward image thinking, let me address briefly three key ideas to this method that will clarify its power to ask the questions we need.

The first idea essential to understanding depth psychology is that it privileges the imagination. In the contemporary mainstream world of ideas, not to mention the culture of materialist and capitalist America, this assertion continues to be met with derision and scorn. Witness the place of art in our public schools. It is a radical idea, even for psychology. It says, in Hillman's words, that depth psychology is a theory of mind that "starts neither in the physiology of the brain, the structure of language, the organization of society, nor the analysis of behavior, but in the processes of imagination" (1985, p. xi). Jung put it even more succinctly when he said that psyche is image; it is the imaginative possibilities in our nature. The imagination, not our ideas about it, is the well out of which our experience flows. If we are going to dissolve psyche in her own water, then what this tells us is that we must cross the threshold into the underworld clothed in images if we have any hope of returning. I will return to this notion later.

A second idea crucial to the depth psychological perspective is that in some deep and mysterious way, we are divided against ourselves. Perhaps St. Paul said it most succinctly, "For I do not do the good I desire, but rather the evil that I do not desire. Now if I should do what I do not wish to do, it is not I that do it, but rather sin which dwells within me." Now here is an image of estrangement, what Paul called "sin," that accounts for many of our strange behaviors. How often do we commit an act in perfect consciousness, but with the shocking sense that we are being controlled by an alien being within ourselves? (Tillich 1948, p. 159) And how can we claim to know much about the motives of other human beings, much less the intentions of the body politic or even the cosmos, if we cannot even know why we do the things that we do? This "I" that thinks it knows what it is doing depth psychology calls the "ego," and that strange force in my limbs that compels me to do things I do not understand it calls "the unconscious." Depth psychology is the study of the relationships between the ego and the unconscious. Its goal is for the ego to establish a conscious relationship with the unconscious. When this happens, forces are released from within the unconscious that guide the individual to individuate, that is, to fulfill his or her destiny by becoming the person s/he was always meant to be. Jung said that this goal is an essentially religious concern because it restores us to our rightful place in the world. It gives us an identity and a cosmos in which we belong. So while the unconscious is the repository of the best and worst of ourselves, it is also the place wherein we meet and converse with the divine. I will return to this notion later.

And third, depth psychology asserts that the push of the unconscious into the affairs of the ego has an intentionality about it. Random thoughts and images do not simply appear on the screen of awareness. What "shows up" in our minds is regulated by an intelligence that informs the core of our being. That intelligence is akin to the ancient Greek notion of the *logos*, one of the most enduring and generative principles of Western thought. According to Richard Tarnas, the historian of ideas, the idea of the logos assumes that "the universe possesses and is governed according to a comprehensive regulating intelligence, and that this same intelligence is reflected in the human mind, rendering it capable of knowing the cosmic order" (1991, p. 47). Different religious and philosophical traditions have different names for this intelligence. Mainstream Christians use theological categories and call it God or the Holy Spirit. Esoteric Christians personify it and call it Sophia, or holy wisdom. Scientists objectivate it and call it cause and effect. Jungians psychologize it, calling it the Greater Self. They say it is the driving force behind the individuation process itself. When we live in accord with the promptings of the Self, we are living in accord with "God's will." Phenomena such as synchronicities, dreams, intuitions, visions, and seemingly random thoughts all play a role according to some intentionality that is different from the ego's. This intentionality has plans for us, which the ego has a moral obligation to know and act upon. If we would but listen, every dream is trying to tell us something.

When we take this idea out of our personal orbit and use it as a lens with which to view the world, we see that the bombing of the World Trade Center is a bad dream taking place at the level of the world psyche. And like the bad dream I had last week, it has something urgent to tell me. This ability to traverse from the personal to the collective, to see our own psychology writ large in the world, and vice versa, is a boon of the depth psychological method. It harkens back to the old alchemical formula "as above, so below." Anything we can perceive in the outer world has a correspondence to something in the inner world. It makes it possible to imagine that the personal is intensely political. With an insight like this into the logos of the individual and world soul, it is no wonder Jung spent the last part of his life psychologizing about the nature of the God image and looking for parallels in the religious mythologies of the world. These are rich waters, indeed, and I simply map them out a bit for you so that we can ask a different set of questions than those posed by other methods of inquiry.

So we now have three ideas at our disposal: that psyche is image, that within her there is an ego and an unconscious in dynamic relationship to one another, and that she carries with her a mysterious intelligence that operates both within me and within the world at large. By allowing these ideas to inform the language by which we descend into the darkness of September 11, perhaps we can get to the bottom of this nightmare.

IMAGES OF PSYCHE IN CHAINS

So let's take another turn in and down. Time now to turn from concept to image. Allow me to paint four pictures for you, if I may, four ways in which to imagine that psyche is in chains and seeks to be liberated by us, her heroes (whether we be male or female). Remember that psyche is image, so that the characters and events in these stories are windows into your own soul. These stories preceded September 11, but in my opinion, their power is constellated anew by recent events.

Picture number one: The Wasteland, that indelible image so beautifully drawn by Wolfram von Eschenbach in his early thirteenth-century poem of the Holy Grail, entitled *Parzifal*. Picture this: a desolate and dreary landscape with felled dead trees and gray dust in the midst of which nothing is living. The people who inhabit this place never smile and the king of the grail castle is incapacitated by a wound to his genitals that causes him immense suffering. In this realm, nothing new will grow; there is no song, no dance. There is only lament. We learn later in the story that this condition has been brought about through enchantment. The land and its people are in a trance. The perpetrator is Klingschor, the evil king, who obtained his dark power by castrating himself. His goal is to win the grail for himself. Opposed to him is the figure of Parzifal, a "dull man slowly wise," one of the first characters in European literature who develops psychologically. At crucial turning points within the story, Parzifal encounters grieving women, each of whom has some bit of knowledge to reveal to him. For our purposes, it is enough to imagine that psyche is here pictured as a land that is in thrall to powerful forces that are located within the sexual realm. Psyche is in chains because of distorted love, and all of the evil in the Wasteland is potential vitality in need of transformation.

Picture number two: the story of Orpheus and Eurydice. Orpheus is that figure in Greek mythology who could, through singing and the playing of his lyre, make the rocks and woods move, the animals tame, and streams halt in their courses. Through his sweet speech, Orpheus could bring to civilization men who were insensitive to virtue as though made of stone and those who were crazed and maddened by the pleasures of the body" (Warden, p.90). Perhaps if our politicians and educators knew of Orphic power, they would cut arts programs last instead of first. The story goes that Orpheus's beloved wife, Eurydice, the source of his inspiration, was bitten by a snake and her soul was sent to Hades, the underworld. The grief of this separation from his soul mate was too great. Orpheus was determined to get her back. Using his musical power, Orpheus descended into the underworld, first taming the three-headed dog Cerberus, who guarded the entry to Hades, then cajoling, for a song, a ride across the river Styx by Charon the ferryman. Once he arrived before the lord of the realm, he charmed the king and queen with his music and won the release of his dead wife's shade. There was only one stipulation. Orpheus could not look back at his wife during the ascent back to the world of light. The return was long and arduous. When Orpheus stepped past the entrance to the threshold of the underworld and into the light, he could contain himself no longer. Her turned to embrace his wife, who, unfortunately, had yet to step into the light. Orpheus lost Eurydice a second time. Despite the tragic ending, we learn something in this story about the power of music in the realm of the underworld. Psyche, the source of our inspiration, is held prisoner there. Navigating in the underworld is not accomplished by ideas or by beliefs. To get to her we must use the imaginal arts. For our purposes, it is the redemptive power of the imagination that is the central motif of this story.

Picture number three: the Omelas story. This is a parable told by Ursula LeGuin, one of our great Northwest writers (see Abrams, pp. 108–14). She speaks about a shining city named Omelas, "bright-towered by the sea." Here everyone is happy, the streets are clean, the public buildings proud. In Omelas there is no monarchy, no slavery, no advertising, no television, no secret police. The people are mature, intelligent, passionate adults who love their children and their city. Great parades are a source of civic pride, and joy abounds in all parts of life. Except one. Apparently everyone knows that it is there, but most quickly overlook the fact. It seems that in some small, dark room beneath one of the beautiful public buildings there lives alone a child of nine or ten. This child survives in abject misery. Its naked body is covered in filth, and it is fed a thin gruel of cornmeal and grease. No one ever speaks a kind word to it. Those are the rules. The child used to scream for help at night and cry a good deal, but now it only makes a kind of whining noise and speaks less and less often. It is so thin there are no calves to its legs; its belly protrudes; its buttocks and thighs are a mass of festered sores, as it sits in its own excrement continually. And this is the way it must be, for everyone in Omelas understands that their happiness, the beauty of their city, the tenderness of their friendships, the health of their children, the abundance of their harvest—all depend wholly on this child's abomination. They are not without compassion. It's just that they know that without that wretched child sniveling in the dark, they would not be able to love their own children as well, nor would their music be as profound, their architecture as noble. It is a harsh picture, but accurate in its depiction of the dilemma of the American conscience. But the story is not finished. It seems that every once in a while, after viewing the child through a slit in the dungeon door, a man or a woman will fall silent for a few days and then will leave home. The viewers walk alone or in pairs down the silent streets at night, past the beautiful buildings, the warm-lit houses, the fields outside of town. They walk ahead into the darkness and do not come back. They are the ones who leave Omelas, and where they are going is into the unknown. They are the ones who, through compassion for a child in chains, have found the will to renounce the thralldom that binds privilege to oppression.

And lastly, a dream. One of my own, dreamed ten years ago, but which is still teaching me today. It goes like this. A dinner party is being prepared in a large room at the United Nations. I am seated at one of the tables. In the front of the large room, there is a table of dignitaries. The people in charge of this event are quite concerned that everything proceed smoothly. Before the main speeches, the entire room pauses to honor those U.N. soldiers who have died in the line of duty. I see a picture of a young woman in her uniform, holding her baby. Then I see another picture of two young men with their families. The camera seems to back up as more and more pictures of soldiers who have died are revealed. The emotion in the room becomes palpable; the grief is strong. People are crying. Finally, a well-respected U.N. leader stands up and speaks in a poignant voice. His words are these: "We are all, myself included, held in bondage by forces we must begin to identify and break free of, that we must give form to and consume. The time is now for huge international shifts of consciousness!" He says one more line, which is a real zinger. And then the lights go out. When they come on again, there is loud music and confetti flying through the air. Champagne fountains begin to flow. The people at my table all look toward one another, wondering if what they had heard really happened. When I am asked about it, I say simply, "I think this is part of some larger lesson plan." This dream has much to tell us about the nature of psyche's thralldom. It says that we are all held in bondage and that the key to our freedom lies in identifying the forces that hold us there. But the lesson does not stop there. It says that upon giving form to these oppressive forces, we must consume them, take them into ourselves, digest and assimilate them. Now this is an image that has great depth. Let us hold it as our work proceeds.

So now we are armed with four images of psyche in chains. She is the land, held under a spell that has been generated by distorted desire. She is in the underworld awaiting her liberator, who can navigate that realm only through the imagination. She is a miserable child in a fetid room awaiting those strong enough to renounce their privilege. She is our self, held in bondage, trying to separate from its trance so that we can help to bring about a different future than the one predicted by our current path.

ENTERING THE IMAGINAL LANDSCAPE OF 9/11

Time now to enter directly into the imaginal landscape of September 11. I propose to do this in two steps, being ever mindful of the powerful forces that swirl around this subject. A mighty wind blows in the land of 9/11 and we must approach it with care. In the first step, I would like to jar your own memories of that day and its aftermath by telling something of my own story. Then I would like to invite you to enter fully into that landscape by means of an imaginal exercise. But first, my version of events.

I have often thought that where you were and what you were doing when you first heard the news of September 11 may reveal something about your destiny and the role you are being asked to play in the healing process. As I tell my story, I invite you to remember back to your own situation, remaining curious about how the context in which you heard this news might carry some clues for you about the role that destiny has assigned you. It is as if, in addition to a time stream from the past that pushes us into the present, there is also a time stream from the future that is reaching back to pull us into our destiny. In special moments, such as presidential assassinations, near-death accidents, and major catastrophes like that of September 11, we are given a brief glimpse into the formative forces of our own future, as well as those of our country.

Such was certainly the case for me. On September 11 I was a forty-five-minute drive to the nearest phone, camped in a wilderness area on the east side of Mt. Rainier. I was one of four guides leading a vision quest experience for eight brave souls who were planning to sit in their ritual circles seeking a vision with which to illuminate the purpose of their lives. Using depth psychological language, the vision quest is designed to lead the ego into the underworld, where it is given an opportunity to die to the habitual forms of the day world and be initiated into the gifts of the Greater Self. For indigenous people, this right of passage was meant to serve as an initiation into the mysteries of death, for they knew that only by living in a conscious relationship with death could they walk a path of beauty. Contemporary rites of passage seek a similar outcome. So after months of ritual preparation, of talking circles, prayer ties, sweat lodges, and all the rest, we arrived at our base camp near Bumping Lake. On the morning of September 11, we set off together on a long hike through old-growth forest to choose our ritual spot in which to sit. At sunrise the next day, each person set off alone to return to that place to seek his or her vision. Each one then created a circle out of prayer ties and sat in the middle, prepared to endure three days of fasting. Meanwhile, back in camp, the four guides who had been dutifully participating in increasingly skimpy meals were ecstatic that they could once again eat. Two guides left to make the long drive to town to pick up supplies, and it was upon their return later in the day that I first learned what had happened.

At first, I thought that my colleagues were joking, and it took some time to establish the relative validity of the information. But in the absence of television images pounding the facts into our consciousness at the rate of 198 replays in forty-eight hours, the four of us were left to allow our own impressions of the facts to do their soul work on us. It took another trip into town the following day to fix the images in our hearts. And what of those who were still in their vision circles? We left them there. Furthermore, the extremity of their emotional state after three days alone and without food suggested that we should not tell them about these events on the first day of their return. It was only after the second day that we initiated a discussion about re-incorporation and the return to civilization after a week of being in the wilderness. We began by telling them that the world they left was very different from the world they were about to rejoin and that the news they were about to hear had a great deal to tell them about their vision quest. Then we told them. I will not speak at this time about the dynamics of how news of this magnitude penetrates a soul that has been open and bleeding for days. Suffice it to say that the psychic experiences that each of these people acquired during their vision quest was considerably deepened in light of the events of September 11. In these matters, there are no accidents, and the quest participants were left to ponder the intersection of their personal rites of passage with their country's.

My own feelings were crystallized in our final sweat lodge. There, in the darkness of the lodge and in the midst of the swirling steam and heat, I beheld a clear image of those individuals who had leapt from the World Trade Center towers to be annihilated on the pavement below. I was right there. Indeed, for a brief moment, I was one of them. Before entering the lodge I had read a short article that suggested that several of those people had carefully composed themselves and then deliberately stepped into space. One man made a graceful swan dive. A couple held hands. A prim lady simply clutched her handbag and stepped off. Something about this image moved my soul in a very profound way and tears of gratitude for these gestures of beauty in the face of death mingled with the sweat and the steam of the lodge. I was transported back to the words of the poet Mary Oliver, whose poem we had used as preparation for the ego death that the questors sought. The poem contains these lines:

> *when death comes*
> *like an iceberg between the shoulder blades,*
>
> *I want to step through the door full of curiosity, wondering:*
> *what is it going to be like, that cottage of darkness?*
>
> *And therefore I look upon everything*
> *as a brotherhood and sisterhood,*
> *and I look upon time as no more than an idea,*
> *and I consider eternity as another possibility;*
>
> *and I think of each life as a flower, as common*
> *as a field daisy, and as singular,*

and each name a comfortable music in the mouth,
tending, as all music does, toward silence,

and each body a lion of courage, and something
precious to the earth.

When it's over, I want to say: all my life
I was a bride married to amazement.
I was the bridegroom, taking the world into my arms.

(Oliver, p. 10)

    The poet captures, as only poetry can, the profound relationship between death and beauty, how the shadow cast by death serves to illuminate life in all its particulars. The close proximity of death to beauty within the human soul accounts for the incredible outpouring of love that followed the 9/11 event. The heart of America was blasted open by the violence, and love poured out like a river. Now everyone knows what is possible and it cannot be taken back, though it can be forgotten. A December 2001 survey reported in the *Seattle Times* (Dec. 9, p. A9) announced "Americans More Caring Since Attacks," and stated that the image of U.S. Muslims had improved significantly in the eyes of their fellow Americans—59 percent of Americans had a favorable view of U.S. Muslims in November, compared with 45 percent the previous March. Interestingly enough, conservative Republicans showed the biggest change in this "compassion index," with 64 percent feeling favorably toward the group, compared with 35 percent in March. But let's not get hung up on statistics. How did this phenomenon take shape in your own experience? I wonder how this relationship between death and the perception of beauty continues to play out in your own heart?

    Let's hold this question in mind as we take our second step into the soul of the September 11 event. This will require some risk on your part. And how could it be any different? How can we hope to break out of the trance, an act that President Lincoln suggested could "save our country," if we do not take risks? Here is what I propose to do. A student of mine by the name of Jon Kennedy has compiled a seven-minute sound collage of the 9/11 event. He is uniquely qualified to do so, not only because he knows how to do it technically, but because he was walking the streets of New York near the World Trade Center towers when the planes struck the building. The pictures he took of the collapsing buildings are incredible. What follows is a seven-minute sound impression of the 9/11 event. But we can't just turn the sounds on and endure what we hear. That would just create more terror. We have to enter this space as imaginal witnesses. When we do so, we transform what could be simply another experience of terror into an opportunity for what Hillman calls "soul making." We "make soul" when we enter into extreme experiences as compassionate witnesses.

I would like to lead us in a simple ritual exercise that will serve as a threshold to the imaginal landscape of September 11. Here is what I propose: I will ring a bell for a moment of silence. During this time I invite you first to relax your body and then to imagine some kind of threshold to cross, perhaps a line in the sand, or a door to a temple, a circle of flowers, or perhaps the entrance to the place in which you meditate at home. If you have been on vision quest, it might be the prayer ties that defined the circle in which you sat. Having stepped over this threshold, imagine yourself in a place in which you feel comfortable and supported. Feel yourself position your body in a way that allows you to be both open and flexible. Then listen to these sounds and allow your imagination to take you where it will. Remember that you are a witness to these events. You yourself are not the events, nor are you any single individual within the events. Instead, you are a compassionate witness to these events. Try not to resist or judge what you experience, but allow it to take shape within your imaginative eye. Following the paths of association, see if your experience of these sounds draws your attention to a particular image of 9/11. When the sound collage ends, I will wait for another minute before I ring the bell to close the meditation. Allow that minute to open your heart to what September 11 has to teach you. Focus on that single image that has presented itself out of the background of multiple images. Try to remember it in all of its particularities. When the bell ends the meditation, we will take some time to process what we have witnessed.

> *A moment of silence is observed, and then the sound collage begins with the voices of young children on a playground, laughing and running. In the distance, faint at first but then getting louder and louder, is the droning sound of an airplane. It moves over the playground and into the distance at which time a loud "Whumphh!"*

sound is heard. The plane has crashed into the World Trade Center. Immediately, sirens begin to converge and a reporter breaks in to announce what has happened. The carnage that is described by the newscaster becomes more and more graphic as the full extent of the disaster becomes clear. The loss of life is catastrophic. There are citizens' voices calling for prayers. An eyewitness survivor from the fifty-fourth floor breaks into weeping when he describes those who were in wheelchairs waiting for someone to carry them down. President Bush is heard making his announcement about the terrorist attacks. More sirens. The sounds of the collapsing building are accompanied by the shrieks of those caught in the clouds of rubble. More eyewitness accounts of people jumping out of the windows. An announcer claims that this may be the worst catastrophe to ever strike America. A voice is heard saying, "America will never be the same after September 11, 2001." The beginnings of a song are heard. The lyrics become clear, "Give it away, today. Perhaps we're on our way, perhaps we've gone too far, perhaps we should slow down and be where we really are, be where we really are. Little by little, be where we really are." There follows a minute of silence.

I invite you now to spend a few moments with your neighbor, preferably someone you do not know, processing your experience and the image that came to you.

DISCUSSION: SHARING DESCRIPTIONS OF THE WITNESSING EGO

Thank you for your hard work. It is not easy to subject one's self to this level of suffering. My thesis is that the only reason to do so is to liberate psyche from her imprisonment. How? By witnessing suffering on such a scale that something in the ego is relativized, its position jarred loose from habitual moorings so that a larger stance outside of the ego is born. This position has the peculiar property of carrying a kind of nonpossessive love for humanity that is very difficult to achieve in any other way. I have seen this kind of love in my study of nuclear nightmares. In those dreams, when a bomb has landed and the people know they have only a few moments to live, the characteristic and recurrent move made by those humans who are present is to form a circle, arms interlocked, heads pointed toward the center, awaiting their annihilation. The images of September 11 have a similar power to penetrate the heart, initiating it into an experience of divine love for the purposes of liberating psyche. Our choice is to seize the opportunity presented by this opening or watch it slowly close until the next tragedy, even greater than 9/11, is visited upon the American psyche.

THE LANDSCAPE OF APOCALYPTIC IMAGERY

When we enter a landscape of massive suffering for the purposes of the transformation of consciousness, we are in the land of apocalypse. I have studied the archetype of apocalypse for many years through my personal encounters with the city of Hiroshima. Allow me to recapitulate a few key ideas.

The word *apocalypse* comes from the Greek *apocalypses* meaning "to reveal" or "a tearing away of the veil, of that which conceals" (*kalyptein*). Embedded in the history of this word is the image of two realities between which exists a partition, a thin veil that conceals something of great value on the other side. Most often, this sense of "passing over" from one reality to the other is understood to be a function of the religious imagination in humans. One lifts the veil that separates the everyday, material, profane world and communes with the extraordinary, spiritual, and sacred world that is "revealed" on the other side. It is also imagined as a two way street—something from the spiritual world can tear away the veil and insinuate itself into the mundane world. When the imagining ego beholds a visitation from "beyond the veil," it is experienced as a revelation. I contend that the events of September 11 qualify as a revelatory experience.

The ideas of depth psychology about which I spoke earlier in my talk can now be expanded with respect to the apocalypse of September 11. First, because psyche is image, we must work with the event imaginally. If we only literalize the images, then we are limited to purely political responses, such as going to war, suspending human rights, and labeling "evil" those who do not agree with the status quo. As we have seen with our little exercise, working with images of 9/11 has the power to open the heart, creating possibilities that cannot exist if we remain solely at the level of the literal. Second, the relations between the ego and the unconscious operate at both personal and collective levels. At the personal level, the events of September

11 have the capacity to liberate each one of us from our habitual modes of thinking, opening our perception to "look upon everything as a brotherhood and sisterhood" and to see "each life as a flower, as common as a field daisy, and as singular." Collectively, 9/11 has the capacity to liberate America from her egocentric provincialism, opening her to new possibilities in the exercise of humane power and compassionate leadership.

But it is the third idea, that there is an intentionality behind all of these events, that I wish to examine more closely as I begin to conclude this presentation. Recall that depth psychology asserts that there exists within our psyche an intelligence that pursues aims and intentions beyond the comprehension of the ego. This assertion is amply documented at the personal level by a century of clinical experience in which dreams and other manifestations of the personal unconscious are seen to have an uncanny knack for pinpointing the precise needs of a one-sided ego attitude. It is as if there is a "sacred other" within our own psyche that knows just what we need to achieve optimum health and well being. This "sacred other" reveals itself in and through unconscious processes such as dreams, visions, body symptoms, illnesses, etc. It is the responsibility of the moral ego to convert these messages into an ethical obligation by acting upon the hints given by the "sacred other." This is not an easy thing to do since the hints given by the intentional psyche often run counter to the aims of the waking ego. It is for this reason that Jung states that an experience with this larger sense of the psyche is "always a defeat for the ego" (*Collected Works*, vol. 14, p. 778). Moving beyond our habitual ego attitudes usually involves a painful crisis of "letting go," which is why it is so difficult to do. Believe me when I say that the theoretical language I am using to describe this process does not do justice to the experience itself. What it actually feels like is closer to the experience of death. Ask anyone who has been on a vision quest and who came back with a sense of renewal. It is not a pleasant experience. However, it does lead to an advancement in personal growth.

The corresponding dynamic at the collective level is even more profound. Perhaps Jung states it best when he says:

> Our personal psychology is just a thin skin, a ripple on the ocean of collective psychology. The powerful factor, the factor which changes our whole life, which changes the surface of our known world, which makes history, is collective psychology, and collective

psychology moves according to laws entirely different from those of our consciousness. The archetypes are the great decisive forces, they bring about the real events, and not our personal reasoning and practical intellect. ...The archetypal images decide the fate of man. (Vol. 18, p. 371)

What Jung is saying here is that from the point of view of the psyche, the transpersonal patterns of images that he calls archetypes are not located within human beings. Rather, human beings are located in and subject to the intentions of the archetypes. Hence, when the archetypal images that have governed the collective body of a culture begin to shift and transform, so moves the fate of mankind. It is my contention that one year after the end of the twentieth century, a lethal century that has left 100 million people dead in massive epidemics of violence, we are witnessing in the apocalyptic imagery of September 11 the transformation of archetypal dominants in our culture. At the collective level, America is being asked to undergo a vision quest, to take an underworld journey, to die to herself in order to be reborn into a more sustainable form. From this point of view, 9/11 was a nightmare sent to instruct us. Like a nightmare, it wants to scare us in order to get our attention. Why? Because it wants to redeem us—tough work in a death-denying culture such as America's. But not only is America being invited to an underworld journey. The suffering inflicted upon the Earth in the form of deforestation, exploitation of resources, poverty, and disease suggests that apocalyptic imagery is calling to the inhabitants of the planet as a whole. Recall the dream voice, "The time is now for huge *international* shifts of consciousness!" No wonder our leaders are using their rhetorical skills to keep us in the same old story of good and evil, of blame and punishment. The reality over which they preside is being severely challenged.

TOWARD A HUMANE FUTURE

Now what kind of transformation of human consciousness is being announced that could account for tragedy of this magnitude and of a global scale? In the waning moments of my talk tonight, allow me to get somewhat cosmic. In his seminal book, *The Passion of the Western Mind*, Richard Tarnas asserts that Western intellectual history has been an overwhelmingly masculine phenomenon. He attributes this fact not simply to the social restriction of women, but to an archetypal process. He says,

> The masculinity of the Western mind has been pervasive and
> fundamental, in both men and women, affecting every aspect of
> Western thought, determining its most basic conception of the
> human being and the human role in the world.... The man of the
> Western tradition has been a questing masculine hero. A
> Promethean biological and metaphysical rebel who has constantly
> sought freedom and progress for himself and who has thus
> constantly striven to differentiate himself from and control the
> matrix out of which he emerged. (Tarnas 1991, p. 441)

This matrix out of which mankind has emerged is pictured by the psyche, for obvious reasons, as being feminine. The implication of this statement is clear: the structure of the questing ego of the Western mind has been founded upon the repression of the feminine in all of its forms, whether as nature, mystery, imagination, ambiguity, emotion, community, or women themselves. The one-sidedness of this position is calling for a compensation. The ego longs for reunion with what has been lost, the ground of its own being. So in words akin to that used by the vision quest, Tarnas goes on to say,

> To achieve this reintegration of the repressed feminine, the
> masculine must undergo a sacrifice, an ego death. The Western
> mind must be willing to open itself to a reality the nature of which
> could shatter its most established beliefs about itself and about the
> world. This is where the real act of heroism is going to be. A
> threshold must now be crossed, a threshold demanding a
> courageous act of faith, of imagination, of trust in a larger and more
> complex reality; a threshold, moreover, demanding an act of
> unflinching self-discernment. And this is the great challenge of our
> time, the evolutionary imperative for the masculine to see through
> and overcome its hubris and one-sidedness, to own its unconscious
> shadow, to choose to enter into a fundamentally new relationship of
> mutuality with the feminine in all its forms. This is the great
> challenge, but I believe it is one the Western mind has been slowly
> preparing itself to meet for its entire existence. (p. 444)

In the light of these words, it is possible to imagine that the outpouring of heartfelt love and connection that was constellated by the apocalyptic nature of the September 11 event was an alchemical *coniunctio*, a fusing together, however briefly, of the masculine and the feminine (Edinger 1985,

211–32). In such a state, values are inverted and qualities of nurturance and compassion are in balance with qualities of heroism and courage. Strangers hold hands and the nation is one. Perhaps it is not meant to last. But once witnessed, it cannot be forgotten. Or can it?

However you choose to react to my words tonight, I know this much is true: we in America are living in a psychic wasteland that has been created out of the manipulation and distortion of desire. The city of Seattle, no less than New York, is a shining city that is built upon tremendous suffering to which we turn a blind eye. We are all, myself included, held in bondage by forces that we must begin to identify and break free of, that we must give form to and consume. We must disenthrall ourselves. Images of liberation abound in the mythologies of our culture. They all demand a sacrifice, an ego death. The shattering reality of September 11 serves as an initiatory threshold into the dark underworld of the personal and collective psyche. Each of us is being called to follow that path down into the darkness in order to seize the opportunity for liberation and love. My faith is this: there is gold at the bottom of that rubble. *There is gold at the bottom of that rubble!*

PART II

Stories of the Journey

WALTER ENLOE

INTRODUCTION

The Genesis of a Single Idea

> *To remember the past is to commit oneself to the future. To remember Hiroshima is to abhor nuclear war. To remember Hiroshima is to commit oneself to peace.*
>
> POPE JOHN PAUL II
> on his visit to Hiroshima, February 1981

> *In this age of nuclear weapons, when their power gets more attention than the misery they cause, and when human events increasingly resolve around their production and proliferation, what must we Japanese try to remember? Or more pointedly, what must I myself remember and keep on remembering? Human dignity...for it is the most important thing I have discovered in Hiroshima.*
>
> Nobel Prize laureate KENZABURO OE
> in Hiroshima Notes, 1981

IT IS EARLY AUGUST 1961—MORE THAN FORTY YEARS AGO. I'm on a British ocean liner sailing from San Francisco to Yokohama, on my way to live in Kobe and Hiroshima for the next five years. I'm talking to a girl named Elizabeth who has lived most of her life in Japan with her parents, who are missionaries for the Presbyterian Church. So are mine. She has just lived a year in Richmond and is on her way back to Nagoya for another five years. We're twelve. She hates the idea of returning. I've gotten over the hating-to-go part, but I don't know what I'm really in for. She does, and I find her fascinating. The more we talk, the more she tells me. She doesn't hate Japan or the Japanese; she just longs to live in America more than anything else.

I was invited to a fourth-grade music recital the other day in Golden Valley, Minnesota. One of my master's students teaches music there. Toward the end of the program a group of children began to sing softly in flawless Japanese "Sadako's Song" written by Michiko. And then they sang in English as the four narrators told her story, the story of a young girl who made the folding of paper cranes an act of peacemaking and a symbol of hope. And as they said, "First she folded one crane and then ten and then a hundred," other children walked out with strings of ten, a hundred, and a thousand paper cranes made of colorful recycled papers. And then the whole choir sang, "One thousand paper cranes, one thousand paper cranes, spread your wings way up high. Sadako, we will carry on, we will carry on."

I first moved to Japan in 1961 and then in 1963 to Hiroshima, where my parents were to live almost thirty years as a minister and a teacher working for the Presbyterian Church. I don't think I ever heard of Sadako during those initial years I lived there. We were a mile from Hiroshima Peace Park, next to Hiroshima University and across from the Red Cross Hospital and its atomic bomb wing. I spent a lot of time hanging out with my Japanese friends in Peace Park, and I remember vividly the Children's Monument and its millions of paper cranes. But if I heard Sadako's story, it held no significance for me at the time.

I came to Japan prejudiced. I knew the Japanese only as the "other," as former enemies who were caricatured in films and especially comic books as "yellow vermin," "buckteeth rats," and "Nips and "Japs." And there was my own conjuring up of them as people needing to hear the "Good News," as "heathen" needing to be saved. I was coming to Japan from the segregated South and had no idea how soon I was to become the "other."

My parents were the most just, reasonable people I knew. While our surrounding culture in 1950s Louisiana and Georgia was infused with racism and separatism from playgrounds to theaters and public bathrooms, in our home no racist behavior or talk was tolerated. Nevertheless, in my dreams I imagined in the months before boarding a ship in San Francisco to head for Japan that the men were all Samurai warriors and the women looked like petite Minnie Mouses in kimonos and heels.

I still have the dog-eared *World Book* circa 1961 that I read and reread before moving to Japan. It provided the "true word" about Japan, which inhabited my imagination before we arrived in Yokohama in the summer of

1961. Remnants lingered on, framing some of my interpretation of people and things Japanese. "The Japanese follow many customs that seem strange to people from Western countries. They pride themselves on being particularly polite…They tend to be short and stocky, and their legs are usually short in proportion to their bodies…They often eat raw fish…Many live in bamboo houses…The most popular places for recreation for many Japanese are the theater and the public baths…" I pictured them as monkey-like people who ate raw fish, slept in bamboo huts, and enjoyed taking baths naked in public. And because of the atomic bomb and Godzilla, I thought Hiroshimans must be mutated forms of the living dead.

The bomb had affected everyone. My grandparents lived close to Oak Ridge, Tennessee, and I had imagined and reimagined Armageddon and the end of the world. In Atlanta I had a friend whose father had built a bomb shelter in his backyard. It was a concrete vault ten feet underground. We were forbidden to go into it, and of course we found a way to open it up and descend the ladder into the concrete room. A couple of times we used flashlights to locate the c-rations. We would not have been caught if my friend's dad hadn't been fastidious in following the Civil Defense Department's orders for replenishing food and water. We were interested in the bomb because we were embedded in the doom and dread of the Atomic Age. (I read Madame Curie's biography the week I had my first X ray for a possible broken arm.) The Cold War tensions, the building of the Berlin Wall, and later the Cuban missile crisis prodded us to prepare for a third and probably last world war.

We kids spent more time in the school basement practicing for the impending nuclear attack than we did talking about the United Nations and peacemaking. We marched silently to the basement to the screams of the air-raid siren, which was supposed to give us a twenty-minute warning, and lay prostrate on the cold concrete floor. For surprise attacks when we would have less than five minutes until doomsday, our teacher drilled us to crawl under our desks, put our hands over our heads, and turn our backs to the windows from whence would come the flash of radiated heat after the explosion.

In my dreams, the little black-and-white cartoon figure on the Civil Defense film sang a jingle about being prepared for nuclear war and then ran and hid, away from the windows. We were good twelve-year-old soldiers, good Americans preparing to survive whatever the "godless pinko communists" threw at us. I did not know much more than that about the bomb. My uncle had been a paratrooper stationed in Germany a few years earlier. He told my brother and me stories about his training and about films he had watched on nuclear warfare. I remember his admonishment before we left for Japan: "Don't drink the water and don't eat the fish."

In 1963 I was in the ninth grade and too old for the American School in Hiroshima City, which my sister attended. (Years later it would become the International School and I would become the principal.) So I rode a streetcar and a bus and I walked (it was more than two hours each way) to attend school on a U.S. Marine Corps Naval Air station. I was one of three in the ninth grade.

It was a lonely time, for we were so isolated. None of my school friends ever visited my home, because U.S. military personnel and their families were not allowed into Hiroshima, in part because of the continued hostility and demonstrations throughout Japan and at the gates of the Iwakuni airbase against the renewal of the U.S.-Japan Defense Treaty. I never discussed Hiroshima with my friends, and school lessons never touched the subject. Peace through armed strength was the ethos of this base, where despite treaty agreements, there was considerable controversy over whether U.S. bases and warships had nuclear weapons on Japanese soil.

The American kids hated being in Japan, though there was a hybrid American culture on the base where they could use U.S. currency to buy American items. There was a teen club, a snack bar, a bowling alley, a movie theater, and a nine-hole golf course. I thought they had it made; I would have done almost anything for an American candy bar after three years in Japan. I was not allowed to exchange yen for American currency since I was not U.S. military. All I had from America was the Far Eastern Radio broadcast, which I could pick up weakly in Hiroshima. The kids on the base complained about missing out on what was happening in the States, and they had no interest in anything Japanese.

I left Iwakuni's school for a year to attend an international boarding school, then returned to Iwakuni in 1965. I was in the eleventh grade and the high school now had twenty-nine students and six teachers. Our basketball team of eight players was sponsored by the base's operations officer, Colonel Don Conroy (the "Great Santini" in a novel by his son Pat Conroy).

The number of students had been depleted as the fighter squadrons joined the growing war in Vietnam.

I hated this school and what it stood for, its ethnocentrism and warrior culture, and I found myself drawn more and more to the streets and people of Hiroshima. But even though I was to meet and respect many peacemakers, pacifists, public servants, and bomb victims, Hiroshima didn't mean much to me at the time in terms of the greater issues of humanity, justice, and the world's future. It was only years later that I understood Hiroshima as a symbol of humans' inhumanity to others. In Hiroshima there were few foreigners at that time. I could walk or ride my bike for hours and never meet another foreigner. The whole place belonged to me and yet I was not part of it really; I was more than a sojourner, more than a visitor. I wanted to belong, but in the final analysis I was *gaijin,* though even the more formal term *gaikojin* was distasteful.

At sixteen I was fair skinned and rather tall; I stood out among any crowd of Japanese. In the streets, playgrounds, and coffee shops I collected many friends, as one might collect butterflies on a spring morning. Some people wanted an American friend for personal status; others collected Americans as curios; others wanted an American with whom to practice their (usually weak) English conversation skills. At Hiroshima University I was able to make some real friends by playing on a soccer club and joining the English Speaking Society. Only occasionally, and always by older men, was I treated rudely. I took their banter and angry comments about "bad Americans" on my lean, inexperienced shoulders.

My friends and I talked about music and movies and had the kinds of real conversations that grow out of comfortable relationships. I developed a close friendship with a girl a year older than I, and years later she reminded me that our friendship improved her English so much that she became a stewardess for Japan Airlines. Her father hated me because I liked his daughter and I was American and he was *hibakusha* (A-bomb survivor). We met secretly. Once we went to a movie to see *Hiroshima Mon Amour* and together for the first time held hands and cried. The movie had been filmed down the street from our homes in front of the Red Cross Hospital. We understood but did not accept the politics of adults.

The next year I had a bit role as an Australian swimmer in the popular film *Umi no Wakadaisho,* starring the "Elvis" of Japan, Kayama Uzo. When my friends found out I was in the movie and had been paid the huge amount of ten thousand yen for two days of filming (I appeared for less than two minutes), the word quickly spread. I probably signed a thousand autographs in the next few months, usually with an illegible "James Dean." Hero and victor, barbarian and outsider, movie star and murderer, that was the schizophrenia of those days in the early sixties in Hiroshima for an American teenager. What stands out as the only noteworthy controversy in my early days in Hiroshima was the role of the Atomic Bomb Casualty Commission (ABCC). I was aware of it probably because of the Americans who worked there as radiologists, biostatisticians, and medical personnel.

Hiroshima literally means "wide islands," and it is situated where the Ota River flows into the Inland Sea. Over hundreds of years, islands—some flat and some mountainous—have become part of the cityscape as land has been filled in between the islands to become Hiroshima City. One of these old islands is Hijiyama, which overlooks and dominates the central city. At its summit, built partly on a Buddhist military cemetery, sits the ABCC. The American Culture Center and American school sat conspicuously on Peace Boulevard at the base of the mountain.

Many Hiroshima bomb victims saw themselves as guinea pigs because the Americans and Japanese who worked with them diagnosed their illnesses, chronicled their sickness and death, but neither prescribed for nor treated them. This was the largest population ever to be part of a systematic, long-term medical study whose results were used to set the radiation dosage levels for dental and medical clinics the world over. In 1962 on a clear winter day you could face east and look up from Peace Boulevard, from the steps of the Baptist Church in whose basement was the American School, to Hijiyama Mountain to see between the treeless branches the metal roofs of the Atomic Bomb Casualty Commission. Facing west down the hundred-meter-wide boulevard you could see in the distance the Atomic Bomb Museum and Peace Park.

It was only in America in college that I discovered that my sense of being the "other" gave me greater empathy for others and a strong sense of justice and equality for all. I worked in Upward Bound as the only "white" tutor for three and a half years, was arrested in a Civil Rights march with thirty-seven others, was an active Vietnam draft resister, and believed with my hero Martin Luther King Jr. that war and poverty and human rights were inevitably and inextricably linked. As president of my student government, I organized not only demonstrations and marches, but also dialogues with members of the community in civic forums and churches. I spent the summer of 1971 working to help establish the Clearwater Florida Free Clinic. Also in that year I was accepted both to Princeton University's theological seminary and social work program and into a graduate program in American Studies at Emory University.

Not finding much to aid my identity quest in American Studies, I switched to humanities and human development. I refused to be drafted and spent much of 1972 fighting the government bureaucracy as it threatened me with arrest. That year I also discovered teaching and for several years taught kindergarten as a formal student of human studies. In 1975 I taught my first high school course in social studies using Richard Minear's book *Through Japanese Eyes* (1974). I can remember exactly the time I opened the book and found this paragraph, which elucidated for me for the first time the inarticulations of my soul:

> The atomic bomb fell on Hiroshima and Nagasaki on Japanese territory and on Japanese people. But the Japanese people were not alone in their suffering. In a very real sense, we were all there…Together with the Japanese we are all survivors of Hiroshima and Nagasaki. Hiroshima in particular has become a symbol to the world, a symbol whose relevance goes far beyond World War II and the Japanese. It has become the chief symbol of the nuclear age, of the holocaust that man's scientific genius has made possible. It has become a symbol of the potential consequence if man does not develop alternatives to war. It has become a symbol—one of the most recent in a long, long series—of man's inhumanity to man.

My high school students were very interested in the bomb; they too had been born under the glowing sign of the Nuclear Age and the Cold War. So I began rereading for the first time since high school John Hersey's *Hiroshima*, and then through a literature search I found Norman Cousins's seminal essay from August 1945, "Modern Man Is Obsolete": "Whatever elation there is in the world today because of final victory is severely tempered by fear. It is a fear of the unknown, the fear of forces man can neither channel nor comprehend…While the dust was settling over Hiroshima, he was asking himself questions and finding no answers. The biggest question of these concerns the nature of man. Is war in the nature of man? If so, how much time has he left before he employs the means he has already devised for the ultimate in self-destruction—extinction?"

Barbara Reynolds, Mary Macmillan, Rev. Tanimoto, and Norman Cousins were all peace activists I had met in Hiroshima, and now ten years later I was attentive to their lifework and messages, though previously I had paid them little attention. Now they meant everything, because I finally was able to transcend the American adolescent who lived in Hiroshima, where my parents continued to live, and become a young man who believed in the words of Martin Luther King, "The world is more of a neighborhood, but is it any more of a humanhood? If we don't learn to live together as brothers and sisters, we shall perish to together as fools." Now racism and ethnocentrism and Hiroshima were forever linked in me and my lifework.

After completing graduate school I returned with my young family for two years to be teacher and the principal of what was now Hiroshima International School. From the beginning, my sixth-seventh-eighth-grade class began studying Hiroshima from Paleolithic times up to the present, using a project method to integrate all the subjects. (The story of those several years of interdisciplinary learning and teaching is told in *Lessons from Ground Zero*.) I began to focus on the politics of Hiroshima, and what was at first a two-year commitment grew into eight years.

While Hiroshima was the International City of Peace and Culture, its international school contributed only indirectly to its mission. The school had the same legal status as a barber or cooking school; it did not even have the quasi-nonprofit status the North Korean School had in Hiroshima or the status of the twenty-three other International Schools in Japan. It took six years to convince business, governmental agencies, and the public that a nonprofit international school in a school building was good for Hiroshima. It might attract foreign business as well as contribute to Hiroshima's goal. We needed an attractive, functional school building instead of the warehouse the school then occupied. When we finally achieved the status we sought in 1986 and were seen by the greater community as the International School (and not the Americans' school), I realized that the 1000 Cranes Club was a great benefit. The work of the foreign children and their 1000 Cranes Club, particularly with their early publicity on TV and in the press, had helped the cause immensely. Hiroshimans saw the gaijin children—foreign, outsider, American children—working for peace and contributing to Hiroshima's image. This idea that the foreign children living in Hiroshima (usually not by choice) could not only learn about this place but even contribute to its legacy was in fact an idea that helped resolve my own mixed sense of culpability, indifference, and desire to be accepted, which grew out of my adolescence at the A-bomb epicenter.

The first time I visited Nagasaki was in 1966. My brother and I lived in Hiroshima and attended Matthew C. Perry High School on the U.S. Marine Air Corps Base at Iwakuni, about an hour and a half from Hiroshima. My brother was in the tenth grade, and I was in the eleventh; we composed 25 percent of the boys' basketball team. We traveled to play several games at Sasebo Naval Base, about an hour north of Nagasaki. Instead of attending a social function in Sasebo, John and I took off, as we were wont to, to explore Nagasaki for an evening. Together we had explored much of Hiroshima and other areas of Japan. Unlike in Hiroshima, we felt welcomed in the little shops and food stalls around the station in Nagasaki. Years later I returned several times with my family as we explored southern Kyushu Island and Nagasaki's Peace Park, Urakami Cathedral, and the museum for the Christian martyrs. I asked then and continue to ask, Was the Hiroshima bomb necessary? Perhaps. But three days later was the Nagasaki bomb necessary? I didn't think so then and firmly believe not today. But it happened. Let us—the world—learn from our history so not to repeat this evil.

The essays that follow, both my own and those written with colleagues who have been touched by their Hiroshima and Nagasaki encounters, portray the genesis of a single idea. Peacemaking is ongoing, a construction, an evolution in the hearts and minds of people that must be continually maintained and sustained. Sadako Sasaki and her friends, and the helping hands of Mr. Kawamoto and the foreign children living in Hiroshima, and the many others who have followed and are yet to follow, have made the folding of birds of peace from scraps of paper a symbol of hope and peacemaking. When you speak with children who have become one with a simple piece of paper as it is folded into a crane or dove, and you ask them how is learning to fold a peace bird like becoming a peacemaker, they are often quick to answer: "It takes time," "It's difficult," "You have to start over," "You can't do it alone," "You learn from others," "You try and try again," "When you're successful you know it." Let's continue to help more children grow as we grow in the artistry and understanding of building peaceful relationships, solving problems reasonably, and tolerating difference based upon an ethic of cooperation and mutual reciprocity. For we are their teachers and mentors. And as these stories exhibit, they have become ours.

9

Mama's Birthday at the Beginning of the New Millennium

> *Give back my father, give back my mother,*
> *Give grandpa back, grandma back,*
> *Give our sons and daughters back!*
> *Give me back myself, give mankind back,*
> *Give each back to each other!*
>
> *So long as this life lasts,*
> *Give peace back to us,*
> *Peace that will never end!*
>
> —Sankichi Toge
> *A-bomb poet*

YEARS AGO, WHEN I WAS THE PRINCIPAL and a teacher at Hiroshima International School, my middle school students, mostly Americans, Australians, and Europeans, were interviewing peace activists and bomb victims in Hiroshima as part of their thematic project study on the aftermath of the A-bomb (as retold in *Lessons from Ground Zero: A Hiroshima and Nagasaki Story*). Immortalized in John Hersey's *Hiroshima*, Rev. Tanimoto was the senior pastor of Nagarekawa Methodist Church and a leader in the "No More Hiroshimas" movement. A student who was interviewing him asked if all the hurt and pain had ended after so many years. "Forty years is not an eternity," he said. "The bomb was yesterday. Not only are you living with the bomb as it has consumed you and become part of your being with all the horror and evil; part of you has died as you watched others die and imagined them dying. I hurt every day for all the souls of the dead. But

---

This chapter was developed from an article titled "Lessons from Ground Zero: Pearl Harbor to 9/11," written with David Willis.

today I hurt most for the orphans who live on somehow without their mothers who can't teach them and can't watch them grow."

Hundreds of times over the past forty years, I have stood at the hypocenter, Ground Zero, of the atomic bombings of Hiroshima and Nagasaki, and each time has been a somber and sobering experience. It was there in Hiroshima Peace Park that my mother first saw me cry as an adult. My mother taught me well. September 11, 2001, was her seventy-fourth birthday. She and my father were Presbyterian missionaries in the Hiroshima area for some thirty years and I spent a considerable part of my youth there as well as eight years as an adult. My father was a Marine during World War II on Iwo Jima and Guam. In the aftermath of the World Trade Center Towers disaster, he might have reimagined Pearl Harbor as many older Americans did, but more probably he imagined Ground Zero. My mother did, and so did I. "We're all a-bomb victims," she once again reminded me. My nineteen-year-old daughter, Serene, who was born in Hiroshima, conjured up images of the Persian Gulf. For me, it could have been—but wasn't—Vietnam, although that war had touched me deeply as both a witness to its destruction and as a victim of anti-draft-resister government policies. In those first horrific hours of September 11, I imagined and reimagined Ground Zero itself, where, often psychically numbed, I've prayed for peace and tolerance and justice many times.

Today with a war on terrorists at hand, an unprecedented opportunity, which provides hope for the future, is developing across the planet. It is a call to use human arms and hands to build a world based on tolerance, justice, and respect for all members of the human family, and even an understanding of those who wish for our demise. Based on the appeal of every living Nobel Peace Prize Laureate, the United Nations General Assembly declared the decade 2001–2010 as "A Decade for a Culture of Peace and Nonviolence for the Children of the World," asking that all nations and communities teach peacemaking, conflict resolution, and nonviolence in their schools, neighborhoods, and workplaces. We must work purposefully, individually and collaboratively, to overcome apathy, indifference, and even opposition toward initiating and sustaining such an effort. We must also understand that the sentiment "We Are the World" is largely a Western, even American, dream. Political totalitarianism, religious zealotry, and tribal consciousness define the lives of people in most of the world. However, as

John F. Kennedy said, "If we cannot end our differences, at least we can help make the world safe for diversity. For, in the final analysis, our most basic common link is that we all inhabit this small planet. We all breathe the same air. We cherish our children's future. And we are all mortal."

As we begin a new millennium, let us remember the human behaviors and productions of the twentieth century. The scientific and technological achievements at the end of the industrial age, whether with light, matter, or the human body, are powerful phenomena. The dawning of the postmodern information age holds unimaginable promise. In Martin Luther King Jr.'s view "we have dwarfed space and chained time." But what characterizes an essential essence of the past hundred years is a paradox of the human spirit and human conduct. In the words of Dr. King, days before his 1968 assassination, "The world is more and more a neighborhood. But is it any more of a brotherhood? If we don't learn to live together as brothers and sisters, we shall perish together as fools."

On the one hand, the past century has seen a great deal of human introspection and understanding. Our biological, social, and human sciences—from genetics to developmental psychology and from narrative to cross-cultural studies—have allowed us to construct an understanding of ourselves, from the inner particles of a molecule to the outer edges of our universe. We can alter genetic material to constitute new life structures, and we can construct communicative forms from novels to films to musical scores that can be reconstituted and valued by others. Through an image of Earth as seen from the moon to planetary satellites, global communication, and economic interdependencies, and through organizations like the United Nations and our Universal Declaration of Human Rights, we have a greater sense of the interconnectedness of the world's people and places.

On the other hand, this past century has been the century of death, a century of human destruction and environmental degradation unparalleled in scope in human history. Through two world wars, and continuing ethnic, religious, and sociopolitical conflicts, more than 90 million noncombatants, including millions upon millions of children, have been murdered in the last hundred years. Add to those innocent dead the millions of dead and wounded combatants. We must acknowledge that the Earth has been a global killing field. And what of those millions and millions who died of poverty and preventable disease years before their natural passing time?

While the innocents continue to die today alongside the warriors of civil and regional conflicts from the Middle East to central Asia, so too do many, many thousands die yearly from violence in our own local towns and neighborhoods. In our own backyards and streets we do not enter after dark; we are increasingly distancing ourselves from each other through fear and intolerance as we build walls of separation.

Fifty-five years ago, Hiroshima and its forgotten sister Nagasaki became atomic wastelands. Along with the Holocaust, they signaled the dawn of postmodernity and joined the long litany of stories of human beings' inhumanity to humans. What is significant about Nagasaki, as the last place to so experience atomic war, is that her spirits are global and struggle to tell us that the nuclear bomb has changed the very nature of human destruction. Time and space have been transformed so that the whole planet is threatened by nuclear toxins (and potential terrorists) as well as a radioactive winter that could last thousands of years. In a sense, we are all survivors of Nagasaki and, with our children, victims of our murderous streets, schoolyards, and media worlds.

For me, Nagasaki has become a symbol of our present world. Its significance lies not only in its image as a holocaust initiating the postmodern age, a possibility made real by our scientific genius, but also in its reality as a symbol of our self-destruction if we do not develop alternatives to war and resolve the conflicts that ignite them. What does Nagasaki, the last place of nuclear war, reveal to us about the state of the world and of humanity's place in it? And what do the spirits of Nagasaki reveal to us as we prepare the next generation to live in the twenty-first century? For one thing, the instantaneous death of thousands of innocent people implores us to come to terms with a new paradigm, developing in the collective and personal psyche, of what it means to be human. As if in direct compensation to the horror of Nagasaki, this new image of humankind was inaugurated in the psyche, first by the messages of World War II holocausts, then by the threat of nuclear extinction, and finally when human beings glimpsed a holistic image of the Earth as seem from our moon.

The sheer beauty of the living reality of Earth itself, devoid of political boundaries and cultural landscapes, conjured up a new sense of hope and urgency that acknowledges and yet transcends cultural, racial, and civil differences. The image is one of the whole of humanity in interdependent relationship and intertwined with the whole of nature. It is a spiritual view of the world that radiates the interconnectedness of life. In this context Nagasaki's spirits remind us of the fragility of human and natural ecosystems and of the fact that the apocalyptic problems our planet faces, other than natural disasters and direct encounters with physical fragments of the universe, are specifically human problems.

Ours are problems of human values and human conduct. Nagasaki reminds us that for the first time in human history, we have the ability to terminate the consciousness through which creation can apprehend itself. Who is going to bear the responsibility for this power? If not we adults, then who? Our children? If not you, then who? Clearly, if we are to leave a world to our children that is both safe and productive, based upon the sanctity of the Earth and her peoples, then we must respond to the basic question of how we are to improve the quality of human life in the face of diminishing resources, global pollution, the threat of nuclear annihilation, and the increasing separation between the haves and the have-nots. But the spirits of Nagasaki draw us deeper. They force us to realize how and to what degree we are dealing with the tendency of social groups and individuals to perceive themselves as other than and superior to their fellow human beings. The social psychologist Erik Erikson labeled this tendency "psuedo-speciation," a tendency whose dynamics lie at the root of state, cultural, and racial conflict. Are we learning honestly about the nature of the human imagination and its hostile and dark dimensions, how we tend to project our own fears, frustrations, and misunderstandings onto the other—the enemy, the immigrant, the foreigner, those "others"?

Many of us are shaken by the world we have created or have allowed to be created for ourselves and our children and their future. Paul Bianchi, headmaster of the Paideia School in Atlanta, Georgia, speaks eloquently to the fundamental issues: None of us is immune to violence and the threat of violence. We are all threatened and we are all vulnerable. What's happening to our children and what can we do about it? Against all reason we hope that the places our children play and study will be safe havens from the violence permeating the rest of society. That hope is an illusion or perhaps a dream. Whatever exists in the larger society is going to be part of our children's lives one way or another. We have created an ethos of human violence that either we do not have the collective will to stop or we do not know how to stop. Our response so far to the desperation we feel is to go for the quick fix. The bigger the problem, the quicker the fix. Our first tendency is to arm ourselves, give guns to teachers, place metal detectors at the school doors, or build homes with high walls and armed guards. Or we can blame others— parents, Hollywood, media and technology, teachers and schools, even the kids. By blaming others, we seem to absolve our own culpability as well as our responsibility to help fix the problem. If it is someone else's problem, somebody else's fault, all we have to do is make them change, and not look at ourselves.

When 20 percent of children living in the richest and most powerful country in the world live in poverty, is it not all of our responsibility to respond? When, according to UNICEF, 40,000 young children die each day throughout the world from preventable disease and malnutrition, is it not our responsibility to find a global solution? To take responsibility, we must understand how much the world has changed over several generations. The child's world, with its opportunities, pressures, and temptations, has changed drastically compared to how little our institutions and support systems have changed (and in some cases change has meant deterioration). Many children grow up in families different from those their parents grew up in. Parents are busier and work more hours. The culture is faster paced. The child's environment is more electronic, more toxic, and more intrusive. Children are exposed to more, at an earlier age, than their parents were. We can argue forever about whether the world is a better or worse place. Certainly it is different.

We adults, parents or not, must all assume responsibility for failing to insist on the changes that are needed for the times we live in. We are going to have to solve our problems, like the toxins in our water and the unstable piles of nuclear waste, by expecting and giving more. To take responsibility, we must each ask ourselves, How much longer am I going to be a perpetuator and witness to the harm we bring our children and future generations? Who is going to stand up and take responsibility? It begins with me and you, with each one of us. We must take personal and collective responsibility as we encourage our children to learn through service and active citizenship.

Having brought some consciousness to our culpability in the woes of the last hundred years, we need to invoke a healing image for the future millennium, only possible in a post-Nagasaki age. Years ago Jonathan Schell, in his brilliant book *The Fate of the Earth*, elaborated the concept of "universal parenthood." After the systematic destruction during the past century of innocent beings at Nanking, Guernica, Aushwitz, Hiroshima, Nagasaki, and others (including the World Trade Center), the very idea of human extinction makes all of us, whether we have children or not, parents of the next generation. This is so because any generation that holds power in the post-Nagasaki age has a choice regarding annihilation. Each subsequent generation is thereby indebted to past generations for having allowed them to exist. As the humble peace activist Dr. Takashi Nagai argued in the days before his A-bomb-related death in 1951, the living can look at the gift of life as a temporary trust for the common good. It's going to take purposefulness, resolve, and greater resources to work together for a common future.

On the occasion of the fiftieth commemoration of the bombings of Hiroshima and Nagasaki, which ended the Second World War, an eyewitness observed, "At Hiroshima, there was much bitterness, much ado; it was very political. . . . The symbol for it could be a fist raised in anger. At Nagasaki, there was sadness, but also tranquility, reflection; it was not political—we prayed. We do not blame the United States; rather we wept over the sin of war, and more particularly, nuclear war. The symbol: hands joined in prayer."

We must join hands, not only in informing the people of the world about the horrors of nuclear weapons, but also in solving other problems threatening world peace, such as lack of fundamental human rights and freedoms, discrimination, environmental destruction, starvation, and poverty. Mahatma Gandhi understood: "If we are to reach real peace in this world, and if we are to carry on a real war against war, we shall have to begin with the children."

When events are framed in absolute terms as "good" or "evil," and causes are seen in purely black and white terms regarding the "other," we each suffer a loss of opportunity for moral culpability and responsibility. We are all victims. And we are all actors, both witnesses and perpetrators, on the local and global stage. We are the ones to make the difference through mutual respect and collaboration for the common good. To respond to evil with evil is evil. As Thich Nhat Hanh teaches, "True understanding comes from true practice. Understanding and love are values that transcend all dogma."

10

Ground Zero: Nagasaki Spirits, Hiroshima Voices

Ground zero, as defined in *Funk and Wagnall's:* the point on the ground vertically beneath or above the point of detonation of an atomic or thermonuclear bomb; the hypocenter.

ROBERT OPPENHEIMER, U.S. lead scientist for the Manhattan Project to develop nuclear weapons, on July 16, 1945, at the planet's first "ground zero" (White Sands, New Mexico), recalled the world's first humanmade nuclear explosion: "We waited until the blast had passed, walked out of the shelter, and then it was extremely solemn. We knew the world would not be the same. A few people laughed; a few people cried. Most people were silent. I remembered the line from the Hindu scripture, the *Bhagavad Gita*: Vishnu is trying to persuade the Prince that he should do his duty, and to impress him he takes on his multi-armed form and says, 'Now I am become Death, the destroyer of worlds.' I suppose we all thought that, one way or another." Several months later he wrote, "When it went off, in the New Mexico dawn, that first atomic bomb, we thought of Alfred Nobel, and his hope, his vain hope, that dynamite would put an end to wars. We thought of the legend of Prometheus, of that deep sense of guilt in man's new powers, that reflects his recognition of evil, and his long knowledge of it. We knew that it was a new world, but even more, we knew that novelty itself was a very old thing in human life, that all our ways are rooted in it" (Richard Rhodes, *The Making of the Atomic Bomb*, 676).

Oppenheimer chose Trinity as the code name for ground zero, the detonation site of the first humanmade nuclear explosion in the New Mexico desert south of Los Alamos; several weeks later Hiroshima and Nagasaki became the first ground zero demonstrations of humankind's means for its own destruction. Years later, when asked why he chose such a name, Oppenheimer recalled a favorite poem, John Donne's "Hymne to God, my God, in My Sicknesse":

> *As West and East*
> *In all flatt Maps—and I am one—are one,*
> *So death does touch the Resurrection.*

Though Oppenheimer's choice of "Trinity" is not clear even to him, this fragment of Donne's poem perhaps captures his paradox of conscience: dying leads to death but might also lead to rebirth; it is a metaphor or analog that this new weapon of death might end the war and redeem humankind in the future (Rhodes, p. 572).

Hiroshima honors the spirits of its dead with a strong voice. But "No More Hiroshimas" has also been the rallying cry for numerous peacemaking individuals and groups, often in conflict with one another, often loud and self-serving—the right, the left, the center, braying and shouting, proclaiming and finger pointing. Nagasaki, the second to be bombed, the stepchild, the little sister, turns inward, toward itself. A Jesuit priest who lived in Hiroshima before moving to Nagasaki in 1961 wrote, "In Hiroshima, they became angry. In Nagasaki, they prayed." In Nagasaki, ground zero of the apocalypse, the evils of world war and total human destruction intersect with hope and faith in salvation and eternal life.

Once, while I was standing at the Children's Monument in Hiroshima Peace Park, a Zen priest told me that in Buddhist belief, spirits are known to occupy—for forty-nine years—the places where they (as humans) suffered and died, before moving on. Within Christianity there is also a tradition in which spirits both occupy an eternal place and revisit the places of loved ones. My own work has been motivated in part by the example of Thich Nhat Hanh. He said,

> In *Crossing the Threshold of Hope*, Pope Paul John II wrote, "The Pope prays as the Holy Spirit permits him to pray." For me, the Holy Spirit is mindfulness itself. How can someone pray without mindfulness? He also wrote, "Man will not cross the threshold of truth without the help of the Holy Spirit. Prayer for the suffering and with the suffering is therefore a special part of this greatest cry that the Church and the Pope raise together with Christ." I believe

that if anyone, Buddhist or Christian, embraces suffering with his or her own mindfulness or allows the Holy Spirit to work within himself, he will come to really understand the nature of that suffering and will no longer impose on himself or others dogmas that constitute obstacles for working toward the cessation of that suffering. (*Living Buddha, Living Christ*, 1995)

Of all the visitors I met in Hiroshima, Robert and Betty Jean Lifton had the greatest impact on my growing understanding of what I define as Hiroshima and Nagasaki. It was the early sixties. Robert Lifton was a psychiatrist and psychologist, a close friend of one of my two life-work mentors, Erik Erikson, who was researching the *hibakusha* for his monumental work *Death in Life: Survivors of Hiroshima* (1967). Betty Jean was a writer and poet whose early ideas for meaningful exchanges between children in Hiroshima and the rest of the world foreshadowed the 1000 Cranes Club by some twenty years. I met them in Peace Park when I was fourteen and had what was no more than a five-minute conversation. It was only some years later—at a time when I wrestled with the deaths of Martin Luther King Jr. and Robert Kennedy, the growing war in Vietnam, the resonant clamor for justice and civil rights, and the depth of enslaved poverty—that the Liftons' work helped me understand that everything following my first contact with Hiroshima and Nagasaki was colored by the awareness of death, destruction, and human suffering, as well as hope and salvation.

Years later, Dr. Lifton concluded his *Hiroshima in America: Fifty Years of Denial* (1995) with a Coda. Its last paragraph captures the spirit of our initial efforts with the Time of the Dove (1995) events in the Twin Cities as well as the somber tenor of our present times following September 11, 2001:

> Americans are strongly aware of 1995 as a year commemorating the fiftieth anniversary of significant events connected with World War II: the liberation of the Nazi death camps, the atomic bombings of Hiroshima and Nagasaki, and the Japanese surrender ending that country's brutal aggression. Our plea is for all to draw upon these commemorations to confront violent and destructive behavior of every kind. We write this book during difficult days for Americans, a time when many wish to ignore searing human problems of violence, poverty, and general hopelessness, in favor of shallow reassurances and patriotic slogans. We offer this volume as a

different kind of patriotic contribution, as an appeal to our better angels, for the renewal of what is most compassionate and open and honorable in the American spirit.

But it is Nagai—teacher, pacifist, lover of humanity, and servant of God—who speaks most powerfully to and through me.

When the atomic bomb was dropped on Nagasaki, it fell near Nagasaki Medical School, where Dr. Takashi Nagai was a dean and professor of radiology and a nuclear physicist. He was also head of the Eleventh Medical Corps. The students and teachers in the medical school were divided into teams and assigned to different areas of the city whenever there was an air raid or natural disaster. While the bomb destroyed much of the medical school hospital and injured and killed many of the staff, students, and patients, and while Dr. Nagai was severely cut on the head by glass, his team was able to make it to the Urakami district, where they worked twenty-four hours a day until they were exhausted. After many days, Dr. Nagai, who was exhausted emotionally and mentally and was gravely ill with leukemia, returned to his home only to find it destroyed and his wife incinerated; he found only a few of her small bones. His young daughter, Kayano, and son Makoto were living in the countryside with relatives at the time and so were not injured. At that moment Dr. Nagai made a commitment to his family and to God that he would work for peace for the future of all children.

Takashi Nagai had been born into a medical family that had served for generations as physicians and herbalists for the imperial family. He had been a good student and could have attended the Imperial University in Tokyo or Kyoto but decided to go to Nagasaki, where the university was known for its excellent and unique studies of Western science and medicine. Though Japan was closed for more than 230 years until the mid-nineteenth century, Nagasaki was a port open to trade only with the Dutch and on occasion with the Chinese. Through that opening of a door to the outside world, Japan was able to keep apace to some degree with advances and discoveries in science, technology, global exploration, governance, and individual status. In Nagasaki, Takashi Nagai boarded with a Christian family, members of a group known as the "hidden Christians," living in the Urakami district. The family's daughter, Midori Moriyama, would later become his wife.

Christianity had flourished in the sixteenth century thanks to the influence of Francis Xavier and Portuguese Catholic priests. There were several hundred thousand converts, particularly around Nagasaki. This very "un-Japanese" religion eventually led to a rebellion against the imperial administration, which led to the massacre of thousands of Christians and the closing of Japan in 1636 to all nations except the Dutch, who were Protestants but were more interested in trade (e.g., Chinese silk for Japanese silver) than in saving souls. Christianity was banned, and for several hundred years hundreds of families outwardly lived Buddhist and Shinto lives while secretly practicing their Christian faith. That tradition continues today.

At the time Takashi Nagai became a doctor, he joined the Imperial Army and was assigned to Manchuria. He found a copy of a Catholic catechism, studied intensely, and upon his return to Nagasaki was baptized, took the name Paul, after St. Paul, and soon after married Midori. He returned to China for a year, then returned to Nagasaki in 1940 and became a professor of medicine. In June 1945 he was diagnosed with leukemia (from his radiology work) and was given three years to live.

In 1946, though obviously weak and sick, Takashi Nagai continued his teaching and studies of the atomic bomb disease. One day he was at the railroad station when he collapsed and had to be carried home by a friend. Confined to bed, Takashi Nagai's condition worsened. He wrote in his book *Leaving These Children Behind*, "From that day to the present the illness has gradually gained momentum. Now I have to rely on other people even to fetch pieces of paper for me. I barely have the strength to look into a microscope, let alone to examine patients. Fortunately, though, my topic of research—atomic bomb disease—is right here in my own body."

In 1948 people began moving into the atomic wasteland in the Urakami district. Dr. Nagai had a shack constructed close to the cathedral. He put two tatami mats (about four square meters) inside. He named it with a sign outside the entrance Nyoko-do (As Yourself Hermitage), after the Christian maxim "Love others as you love yourself." In that tiny space, within reaching distance around his bed were writing paper, brushes, paints, reference books, and daily articles. The second mat was for his children; the cooking area and the bathroom were outside.

Here Dr. Nagai began writing books and creating paintings as a way to encourage the people of Nagasaki to hope, live, pray, and work together for a better future each day, each hour, each minute. His first book, *Nagasaki no Kane* (Bells of Nagasaki), written less than a year after the bombing, was banned by the U.S. occupation forces in 1946. He was allowed to publish it in 1949 only if he included an appendix describing Japanese atrocities in the Philippines. (The appendix was dropped in the late 1950s when the occupation forces left.) The *Bells of Nagasaki* was controversial, I believe, not because of its descriptions of the suffering caused by the bomb, but because of the fact that Dr. Nagai was a deeply religious man. His book tells the story of one man's inner struggle to reconcile the destruction and misery of innocent people with his belief in a loving God. Near the end of the book, Dr. Nagai writes,

> Before this moment there were many opportunities to end the war. Not a few cities were totally destroyed. But these were not suitable sacrifices; nor did God accept them. Only when Nagasaki was destroyed did God accept the sacrifice. Hearing the cry of the human family, He inspired the emperor to issue the sacred decree by which the war was brought to an end. Our church of Nagasaki kept the faith during four hundred years of persecution when religion was proscribed and the blood of martyrs flowed freely. During the war this same church never ceased to pray day and night for a lasting peace. Was it not, then, the one unblemished lamb that had to be offered on the altar of God? Thanks to the sacrifice of this lamb many millions who would otherwise have fallen victim to the ravages of war have been saved. How noble, how splendid was that holocaust of August 9, when flames soared up from the cathedral, dispelling the darkness of war and bringing the light of peace! In the very depth of our grief we reverently saw here something beautiful, something pure, something sublime. Eight thousand people, together with their priests, burning with pure smoke, entered into eternal life. All without exception were good people whom we deeply mourn. Let us give thanks that Nagasaki was chosen for this sacrifice. Let us give thanks that through this sacrifice peace was given to the world and freedom of religion to Japan. May the souls of the faithful departed, through the mercy of God, rest in peace. Amen.

Dr. Nagai's other writings included *Seimei no Kawa* (River of Life), *Rozario no Kusari* (The Rosary Chain), and *Kono Ko wo Nokoshite* (Leaving These Children Behind), which became a well-known film. It was the thought of his children losing their mother and soon himself that motivated him to write so prolifically. In *Leaving These Children Behind* he wrote of his children, "I have to postpone the moment when these children become orphans, even by one day or one hour. Even if it is only one minute or one second, I want to reduce the length of time they must suffer loneliness." In the year before his death he was visited by an emissary of the Pope, received a visit from Helen Keller, and finally, in the months before his death, was visited by the emperor and received a commendation from the prime minister. He died June 1, 1950, at age forty-two. His funeral was held in the ruins of Urakami Cathedral.

Many children had lost their parents, and much of Takashi Nagai's income each month went to help neighborhood children with food and clothing. As in Hiroshima and much of Europe and Asia, there were thousands of orphans. Dr. Nagai created a library and named it "Our Book Case," where children could read and play. He lived his philosophy of "love others as you would love yourself." In the last chapter of *Leaving These Children Behind* Dr. Nagai writes from his bed pallet: "From here I can see Makoto preparing to carry away broken roof tiles in a straw basket, and Kayano playing house by herself and using the fragment of an Arita vase to arrange flowers. I wonder how these children will comment on my way of thinking after they grow up. In fifty years' time they will be much older than I am today. Perhaps when they read this book they will sit together and rattle their false teeth, saying things like, 'Dad certainly had a youthful attitude.'"

Powerful testimonies to the Nagasaki experience are two collections of children's stories, *In the Sky over Nagasaki* and *Living beneath the Atomic Cloud*, compiled by Dr. Nagai. These peace readers published in 1949 were later later translated with the help of the Nagasaki Appeal Committee by the Wilmington Peace Resource Center in Wilmington, Ohio, a Quaker college where Barbara Reynolds retired after living in Hiroshima and founding the World Friendship Center. One of the stories is by Dr. Nagai's daughter, Kayano, who was five at the time of the bombing and age nine when she told this story, "I Hope My Father Can Walk Soon":

> My brother and I were staying at a house in Koba near the
> mountains for safety. When Mother came from Nagasaki to see us, I
> asked her, "Mama, have you brought my clothes?" "Yes, of course.

I've brought a lot of your clothes," she said, patting me on the head. "Come back to Nagasaki when the air raids have finished," she said, and went back to Nagasaki in a hurry. After the atomic bomb was dropped, it was Father who came up to the house in Koba. His ears and his head were bandaged. All of us went down to Nagasaki together after Father's wounds were healed. My house had been large and Mother used to be there, but now I found everything in ashes and nothing remaining. We built a house of tin in the ruins. We put in two rooms. We slept there, but it was so cramped that I was troubled by my brother kicking me. Though our house was completed, Mama didn't come back to us. Now father is sick in bed all day. He can move his hands, but the rest of his body is unable to move. When he goes out, he must be carried on a stretcher. I hope Father can walk soon. Then I'd like to go the mountains hand in hand with my Father, to draw pictures.

There were three schools within a kilometer radius of the hypocenter, or ground zero. Fuchi Citizen's Junior High School, 1,500 meters from the hypocenter, officially had more than 1,400 students and some fifty teachers, but all of the students were working in factories in place of the older teenagers who had been drafted into the military. Most of the teachers had become work supervisors. The children at Yamazato and Shiroyama Elementary Schools, 700 meters and 500 meters from ground zero, had been sent home for their "safety." Instantly, in the moments of the explosion, the area became an inferno that turned buildings into rubble and created a blackened, leveled field as far as you could see. Of the 1,400 students in this school district fewer than seventy-five survived. When the schools were rebuilt, peace education became a priority.

Teachers continue to nurture the growth of peace consciousness by helping children understand that peacemaking begins with each of us. Practicing peace in daily life includes tolerance and cooperation with others, conflict resolution without fighting, dealing with "ijime" or bullying, kindness to animals, and growing and caring for plants. Teachers emphasize "teaching others what we have learned" rather than "learning what is taught." Teachers see their job as helping children become ambassadors for peace.

Shiroyama Elementary reopened in 1948. Beginning in 1951, a peace ceremony has been held on the ninth day of each month as a way of remembering August 9, 1945, and as part of the school peace program in honor of

Dr. Nagai. The peace curriculum is known as the "Takashi Nagai approach to peace." On the fiftieth anniversary of the bomb, the school unveiled its peace monument, which consists of two hands holding three interconnected rings symbolizing boundless hope, an open heart, and deep love. The fiftieth anniversary of the bombing, 1995, became an opportunity for the school to adopt the slogan "Peace from Shiroyama," signifying that the school should become a source of inspiration for peacemaking. The school has produced a "Shiroyama Peace Map" and created around the school grounds five areas as part of its "Shiroyama Peace Zone Project" to promote feelings, images, and thoughts related to peace: "Peace Entrance Zone," "Relaxation Zone," "Atomic Bomb Study Zone," the "Nature Zone," and the "Prayer Zone." Students have made signboards with written explanations and illustrations in each zone, and older students serve as guides or docents.

At Yamazato Elementary School there is a small hill within the school grounds on top of which sits a stone monument known as the "Memorial for Those Children." The memorial, envisioned by Dr. Nagai, was built using the royalties from his book *Living beneath the Atomic Cloud: Testimony of the Children of Nagasaki*. The school's peace program, based on Dr. Nagai's loving approach, includes an exchange program with the elementary school Dr. Nagai attended, Iiseki Elementary School, in Mitoya, Shimane Prefecture. Every two years on August 9, students from Iiseki visit Yamazato to take part in a peace ceremony, play games, and have discussions and a special dinner in the school gym. Students at Yamazato keep "peace notebooks" from grade one through grade six, in which they write observations, comments, and essays and create drawings around the theme of peacemaking.

Perhaps, as my parents often said, real peace will come to the world only when all religions learn to respect and appreciate each other. Perhaps then there will be authentic peace, but we must still work at it, person to person, as Takashi Nagai did, day by day, hour by hour, minute by minute. For him, it was an attitude, a way of living, and through his example we come closer to understanding the task laid before us, the task Thich Nhat Hanh describes as "being peace."

11

A Thousand Paper Cranes

Spread your wings, and we'll fly away.
—S<small>ADAKO</small> S<small>ASAKI</small>

T<small>HIS STORY STARTS IN</small> 1945. A girl named Sadako Sasaki was living in a Japanese city called Hiroshima along with about half a million other people. When she was two years old the first atomic bomb ever to be used against human beings was dropped on Hiroshima. Most of the city was completely smashed and burned to the ground. Sadako was about a mile and a half away from where the bomb exploded, but she wasn't burned or injured at all, at least not in any way people could see.

A few weeks after the bomb was dropped, people in Hiroshima began dying from a sickness even the doctors couldn't understand. People who seemed perfectly healthy would suddenly get weak and sick and then just die. It was so strange and new that no one knew what to do to treat a particular person.

By the time Sadako was in the seventh grade, she was a normal, happy twelve-year-old girl going to a regular school and studying and playing like everyone else. Ten years had passed since the nuclear explosion, and Sadako was thinking about other things. One of the things she thought about most was running.

One day after an important relay race that she helped her team win, she felt tired and dizzy. After a while she felt better, so she thought it was just that she was so tired because of the race. Over the next few weeks she tried to forget about it, but the dizziness kept coming back, especially when she was running. She didn't tell anyone about it, not even Chizuko, her best friend. Finally, one morning, it got so bad that she fell down and just lay on

---

This chapter is an excerpt from a booklet written and published by pupils of Hiroshima International School, Japan.

the ground for a while. This time everyone noticed. They took her to the Red Cross hospital to see what was the matter. No one could believe what they found out. Sadako had leukemia, a kind of cancer of the blood. At that time quite a few children about Sadako's age were getting leukemia, which the people then called "the A-bomb disease." Almost everyone who got the disease died and Sadako was very scared. She didn't want to die.

Soon after Sadako went to the hospital, her best friend, Chizuko, came to visit her. She brought some special paper and folded a paper crane. Chizuko told Sadako about a legend. She said that the crane, a sacred bird in Japan, lives for a thousand years, and if a sick person folds a thousand cranes, that person will get well. Sadako decided to fold a thousand cranes. Because of the leukemia she often felt too weak and tired so she couldn't work all the time, but from that day on, whenever she could, she folded cranes.

Sadako actually folded her thousand cranes, but she wasn't getting any better. But instead of getting angry or giving up, she decided she would fold more cranes. She started on her second thousand. Everyone was amazed by how brave and patient she was. On October 25, 1955, surrounded by her loving family, she went to sleep, peacefully, for the last time.

But this story doesn't end with Sadako's death. She had a lot of friends who loved her and who missed her very much. And they didn't only feel sad about Sadako. Lots of other children in Hiroshima had died or were dying of the A-bomb disease. Her friends wanted very much to do something for Sadako. So thirty-nine of her classmates formed a club and began asking for money for a monument for her. The word spread quickly. Students from 3,100 schools in Japan and from nine other countries gave money, and finally, on May 5, 1958, almost three years after Sadako died, they got enough money to build the monument. It's called the Children's Peace Monument and it is in the Peace Park, which is in the middle of Hiroshima, right where the atomic bomb was dropped.

The movement to build this monument became so famous and popular that a movie called *A Thousand Paper Cranes* was made about it. About sixty children from Hiroshima and about twenty children from Tokyo helped make the movie, and when it was finished they wanted to stay together as friends, so they started a new club called "The Paper Crane Club." The purpose of this club was to help children get together to think and work for peace. This club has continued to exist for almost thirty years. The members take care of Sadako's monument, visit atomic bomb survivors, people who were in Hiroshima when the bomb was dropped and who are getting sick and old or who just need help for some reason.

One other thing they always do is fold cranes. They use the cranes in many ways. Sometimes they hang them on Sadako's monument and other monuments in Hiroshima's Peace Park. Sometimes they send them to world leaders as a way of reminding those leaders that the children of the world want to get rid of nuclear bombs. And whenever world leaders or atomic bomb survivors or people working for peace come to Hiroshima, members of the Paper Crane Club greet them and put a wreath of cranes around their necks to welcome them and to help them think about the meaning of Hiroshima.

But the meaning of folding cranes and the meaning of Hiroshima and the Paper Crane Club are perhaps best summed up in the words carved on the granite base of the Children's Peace Monument:

> *This is our cry*
> *This is our prayer*
> *To build peace in this world.*

12

Hiroshima and the 1000 Cranes Club

For us all, and for all people in the world, Hiroshima is, today, already both myth and reality.

OLAF PALME
Chair, Independent Commission on Disarmament,
United Nations, 1981

That is true culture which helps us to work for the social betterment of all.

HENRY WARD BEECH

THE WHITE CRANE IS THE SACRED BIRD OF JAPAN. Legend tells that it lives for a thousand years and that anyone who folds a thousand paper cranes will also live a long life. Most Japanese children also know the life story of Sadako Sasaki and the Paper Crane Club, which helped to make the paper crane a vibrant symbol of the hope for peace.

Sadako was two years old when the atomic bomb was dropped on Hiroshima on August 6, 1945. She was not burned, but radiation poisoning caused her to contract leukemia at the age of twelve. Hospitalized, she began folding paper cranes; she folded more than a thousand cranes with the help of friends, hoping she would get well. She died several months later.

Her seventh-grade classmates wanted to build a monument to Sadako and the thousands of other children who had died or were still dying from the bombing. Largely on their own, they organized a fund-raising campaign. They asked children in Japan and thirteen other countries to donate the equivalent of five cents each. More than three thousand Japanese schools

---

This chapter first appeared as the last chapter of the book *Linking through Diversity*. It is a condensation of journal entries made by Walter since leaving Hiroshima in 1988.

and hundreds of foreign schools participated in fund-raising drives, and in 1958 they had raised enough to build a child-spirited structure in the middle of Peace Park, topped by Sadako's statue holding aloft a crane. People place millions of cranes at the base of the monument each year. Sadako's classmates also formed the Paper Crane Club, which continues today and involves students in keeping the area around the monument clean and bestowing necklaces of cranes on visitors.

Years later I held the position of principal of Hiroshima's International School. One August morning, the foreign children at the school and I were stringing together cranes at the monument when Kim Blackford said, "Kids don't start wars. But what can kids really do for peace?" Sitting as we were, surrounded by paper cranes, the students were beginning to find an answer, and so was I. Perhaps I would actively support the telling of Sadako's story to children in the United States and around the world. I would resolve my personal anguish over the inability to help, to do something constructive for Hiroshima and the bomb victims. What we uncover from the past is a reconstruction that somehow is embedded in the present of our meaning-making. The message of Hiroshima and of Sadako is not simply in the past; it is the past in the present as the future.

Late that afternoon I took the strung cranes to the Children's Monument and laid them atop millions of other brightly colored paper lights of hope. The park was alive with tourists, lovers, friends, and little children who were feeding hundreds of little doves. A group of Native Americans in full headdress were drumming a day-long prayer vigil with the participation of a Buddhist priest and a South African "witch doctor."

I walked past the Peace Museum, which sits twenty-five feet off the ground on huge columns, like a tomb perched toward the sky. Underneath there was much activity. Small groups of two or three gathered. Elvis played from a stereo blaster as six Japanese "Fifties" twisted away. A young Japanese man with cerebral palsy and severely twisted hands parked his wheelchair at the steps descending from the museum to collect signatures and contributions to rid the world of nuclear weapons. "Was he a bomb victim?" foreign tourists invariably wondered.

Two young men with burr haircuts rode skateboards, and another, wearing a red-white-and-blue cape, rode a unicycle. They were U.S. servicemen on leave from the marine air station where I had attended school twenty years earlier. What is sacred, and what is commemorative? For whom? Were they exporting America's carefree abandon in the face of inevitable catastrophe? Were they just ignorant, senseless, ugly Americans desecrating the sanctification of Hiroshima? German soldiers skateboarding at Auschwitz? Japanese sailors playing Frisbee at the Pearl Harbor memorial? Twenty years later, no longer banned from Hiroshima, these nineteen-year-old ethnocentric U.S. teenage soldiers were, if not welcomed, at least tolerated performers under the world's memorial to nuclear holocaust, part of the deep ironies and contradictions of and within Hiroshima.

THE 1000 CRANES CLUB AND A THOUSAND POINTS OF LIGHT

I started thinking, maybe we could start a club. Why not contact kids around the world and tell them the stories of Sadako and the Paper Crane Club? We could ask them to send cranes to be placed at the base of the Children's Monument. Maybe it would be the start of an activity that would help keep Hiroshima's message and peace in the minds of children all the time, not only on special anniversaries. One of the most compelling concerns of my children was that the world media paid undue attention to Hiroshima during the week of the fortieth anniversary of the bombing, but what the media failed to tell was the story of the weeks after. Would there be any interest on the forty-first anniversary or would the fiftieth commemoration be the only newsworthy date?

A club would give us foreigners living in Japan a chance to take part in the global community, communicating with students from other countries, finding out what they were thinking and doing, all linked together by a common project. It seemed like a good idea because like Sadako's original cranes and the response of her classmates, it sprang spontaneously from a sincere wish to do something about a situation that seems hopelessly beyond a child's influence. It was a manifestation of social concern, of creativity, and of the urge to reach out across barriers of space and culture to become part of larger community. It held the promise of taking the children beyond themselves.

Eleanor Duckworth, Piaget's translator and a brilliant educator, wrote an essay in the 1960s titled "The Having of Wonderful Ideas" in which she described good teaching as empowering children to have wonderful ideas and supporting them to follow through and actualize those ideas. That was our philosophy at the beginning of the school year in September 1985. The Hiroshima International School community voted that the 1000 Cranes Club would become an integral feature of each class and of the school as a whole. Teachers would provide class time for the project, be open to expansion and integration into other domains, and would facilitate, but not dictate, what would happen with the activities and direction of the project. As much as possible the club would be "living social studies"—through hands-on project extensions, cross-age work and teaching, discussion of moral and social dilemma, role-playing, and arts and crafts.

We decided as a community that each member would learn to fold a crane, at least as a Japanese craft. No one had to fold cranes "for peace" (interpreted as folding cranes to go into the 1000 cranes booklet). We decided as a staff that active discussion of war, peace, and the nuclear debates would arise only from the concerns of students themselves. The horror of Hiroshima and the anxieties of a potential holocaust would not be initiated by teachers. We would fervently support any discussion and exploration initiated by the students. However, the concepts of conflict and conflict resolution would be active and prominent features of our program, as would the study of critical thinking, debate, advertising, and propaganda.

Part of our reluctance to take a nuclear-horror approach to peace studies was that it was an emotional and cognitive imposition. Hiroshima City's Peace Curriculum, which we were invited to adopt by the city's teachers' association and which was required in all elementary schools, begins in first grade with a typical lesson of showing children drawings of the horrors of war, including bodies in flames, with the admonition, "War is terrible! War is wrong, isn't it?" While we agreed with the evil and inhumanity of war, we were bothered by the admonish-and-scare-them-to-believe-in-peace tactics.

On the other hand, we weren't living survivors of the atomic firebomb as were the writers of the curriculum. From our limited (and perhaps naive) perspective, peace was not the simple abolition of war and conflict. Peace was a way of life, an attitude toward self and others. How can we help children to resolve conflicts more reasonably and humanely? If conflicts and problems are essential for growth, then collaborative conflict resolution and problem solving would become essential activities of our "peace club." Our greatest concern was to avoid talking about peace but to actualize it within the cooperative and collaborative ethos of our community. Preach little. Practice what we value a lot.

The students agreed that the senior-level classes would learn to fold three kinds of cranes, and these students in turn would teach the intermediate-level students, who would instruct the primary-level students. Peer pressure, perhaps, but the teacher insistence insured that all students and staff participated. Students at the senior level also spent more than a month researching and planning their 1000 Cranes Club booklet, which contains letters to students and teachers, the story of Sadako and the Paper Crane Club, and a bibliography of all materials on Hiroshima written in English. The younger classes made booklets and drawings, created murals for the club, and set up display areas for anticipated letters and cranes. Throughout the school, class discussions of actual and simulated socio-moral dilemmas, cooperative games, collaborative school chores, and the daily folding of cranes for each booklet defined the ethos of the school.

To publish the booklet and to pay for the initial mailings, the students organized bake sales and a walk-a-thon. At a weekly school meeting they voted to divide their substantial funds ($6,000 a year) three ways: 33 percent to the 1000 Cranes Club, 33 percent to schoolwide projects (e.g., camping), and 34 percent to UNICEF. (Five years later, their commitment to giving to others continues.) On October 25, the thirtieth anniversary of Sadako's death, the club was born. Hundreds of booklets were sent to important leaders and organizers and to Sadako's parents and members of the Paper Crane Club who were present. Then we waited.

The story of Sadako and the Paper Crane Club is powerful on many levels. It illustrates a grim truth about nuclear weapons and symbolizes a fear of nuclear war that has been a part of many children's and adults' consciousness for more than two generations. It is also the story of a young person's patience, courage, hope, and creative activism in the face of the ultimate fear of pain and death. Sadako's story is the tale of the power of children working together in partnership for a common cause. Groups of students folded cranes, created a movement, raised funds, built a monument, and established paper cranes as a globally recognized symbol of hope and the wish for peace. The story thereby opened a channel for the creative, peaceful expression of fear about nuclear war in particular, and more generally, it provided a channel to express deep-felt concern about peoples' inhumanity toward others, as well as the hope for a better world.

Sadako's classmates started a project that has lasted thirty-five years and has become a tradition. It is a tradition that has grown primarily for the lived experience of its message. By that I mean that it is a cooperative and collaborative action. It is a nonthreatening, apolitical, humane way for children to express feelings that are extremely difficult to articulate and resolve. And by doing so children can subtly, yet recognizably, let the adults around them know how much they care for each other and their survival. Finally, the work of Sadako's classmates, like that of the International School children's 1000 Cranes Club, has served to give other children around the world a concrete example of peaceful cooperation and the experience of a collaborative project.

Conflict, differing opinions, and even animated arguments are natural phenomena of authentic projects as students actively imagine, organize, plan, research, and implement a collaborative enterprise. Interest naturally ebbs and flows among participants. Ensuring there is a balance between focusing on the "others" the project was created for and on the potential benefits of mutual respect and camaraderie from communal teamwork is often difficult. However, the benefits are truly amazing.

The aims of helping and joining others in a 1000 Cranes project, locally or globally, leads easily and naturally to exploring the relationship between international conflict and peace, between conflict and peacefulness with friends and family, between our personal "internal" conflict and peace of mind. The project provides a natural context for the exploration of human justice and human rights and the environmental and people problems of the world. It provides an ethos for exploring the commonalties and wonderful diversity of being human, in all its interrelated, cross-cultural, intercultural, and multicultural forms. Working together and discussing, role-playing, or getting involved in conflict in order to find reasonable, peaceful resolutions create an emotional paradox that provides an ideal context for significant insights and social bonding in the classroom.

Whether children are six or twelve, folding cranes over an extended period of time provides a wonderful context for discussions and activities of peaceful collaboration. Whether five or ten minutes a day or several afternoon periods a week, to think of Sadako or participation in the 1000 Cranes

Club, or to reason about a classroom issue, is to feel and reason at some point through various mediums about friendship, fairness and justice, prejudice and equality, empathy and reciprocity—in short, a whole range of human values. Crane-folding sessions become a time to work together creatively, to help or teach others, to work for a common cause. And origami involves concrete mathematics (seriation and geometry), fine motor coordination (teaching patience, exactness, and precision), and a wonderful craft of Asia (leading to other origami projects and paper-folding projects that originate in China).

CREATIVE EXTENSIONS AND INTERCONNECTIONS

Over the past seven years, thousands of booklets have been sent to schools and organizations in more than thirty countries. From sixteen countries, hundreds of schools and classrooms have sent a thousand cranes to be placed at monuments in Peace Park.

What is absolutely fascinating are the many wonderful spin-offs of this project, particularly the creative extensions it fosters in children and their teachers, and the interconnections made between groups of people. Besides sending colorful banners to accompany their cranes, groups have sent to Hiroshima hundreds of drawings, dioramas, collages, an original play, several video letters, tapes of songs (including original works), poetry, and stories—all expression of the human spirit to create, to reach out, and to touch others. Numerous classrooms and schools and groups have linked with each other—in some cases classrooms within a building; in others, across town, a region, or a nation, and between nations. Locally and globally—interculturally linked!

In Argentina, various schools throughout the country sent cranes and then began exchanging students and projects with each other. In West Germany a participating school created a cultural information exchange (videotapes, artwork) with a 1000 Cranes Club school in Sweden. In Sweden a children's agency published articles on the club in more than fifty magazines and newspapers. In St. Paul, Minnesota, with a helping hand from Ken Simon, a class of second graders introduced Sadako's story to classes of eleventh graders and taught them to fold cranes. In a number of countries, including Argentina, Brazil, Mexico, and India, groups have translated parts of the 1000 Cranes Club booklet into native languages and shared the story with other students. And in the town of Townsville, Australia, and perhaps in other locales of the globe, the whole town got together, led by the mayor, to have a picnic and fold paper cranes to send to Hiroshima.

Inspired by Sadako's story, third graders at Arroyo del Oso Elementary School in Albuquerque, New Mexico, decided to raise money to erect a "sister" children's peace statue in Los Alamos, New Mexico, the test site for the bomb. Children and teenagers in New Mexico have formed the Kids' Committee to oversee the project. The Kids' Committee had collected $8,957.93 as of November 16, 1992, and they were finally able to build the statue several years later.

In 1986, once the 1000 Cranes project became a part of the school's activities (with endless correspondence and delivery of cranes to Peace Park), I wanted my students to interconnect in new ways with other children. Over the next two years we exchanged culture boxes and arts and crafts with a small school in Pigeon Forge, Tennessee. We exchanged video letters with other international schools in Japan, including travelogues and videos on indigenous folk dances and songs. We exchanged a "how to" video with a school in Australia—we demonstrated Esdee Tennis and Radio exercises; they sent us a tape on Aussie rules of football and the correct way to throw a boomerang and enclosed three boomerangs. From a school in East Germany we received fifty drawings of children and scenes of "Peace," each under half a rainbow. We completed the artwork by drawing scenes under the other half of the rainbows, photocopied them, and sent the originals back to East Germany, where the two halves were displayed. We continued to make tourist guidebooks (for children) to Hiroshima.

Over the years the Hiroshima International School students have raised the funds to translate the Sadako story into Japanese, Spanish, and Russian. In 1987 Premier Gorbachev sent students a telegram of encouragement. Of the many teachers who have written to Hiroshima International School, what is most striking is a common thread—this project encourages children (and adults) to enact social values not often given preference in our competitive, individualistic schooling. By working together in a communal atmosphere of cooperation for a common good and for the joy inherent in the task of creating, children, tacitly at least, showed adults how much they care to work together. It is a lesson for us all. Let me quote the closing paragraph of the 1000 Cranes Club booklet written by Kim and the original group of children (now adults):

> Something we have learned from folding 1000 cranes is that even with a group of twenty-five students, it takes time to fold a 1000. In a class of 25, each student would first have to learn to fold a crane and then fold forty. But once you begin it can be fun. Most important, it is a time to work together, to talk about things like friendship and conflicts. We don't have any particular suggestions other than when we did this, we learned a lot about each other, we helped each other, and now our class is really close. We folded these cranes for peace and in memory of Sadako, but really we helped ourselves. Please join us.

For specific information on joining the 1000 Cranes Club project, send a self-addressed, stamped envelope to: Walter Enloe, Graduate School, Hamline University, 1536 Hewitt Ave., St. Paul, MN 55104, or search for *Hiroshima International School* on the Internet.

From Piaget I hold two recurring images. One is that everything is interconnected and systemic. I look at a photograph of the Earth taken from outer space, and I see a new paradigm for what it means to be human. I'll tell you its secret. It's not the information-processing system the scientistic education establishment wants us to believe in—new machinery in an outdated like-a-machine paradigm. No, our photograph is of an *umwelt* or ecosystem; not simply images of a food web or water-oxygen cycle. Our paradigm includes two children, a boy and girl, one from the United Sates and one from Japan, sitting on the beach on a sunny day, alive and connected, and folding cranes!

Piaget's second image of being human speaks for all of us committed to children as active creators, experimenters, and citizens, locally and globally. We share with him the deep respect he had for children and his conviction:

> The principal goal of education is to create people who are capable of doing new things, not simply repeating what other generations have done—people who are creators, inventors, and discoverers. The second goal of education is to form minds that are critical, can verify, and do not accept everything they are offered. The great danger today is from slogans, collective opinions, ready-made trends of thought. We have to be able to resist individually, to criticize, to

distinguish between what is proven and what is not. So we need pupils who are active, who learn early to find out for themselves, partly by their own spontaneous activity and partly through the materials we set up for them; who learn early to tell what is verifiable and what is simply the first idea to come to them.

In closing, I would like to ask you to join me in Hiroshima's Peace Park. Imagine! We stand facing the Children's Monument, dedicated to all of those thousands of children, who, like Sadako, died from the effects of the A-bomb. We step forward to the monument and place our cranes at its base and read the inscription:

> *This is our cry*
> *This is our prayer*
> *To build peace in this world.*

13

Winged Messengers

A Holiday Peace Project

Pika to Hikkata, Genshi e no tami ni, Yoi-yaga, Tonbe agatte Heiwa, No Hato yo (The atomic ball, loosed sharpest lightening, Yoi-yaga, they fly upward, the doves of peace)

SONG OF HEIWA ONDO (peace dance)
Hiroshima Festival of Peace, 1947

I WAS TEACHING AT THE HIROSHIMA INTERNATIONAL SCHOOL in Japan in 1985, the fortieth anniversary of the dropping of the atomic bomb on that city. The attention given to this event—locally and internationally—got me thinking about how we could approach it in school. I wanted to accomplish two goals. I wanted to convey to my students the urgency of world peace without going into the complex and disturbing details of war. And I wanted to turn that urgency into action by encouraging my students to put the message of peace into practice in their own lives.

I chose as my starting point a story already familiar to my students, that of Sadako Sasaki, a twelve-year-old Hiroshima girl who died in 1955 as a result of radiation from the bomb. Sadako became famous for her determination to fold paper cranes, believing that this would make her well again. By focusing on the young girl's dignity and courage as she faced a slow, painful death, I encapsulated the horrors of war in a context my students could understand. And by involving them in small-group crafting of paper

---

This chapter was written for *Learning Magazine* in 1989 to introduce classroom teachers both to the symbolic stories of Sadako and the 1000 cranes and to the creative and constructive craft and gift-giving possibilities. Responses from elementary teachers around the United States were tremendous.

cranes, I set up a situation in which they would actually experience cooperation and conflict resolution. (In fact, my students themselves took this project much further that I had envisioned—but more about that later.)

Clearly, the message of the paper cranes goes beyond the city of Hiroshima. Especially at this time of year, Sadako's story can provide your students with the same opportunity to learn about peace on both a global and a personal level.

FROM WAR, LESSONS OF PEACE

Sadako, like many small children at the time of the bombing, was exposed to so much radiation that she developed leukemia several years later. Rather than despair over her fate, however, she began folding cranes. According to Japanese legend, anyone who folded a thousand paper cranes would live a long life. Sadako died despite her beliefs and valiant efforts, but her classmates, so inspired by her courage, took steps to ensure that her story would live forever. With money collected by and from students, they commissioned the building of the Children's Peace Monument. Today it stands, ever festooned with cranes, a tribute to Sadako and to children the world over who call out for peace.

Begin your exploration of peace and cooperation with Sadako's story. Older students can read and discuss *Sadako and the Thousand Paper Cranes* by Eleanor Coerr (Dell, 1977)—though you should point out that, contrary to Coerr's book, Sadako did fold a thousand cranes: she died before she reached her second thousand. Younger students can listen as you tell them a shortened version of the story (see the insert "The Story of Sadako: A Child's Plea for Peace"). As the story draws to a close, focus your students' attention on the cooperative effort of Sadako's classmates to erect a monument for her. Then relate another cooperative effort, one that allows your students to participate in the paper crane tradition. Tell them how my students took the story of Sadako beyond their classroom and into the world.

As they were diligently folding cranes, one of my students suddenly mused: Why not create a club to spread the word about Sadako and the paper cranes? The idea flashed like wildfire through the class. Soon the students were busy writing a booklet about their club—the Thousand Cranes Club—and devising a system for displaying at the monument any cranes that were sent to them from overseas. (The insert "Packaging Peace" gives the specifics for sending your cranes to be placed at the monument in Hiroshima.) It was a wonderful idea because, like the effort by Sadako's classmates thirty years earlier, my students' club sprang from a sincere wish to do something about a situation—the need for world peace—that seemed hopelessly beyond a child's influence.

These stories should be inspiration enough for your students to launch their own cooperative crane-folding project.

CRAFTING CRANES

Paper-folding, or origami, has long been a part of the Japanese school curriculum. Not only is it an enjoyable craft activity, but it also develops fine-motor skill, cognitive acuity, and patience. (Some evidence even indicates that it increases mathematical capabilities, such as understanding seriation and moving from the concrete to the abstract.) Most children take to it readily, given the proper instruction. Here are a few tips for your origami adventure:

Choosing an origami book. Origami books are available in the craft section of most bookstores or can be ordered from The Friends of the Origami Center of America (see "Resources"). If possible, study the diagrams and instructions before you purchase a book. (If they're not clear to you, they won't be clear to your students.)

Type of crane. Some origami books include several different cranes. Once your students have learned the standard crane, have them experiment with the plump, slender, and flapping varieties.

Kind of paper. Origami paper is available in most craft stores, but in can be expensive. Sadako's family, friends, and nurses saved many different kinds of paper for her cranes—scrap paper from her father's barbershop, silver foil wrappers from candy bars, even wrappings from medicine packages. Challenge your student to find paper to recycle into cranes. (What about old dittos, magazine covers, holiday wrapping paper?) Just make sure each piece of homemade origami paper is a perfect square, and avoid papers that are too thick (cardboard) or too thin (tissue paper). Also, warn your students never to use the color black because to the Japanese it symbolizes bad luck and death.

Size of paper. The recommended size is 15 x 15 cm (6 x 6 inches), though any manageable size may be used.

Age level. Children as young as 5 or 6 can fold cranes, although the younger the children, the more learning time they'll need (see "Teaching Strategy," below). If your students have trouble with the crane even after several days of practice, substitute a simpler bird. Maryann Murray, a librarian in Pennsauken, New Jersey, uses a swan pattern with younger students.

Teaching strategy. Begin by picking three or four students and teaching them how to fold a crane. These students, in turn, become teachers for their classmates, again in groups of three or four. Have them do the teaching in two stages. The first day, the students fold until they reach the basic "kite form"—so named because it looks like a kite and is used as the basis for several origami patterns. (With first and second graders, you may want to invite students from upper grades to be your helpers. Also, expect the first "day" of practice to last several weeks.)

Folding sessions. Once your students feel secure about making cranes, begin producing them in quantity. Set aside time each day or week to work on the project. Sessions should last at least thirty minutes. Experiment with large and small cooperative groups. (My students worked best in groups of four or five.)

INSPIRING COOPERATION

During the crane-making sessions, a living lesson in cooperation will unfold. Over the course of a few sessions, watch as a range of emotions and values emerges in different groups: envy at others' abilities, competition for the prettiest paper, patience with slow workers, satisfaction at a job well done. In short, the session will become models of conflict resolution, of how people can hold conflicting needs and opinions without coming to blows or losing respect for one another.

In a class meeting, encourage your students to reflect on conflicts that might arise in school or at home. Help them to see that in all situations, one theme rings true: the important ingredients of world peace—cooperation, mutual understanding, and reciprocity—are also the foundations for a peaceful, supportive neighborhood, family, and classroom.

On that note, your students can choose a final roosting place for their paper cranes—strung up around the classroom as holiday decoration or displayed on an international monument halfway around the world.

THE STORY OF SADAKO: A CHILD'S PLEA FOR PEACE

Sadako Sasaki was just two years old on August 6, 1945, when the United States dropped the atomic bomb on her home city of Hiroshima. Although she lived about one and one-half miles from the point of explosion, she was neither burned nor injured—at least not in a way that anyone could immediately detect.

Ten years passed, Hiroshima rebuilt itself, and Sadako grew into an energetic young girl who dreamed of becoming a track star. But inside her a sickness was also growing, and when she was twelve the doctors made a dreaded diagnosis. Sadako began folding, she imagined herself getting better. And the cranes, hanging above her bed on strings, made her feel less angry, less depressed, and, most important, less afraid.

Sadako folded her thousand cranes and had started on a second thousand when she died. Her classmates, determined to let the world know of their friend's brave struggle and of the tragedy of nuclear war, began asking children all over Japan (and later students in thirteen countries) to each donate the equivalent of 5 cents. More than 3,000 schools responded. Today, a child-inspired tower topped by Sadako's statue sits at what was once ground zero in Hiroshima. Since its completion, hundreds of thousands of cranes have been placed at its base each year.

PACKAGING PEACE

Each year, hundreds of thousands of paper cranes flock to the Children's Peace Monument in Hiroshima bearing tidings of courage, hope, and peace. The 1000 Cranes Club, formed in 1985 by my students at Hiroshima International School, invites your students to take part in the international tradition. In return, your class will receive a color picture of the cranes placed at the foot of the monument and a certificate of club membership.

14

Bringing Constructivity to the Classroom

> *Whatever you do for one side, you always have to do for the other.*
>
> Seven-year-old Nick Schnoes'
> algorithm for paper-folding and peacemaking

Much of what we know well is often at an intuitive level—derived from lived experience. Because this knowing is so much a part of being in the world, we often do not examine and reflect on its meaning, but instead take it for granted. We tend to place greater value on those things outside our ways of being in the world, the contrived hypotheses of our empirical questioning.

But those same empirical questions frequently originate in the lived experience itself and such was the case with the study described here. The study investigates a much discussed topic—the evident superior achievement of Japanese students—but treats the question not as a set of hypotheses and data, but rather as a hunch about a uniquely embedded lived experience of Japanese pre-schoolers.

This essay is the result of years of creative teaching and study of paper-folding, gift giving, and the learning gained from teaching children and observing children teach others. It was co-written with Karen Stout, who teaches and learns from educators at the University of Minnesota, and it is written with thanks to the children and staff at the Downtown Open Basic School in Minneapolis. Our hunch about the power of multiple intelligences grows out of the 1000 Cranes Club, which introduced paper-folding dramatically to foreign children living in Hiroshima and subsequently to children in the United States and other parts of the world. In China and Japan paper-folding was originally a part of religious rites, and at temples today, priests write prayers on rice paper that is then folded and placed in trees and shrubs until the paper disintegrates. From the nineteenth-century kindergarten of Froebel to the studio of Frank Lloyd Wright to the German commercial arts course of the Bauhaus, paper-folding has had an intriguing part to play.

The hunch grew out of Walter's experience of spending many years in Japan as a teacher/principal of the International School in Hiroshima. Here he observed that the math performance of the youngest students improved when origami, or paper-folding, became part of the curriculum. He also noted that there is no formal manipulative curriculum in Japanese kindergarten, and yet first-grade Japanese children are more advanced than American children in the logic of mathematics and on measures of spatial reasoning (American youngsters are more advanced only in verbal memory [Stevenson 1986]). Looking closer, he found that Japanese children learn origami at their mothers' knees. The textbook, *Origami* (1976), written for elementary teachers by the Nippon, Japan, Origami Association, argues that the ancient art of paper-folding "stimulate(s) the development of children's intelligence" and promotes a dialogue between parents and children, grandparents and grandsons, and so on. From these observations of an embedded cultural phenomenon, came a hunch that constructive manipulative experiences, such as origami, during the pre-operational stage support later mathematical understandings.

Walter followed up on this hunch when he returned to the United states and had similar experiences with American classrooms. His contagious belief in it drew me into becoming a fellow investigator, and we began our study by compiling an exhaustive literature review that supported our emerging idea that handicrafts are much more than entertainment for young minds. In fact they are a form of schematic learning through the repeatable actions implicit in the routine practice and inventiveness that constitutes songs, hand games, and dance.

PAPER-FOLDING AS A UNIQUE CONSTRUCTIVE ACT

A piece of paper is a three-dimensional whole on which homeomorphically the whole, through folding, becomes transformed into another whole or imitative object that can be reversed to its original form. Manipulatives, such as Unifix cubes, Cuisenaire rods, original Legos, and so on, on the other hand, begin as elements (unconnected whole). Consider Unifix cubes. We can connect them, give them an order, reverse the order by rearranging or removing them, and thereby give intelligent orderliness to them. But perhaps for children there is a fundamental difference in the quality of logical-mathematical experience between acting on conventional manipulatives and transforming through paper-folding. Seriation and reversibility (as only two operations to be considered) are experienced as parts to whole with conventional manipulatives and, in origami, are experienced as whole transformed through second order parts or steps to another homeomorphic whole.

At its simplest, paper-folding involves figurative knowing (Piaget and Inhelder 1956), or physical knowledge such as texture, size, color, and shape. Through folding, figurative knowledge gives way to logical-mathematic operations (e.g., seriation, reversibility) or knowledge derived from coordinate actions on the object of paper but not from the paper itself. Piaget and Inhelder argued that "motor activity in the form of skilled movements is vital to the development of intuitive thought and the mental representation of space" (p. 19). Both the pre-operational and the concrete operational stages are sensitive periods for the learning of movements that become internalized as cognitive operations. The pre-operational stage, ages 4–7, is the stage during which actions on objects become intuitively incorporated into the child's schemas. The stage of concrete objects is the foundation for developing abstract concepts.

The logical-mathematical operations intrinsic to the act of paper-folding involve seriation and reversibility. The movements must be performed in certain orders, not as parts to a whole as in manipulatives (Legos, Unifix cubes, etc.), and the origami object is a whole that can be reversed to its original form through the reversal of steps and not merely the taking apart of pieces as conventional manipulatives. The correspondence of figures and classes occurs because each paper-folding base leads to a different class of objects folded from that particular one. Paper-folding also develops topological and Euclidean space relations through active construction. In short, paper-folding embodies many of the movements vital to the development of intuitive-mathematical thought and the elemental representation of space.

In *The Child's Conception of Space* (1956), Piaget and Inhelder note that the concepts of geometry derive from an intuitive foundation—sublogical—similar to logico-arithmetical ones but on objects. This intuitive foundation is characterized by symbolic (mental or pictorial) images. Spatial and geometric reasoning emerge at an intuitive level—from within the pre-operational and concrete-operational child. Innovations in math education, however, have focused on math from the outside. They have been characterized by ways to teach more, at an earlier age and more efficiently

(Kamii 1985). Paper-folding, however, as an "innovation" with a constructive nature, may promote the invention of logico-mathematical knowledge from within.

A constructivist orientation also respects the social setting as an important element in the construction of meaning. Paper-folding is not typically a skill learned in isolation but rather in a social setting. It has elements of play as children share their construction, and in order to be successful, it requires knowledge that children and adults convey through physical exam and verbal explanations. Through the activity itself, the child comes to know the importance of following directions, being precise, listening closely, giving directions so that others can understand (with checking for understanding implied), and working toward neatness. These social/cultural expectations of schooling are implicit to success in the activity and not teacher imposed.

STUDYING PAPER-FOLDING

To date, the theoretical foundations for our hunch keep accumulating, but early on we had enough to initiate a question-generating study. We acknowledged that origami could not usefully be studied as a treatment or intervention but rather as part of an organismic worldview, where humans are engaged in making meaning of the environment that surrounds them, both by acting on it (assimilation) and by acting on their own mental models of reality (accommodation). In addition we articulated a set of shared beliefs about applied educational research:

1. It should consider a question of interest to both researchers and practitioners;
2. It should inform practice;
3. The merits of an idea should be decided by how well it works in the classroom (Duckworth 1987);
4. The idea should be studied as situated in the context where it must grow and, if it works, eventually live;
5. Everyone (teachers, university personnel, and children) should participate as researchers, practitioners, and learners.

Our methodology sought to make paper-folding not an intervention but rather a part of the lived experience of the school.

Phenomenological research provided the philosophic framework for the methodology. "Its particular appeal is that it tries to understand the phenomenon of education by maintaining a view of pedagogy as an experience of the whole, and a view of the experiential situation as the *topos* of real pedagogic activity" (van Manen 1989, p. 7). Phenomenology asks what the nature of the learning experience is for children as they live it in their everyday life/world. The researcher is not oriented to the object being researched but instead to the subjective experiences of him/ herself and the participants. A tendency to be governed by a set of fixed procedures is replaced by a willingness to let experience do the leading.

Both of us are former teachers and Walter also a headmaster. For one school year we visited the Minneapolis Downtown Open School at least twice a week and initiated paper-folding with individual children, teachers, and groups of children. Teacher and researchers met formally and informally to share perceptions, plan strategies, and discuss results. Classroom observations and notes from these meetings were recorded.

Teachers also were interviewed formally at the end of the school year about their perceptions regarding successes and shortcomings of the project, feelings, pedagogical concerns, and individual meanings, as well as ideas for future research.

WHAT WE LEARNED

Perhaps the stories of the individual children reveal the most about the results. As one teacher put it, "We would not have known some of this about kids (without origami)." She cited seeing Mike as a logical thinker—"he's jumpy otherwise." Initially, Mike stood and watched the origami activities or crumpled other's work. He would act like he wanted to learn but just would not. This attitude permeated all his work. Gradually, he took small steps and learned. Now he's one of the class artisans—patient, shows pride and care, and is focused on his work. This change in Mike has transferred to his other work as well.

Patty was isolated and origami became her "path to joining the class." She became a teacher to others, and her mother reported that origami reinforced a handiwork ethic in their home. Another student, Rachel, became completely lost in the folding. She quickly did her classroom contract for the day so she would have time to fold.

Gary was so proud when he could make the folds on his own. He has the ability to look at something and replicate it. Gary was at a shelter for one and a half months and out of school. He later related that he just kept folding and folding so he would not forget. All of us felt chilled by this disclosure but also speculated that folding was a social connection remembered through the actions, and those actions reminded him of the caring adults at his school. We also recalled that he had been the first male to learn to fold and thus had a position of some special importance in the school, as many children sought his counsel on folding new objects. He may have wanted to retain this position with his peers.

Overall the teachers felt that there was more risk taking in general. Also noted was greater attention to precision, neatness, and pride in other areas as well. One teacher observed that she saw more "sustained creativity" as opposed to "spontaneous self-expression." The teachers all were pleased to see that children who did not star in other places often starred at this. In this multi-age setting, paper-folding also banishes age differences; younger children often taught older children.

Paper-folding was stimulating and enriching for the children. One teacher said, "folding and folding and folding…(they) can't be near paper without folding." She added that some children need their hands busy while listening.

In terms of paper-folding's effects on math, the teachers agreed that the math value is "in the long run." One remembered that when she introduced symmetry, the word was unknown, but the children grasped the concept immediately. She had never found it so easy to teach this concept in the past.

The school declared "Whatever you do to one side, you do to the other" as Nick's Rule, unknowingly articulating a fundamental algebraic rule well before these children will learn algebra. Another teacher felt that doing origami connects math "to something" for the children. The teachers especially noted the value for teaching order or seriation. The school used a hands-on, manipulatives-based curriculum, but the teachers noted that paper-folding took it to another level (i.e., more depth) with its embodiment of construction and transformation.

Teachers also saw value in doing paper-folding for building higher-level thinking skills. The process can invoke "seeing what it looks like as you work," and children feel a thrill at the end. One teacher noted that there are no wrong ways to use manipulatives, but the children discovered that was not the case with paper-folding. On the other hand, children can do something with conventional manipulatives from the start and without instruction. With origami, they must initially be shown. When they know enough origami to discover new forms (or schemas), however, the discoveries are more sophisticated.

The introduction of paper-folding in this school effected changes for the teachers and their practice as well as for the students. The first thing all the teachers noted was that it was "humbling to learn from a five-year-old" and uplifting to learn new schemas from a "poor child." But they felt that these experiences translated into more risk taking for them—more willingness to experiment with constructivity in other areas of the curriculum.

At the same time, teachers and the two researchers agreed that origami had been "hard to teach." Its introduction to the classroom was largely an exploration. At first the children had "Walter passes" that allowed them to see him and learn individually. Both Walter and Karen introduced the crane at first and found that it was much too difficult for most of the children and that interest was fading fast. Karen then gave a large group lesson on folding a kitty, but we all quickly discovered that we had to work in small groups. Fortunately, by the end of this lesson, there were kitties all over the school, and the children were soon making families, coloring their kitties, and naming them. All of us became learners with the children. As one adult put it, "The personal interactions with the kids teach me."

Another important outcome for teachers was that through observing paper-folding, they discovered the children's learning styles in a compelling way: "We would not have known some of this about kids." Teachers also voiced interest in pursuing greater involvement with origami, including teaming with an older classroom or teaming with a classroom in Japan. Related to this was the observation that learning origami made the country of Japan seem so much closer and accessible.

In addition, teachers experienced changes in their teaching. They reported that they now saw children as creators, inventors, and explorers. They set higher standards for work. All are experimenting with using the constructivity metaphor to design authentic assessments for the district's identified outcomes.

Finally, changes in the school reflect the changes in its people. Teachers expressed that the origami project has resulted in a "deepening of the school's direction." They now identify themselves as a "caring, creative, collaborative community." The concept of competence has changed for the school; it has moved beyond "paper and pencil value." Words such as *seriation, constructivity, reflection, operations,* and *reciprocity* are part of the discourse among the teachers—words not commonly heard from elementary teachers. Teachers noted that origami was an entry into constructive ways of "doing school," a metaphor for practice.

DISCUSSION

From our involvement in this origami project, we observed changes in ourselves, the children, the teachers, and the school community. We have come to see these changes in the context of reflective practice, a coming to ideas for the school community itself as well as the larger research community. We started with a hunch that there might be something unique about paper-folding that is learned during a sensitive period of four to seven years, when body-in-the-mind activities lead to the interiorization of logical-mathematical operations. The bigger picture is that we came to recognize the loss of truly constructive activities, specifically handiwork, in both the schools and our culture. This may be in part because American education has never really had a dominant constructive paradigm. Although the progressive strand running through American education embraces an activity pedagogy (Dewey 1916), the prevailing instructional approaches, the way we organize our schools, management techniques, beliefs about children and learning, including the newer cognitive theories, are essentially mechanistic and behaviorist, what Piaget (1969) argues is "passivity against activity."

Other researchers provide a comparative frame focusing on the contrast between the education of American children and children in other cultures. Merry White (1987), who has studied Japanese schools extensively, suggests that we might reevaluate our definitions of creativity. Western educators do not hold that creativity can be institutionally fostered. We see fostering creativity as tied to individual, spontaneous self-expression rather than also including the development of skill through the learning and execution of schemas and forms. "Americans, in short, confuse self-expression with creativity...rather than on taking pains." In contrast, White argues, the Japanese believe "that before a child can be truly creative, or even express himself, he must be taught possibilities and limits of the medium; in short, one learns how to use existing forms first."

Gardner, in *To Open Minds: Chinese Clues to the Dilemma of Contemporary Education* (1989), corroborates her conclusions. He documents that Chinese children, through the learning of the visual arts, develop a vocabulary of schemas (a repeatable action), or formulas that allow them to reproduce representational drawings. The problem is that the Chinese school environment is so constrained that children cannot venture beyond these schemas and create interesting and original drawings. What Gardner calls for is a balance between unguided exploration and spontaneous self-expression (the individuality dimension) and the learning of forms and schemas through routinized practice.

Finally, the experiences at the Downtown Open School emphasize that we need desperately to study the constructive and creative practices of other cultures, as well as the history of our own. This includes looking at both Western and Eastern countries and their arts and crafts from both cognitive and pro-social perspectives. We suggest considering a wide variety of movement and rhythmic activities such as string games, jump rope games, Chinese tangrams, and American Indian arts and crafts (e.g., beadwork, dream catchers). Of course, we believe origami specifically should be studied further in all its dimensions. Clearly, given the new visions of what constitutes learning (Marshall 1992) and the diversity of children in American schools, the time is ripe for a renewed exploration of traditional arts and crafts that promote active construction and collaboration.

15

Folding Ourselves into a Nonviolent Society

Origami, Schools, Conflict Resolution, and the Pedagogy of Action

> *To operate is to co-operate.*
> —Jean Piaget

CONFLICT RESOLUTION IS A PROCESS IN WHICH ALL SIDES in a disagreement work together toward a mutually satisfactory outcome. I study conflict resolution because it teaches me about cooperation, collaboration, peace, and justice. I need to know these four practices in deeply personal and intimate ways as they are essential to the nonviolent society I seek to help build. Conflicts are windows into the social construct of our humanity. By creatively, authentically, and actively practicing pro-social conflict resolution I find myself positively experimenting with equality, respect, emotion, self-expression, and many other facets of healthy human relationships.

I work in education because *school* is one of the most important institutions in our society. Schools are where children learn how to be part of our social system. School is, for most children, the first place they *experience* and *participate* in a civic endeavor. School is the primary platform where children learn how to work with others who are different. And school is a structured environment where young people go to experiment with human rela-

---

The authors of this chapter, Will Pipkin and Walter Enloe, have worked together for years as trainers for Project CREATE, a conflict resolution and community-building project of Metro ECSU, St. Paul, Minnesota. This project originally grew out of Educators for Social Responsibility and their active education programs about nuclear war issues. One area of training that has become more important recently has been the concrete connection between learning the skills of paper-folding and learning the skills of conflict resolution.

tionships. Hopefully, that experiment is a creative, authentic, and active practice of pro-social behavior.

Transforming our violent, materialistic, individualistic, and stratified society into a genuinely peaceful and just society will take many, many more years of work, and on many fronts. I contend that schools have a key, if not essential, role in this effort. If our society is to be saved from self-destruction, schools must, because of their central place in our society, step forward and make intentional choices to make the vital contribution that is so desperately needed.

But how? What exactly can schools contribute? Many progressive school reformists have answers to this question, and mine is but one voice in the chorus. This essay is about how school-based conflict resolution education and a pedagogy of action can be important therapies for social transformation. It is also about a particular way of pursuing conflict resolution education: one that is creative, authentic, active, pro-social, and full of practice. And this essay is about how folding paper birds helps us see these lessons.

Years ago, when I first heard the story of Sadako Sasaki, I decided to fold paper cranes in the ancient Japanese tradition of origami. I folded the cranes for my friend Sue. Her birthday was August 6, which also was the date of the bombing of Hiroshima. I knew she felt sad about this shared anniversary. My crane folding was a gesture of healing, both to Sue and to myself. At first I would enclose a few cranes in the letters I sent her. Later, I'd just mail manila envelopes stuffed full of the brightly colored, smartly folded birds. I folded them on breaks at work, on the bus, and especially while I watched the evening news and its daily accounts of violence. It was a social contract: I folded the cranes to let Sue know how much I loved and appreciated her; I folded cranes to grieve Hiroshima; I folded cranes because people often asked what I was doing and it gave me a chance to talk with them about nuclear war.

As I recall that time I remember feeling very creative. It took me about three minutes to turn a two-dimensional, square piece of paper into a work of art: a three-dimensional sculpture with deep personal and historical meaning. Not only was each crane something I created, each one was a part of the larger creation, a body of hundreds. Even though I was folding the cranes according to a very old pattern, I felt I was creating something special.

The crane-folding process was, for me, authentic. That is, I *authored* it.

It was *mine*. *I* folded the cranes. The idea of giving them to Sue was *my* idea. I loved doing it because it was my project.

I also look back on it as being very active. It was precise handwork that took time, physical action, and concentration. Unlike watching television, or even reading, it was physical activity in which I participated. It was tactile. I *made* things, *real* things, and it was fun.

Years later, I came to understand my little project as pro-social. I did not fold the cranes just for myself, even though I did get something out of it. Instead, I folded them as a gift. The cranes were meant to be shared, and they were meant to be healing. This intention to do good imbued every crease and measure.

Finally, I remember the practice. It was repetitive: after you fold several hundred cranes you get pretty good at it. Traditional origami paper is colored on one side and white on the other. With cranes, one strives to fold so that none of the white shows. I got good enough so that only the smallest slivers of white could be seen. I recall being very focused and driven. I tried hard to improve my folding skills. A well-folded origami object is a very precise work of art. It requires exacting eye-hand coordination. However, I did not sit down to rehearse or study my crane folding in the same way I practiced playing the clarinet as a youngster. For instance, I never threw out an individual crane because it wasn't perfect; even the first cranes, which were lousy, counted in my project. With crane folding, there was no drill before a performance or an event, as with, say, basketball. And while I did practice (verb) my skills, folding came to be a practice (noun) for me. Crane folding became one of the things I did. It became a meditative habit, something I did because it felt natural and right.

I am a staff trainer with a Twin Cities–based conflict resolution program for schools, Project CREATE,* which has been using crane folding in its work with teachers. We're using crane folding as an analog to conflict resolution, a way to illustrate the process and values of conflict resolution.

---

*CREATE stands for "Conflict Resolution Encourages Affirmation, Tolerance, and Empowerment." The program began in 1987 as a project of the Twin Cities Chapter of Educators for Social Responsibility (ESR). In 1994 the Project moved to a new organizational home: the Educational Cooperative Service Unit of the Metropolitan Twin Cities Area (Metro ECSU). Project CREATE provides collaborative training, consulting, and information services to schools throughout the upper Midwest.

But the Project doesn't just train educators in the procedures of conflict resolution; we also help them find ways to teach conflict resolution skills and strategies to their students, which we call *conflict resolution education*. I would like to suggest that the process of learning crane folding compares closely to the process of learning conflict resolution: in this way, crane folding is also an excellent analog for helping schools understand the challenges inherent in setting up effective conflict resolution education programs.

First, let's examine how crane folding is, in many ways, like conflict resolution. With even a small bit of crane folding experience you will readily see that there are steps in the process of folding. And after a few more sheets of paper, even a beginning folder will see that there are different ways to get to the same outcome. Like folding, conflict resolution is a process (though it is less product oriented than origami), a process with steps. While the steps may vary from culture to culture, group to group, generally there appear to be similar patterns. The conflict is acknowledged, the parties agree to work it out, each side tells its story, solutions are planned out and then implemented. As in origami, not all the steps will happen in that order every time, yet the steps eventually do build to a conclusion. Also, as you fold a crane, you might find that you've made a mistake, that you are unhappy with a particular fold, or that you're confused. It can be unfolded and you can go back to the step that went awry and start again from that point. The same is true of the conflict resolution process: if it breaks down, you can cycle back to an earlier step and keep working at it.

In conflict resolution, the people in the conflict solve it themselves. Even when a mediator helps, the process works only when it is owned by its participants, an authentic process. Someone may fold a crane for you and give it to you as a gift, but no one can fold your crane. No one does it for you. You have to do it yourself, or with the help of another person. The only difference in conflicts is that the two (or more) people in the disagreement take collective responsibility for "folding" the solution together, rather than the one person who folds a crane.

Conflict resolution and crane folding are both active, kinesthetic processes. You have to be engaged and focused for either of them to work. If you sit back, the paper will not fold itself. If you are not an active participant, with both body and mind, in solving your own conflict, then it won't get resolved.

Conflict resolution is an essentially pro-social process. When people resolve conflicts with mutuality and in a collaborative fashion, they are building positive social relationships. Conflict resolvers care about other people and about their relationship to others; if you don't care then there's no motivation to solve the problem to the other person's satisfaction (in addition to yours). One of the remarkable things about conflict resolution is that individuality is not lost at the expense of caring about others. It is a mutual process, just as when I fold cranes for you I am also folding them for myself.

Like the folding of flat paper into sculpture, solving human conflicts is a highly creative and constructive process, even though it is a bit more volatile than paper-folding. Hearing the evidence Walter Enloe and others have collected on the relationship of origami to children's constructivity has helped me more clearly see the constructive nature of conflict resolution. Not only does the problem-solving process build stronger social relationships, it unfolds in unexpected ways each time, the outcomes are unique every time, and the people involved in the process *make* their own solutions.

The people who are successful at conflict resolution make it a practice; it becomes part of their lives because they work at it. Now, most people don't go around looking for conflicts in their lives so that they can practice, while most paper-folders will go out of their way to find origami paper. I still avoid dealing with some conflicts (even as I write I am putting off calling a friend who hasn't been speaking to me). But still, what I hear from people who are committed to conflict resolution is that they confront problems more than they avoid them, and they feel a duty to work on the conflicts in their lives.

Hearing Sadako's story and learning origami have both stretched me. Sadako's story forced me to *reflect* on war and peace and my country's role in the bombing of Hiroshima. The process of conflict resolution stretches people in a similar way. It helps them focus on the stories and needs of other people, in addition to their own. It facilitates personal reflection: you have to understand yourself to work on a conflict. It is a collaborative process in which the participants work together toward a mutual goal. For many people, supporting another person's interests as strongly as their own is a radically different approach to problem solving.

As I learned about origami I did something very uncommon to white people in this country, I steeped myself in a cultural practice other than my own. I believe culture and conflict are inseparable, especially in our diverse society. Every culture in the world has ways of resolving conflicts. Those who want to learn new and better ways to handle conflicts will gain by studying the practices of others.

When conflicts come up between people who have different, culturally specific ways of handling problems, the practices are sometimes incompatible, and that can compound the conflict. Here is an example. I am currently working with a group that is made up of Cambodian and Hmong refugees and recent immigrants from the Caribbean and Central America, as well as African Americans, Native Americans, and European Americans. More than the language barrier, the cultural differences are keeping this group from working through conflicts very effectively. Some of the most vexing, ongoing conflicts in the United States are ethnic and cultural in nature. Most notably, conflicts between African Americans and European Americans have indelibly shaped our national identity. Crane folding and conflict resolution have both taught me the importance of valuing other cultures.

Finished paper cranes are marvelous looking things. The sculpture has many different surfaces, each "face" connected to others and all the panels connected back to the whole. It doesn't look like just one piece of paper, but it is, especially if it has been skillfully folded, showing very little white. Conflict resolution, on the other hand, is basically the result of many different skills welded together: listening, self-expression, perspective taking, knowing the steps, appreciating differences, finding commonalities, and so on. These skills are the building blocks of conflict resolution. The more neatly they are put together, the better the problem solving. Of course, paper may often be more cooperative than a person with whom you are in conflict.

Next, let's look at how crane folding works as an analog for conflict resolution education. *Learning how* to do conflict resolution is a lot like *learning how* to fold paper cranes. As schools develop programs in this area, from peer mediation to the teaching of social skills in classroom settings, I contend that they need to embrace the five fundamentals that are illustrated in crane folding. They must be *authentic* programs, efforts that are owned by the participants. These programs must promote and enhance the *active* creativity of participants. To excel they must promote active, *pro-social* behavior. The successful programs, I believe, will keep students and adults *practicing* (verb), and will promote conflict resolution as a *practice* (noun).

It is extremely difficult to learn how to fold cranes simply by reading a book, watching a video, or passively witnessing a folding demonstration. The best way to learn is through hands-on trial and error. To learn how to fold the paper one must touch it and manipulate it. Similarly, it is impossible to learn how to resolve conflicts simply by studying books, listening to lectures, or even group discussion. The only way to "get it" is to do it. One must actively try it out. Students must be active learners if they are to master the skills and strategies of conflict resolution. This active learning must take different forms: games, role-plays, exercises, discussions, drama, writing, and collaboration.

Conflict is experienced in the body. To learn, for instance, how to actively listen in a volatile situation students have got to role-play that situation just to see what it *feels* like. Similarly, a crane cannot be folded well on the first try. Folding is a process for which one develops a *feel*, and it is learned by physically doing it. Kinesthetic learning, or learning by doing, is one of the learning styles that is critical to include in conflict resolution education.

A key way to get students to kinesthetically learn about conflict resolution is through creative dramatics. The connection between drama and conflict is self-evident and this relationship is being mined by conflict resolution education specialists. Creative dramatics not only helps young people understand the process of working through a conflict, it also helps them practice the pro-social relationship skills inherent in conflict resolution.*

I remember a colleague's experiment in teaching a group of teachers how to fold cranes. He had everyone work separately and silently on folding cranes—with the help of a printed handout and after a brief demonstration. No one was able to stay focused on their own work. People looked at each other's cranes. They leaned over and touched other people's cranes. They started talking to each other, and pretty soon chairs were being scooted across the floor. Eventually, the room was abuzz with activity: people mov-

---

*For an in-depth review of this topic, refer to "Using Creative Dramatics to Teach Conflict Resolution: Exploiting the Drama/Conflict Dialectic," by Will Pipkin and Stephen Dimenna, *Journal of Humanistic Education and Development*, vol. 28, Dec. 1989.

ing around, lots of talking and laughing, small clusters of people working with individuals who were having trouble.

To me, this story illustrates another parallel between crane folding and conflict resolution. Both are learned best in lively, collaborative, highly interactive ways. Sure, you can fold all by yourself, once you know how to do it, but learning crane folding, especially for young people, works when students can raise questions together, solve their own problems, and do it together in a collaborative fashion.

This is also how people learn conflict resolution skills—by interacting. Interpersonal conflicts occur between people. Since conflict resolution is entirely about facilitating nonviolent human interaction, learning how to do it has to include human interaction. Students must experiment with how to interact in the conflict resolution steps, by speaking to, questioning, watching, expressing feelings to, listening to, and working with other people. Precisely because conflict resolution is a collaborative process, conflict resolution education programs must emphasize student collaboration.

Learning about conflict resolution is not the same as studying, say, the periodic table of elements. None of us will ever conclude our learning about how to resolve conflicts. A commitment to learning about conflict resolution means a commitment to lifelong personal growth. A commitment to conflict resolution also means a commitment to lifelong personal reflection. Reflection and growth are fantastic building blocks for lifelong learning, and I've found both in crane folding.

Conflict resolution education programs must communicate to young people that they will never be perfect at problem solving, and we as adults must be open with youth about our own imperfect actions. Instead of preaching excellence as a goal one achieves, like climbing to the mountain's summit, conflict resolution excellence should be characterized by a commitment to continued growth and reflection. Sadako may not have folded a full thousand cranes before her death, but her classmates continued the tradition by spreading the practice throughout the world.

For thousands of years, paper cranes have been given as gifts in Japan. They are meant to be given away and circulated. My brother reminded me that he once took some of my cranes to Europe and gave them away to fellow travelers he met. Each person promised to mail the crane to a school where a friend of mine taught. That way, his students would get "crane mail" from all over the world. Sadako's classmates raised the money to build her monument in Hiroshima. Students in that city's International School started the 1000 Cranes Club. Also, the children of Los Alamos, New Mexico, are building a Sadako memorial at the site of the first nuclear test blast. During the Persian Gulf War, students in Redwood Falls, Minnesota, folded 10,000 cranes for every family in the area who had a family member stationed in Saudi Arabia. These are all instances of what I call the *pedagogy of action*: students getting actively involved in their communities, participating in real-world events, engaged with purpose outside of the school walls.

I believe conflict resolution, like a crane, is a gift, meant to be given away. I challenge schools with mediation or conflict resolution programs to find service learning projects that bring students' skills and vision into the community. Kids can teach elders how the process works. Students can identify conflicts in their communities and help adults with efforts to solve the problems. Young people can mediate in places other than schools. Successful student mediators from one school can train their peers at another building. Students can create and tour plays, videos, art shows, books, or games that flow out of their conflict resolution work. The sky is the limit. It is important, however, that young people come up with the ideas and that the young people carry them out (with adult help). Few schools have conflict resolution programs that extend beyond the building grounds. Yet I think it is an obvious and important next step in the evolution of conflict resolution education.

Schools have been far too separate from the rest of our society. They are places where we "send" our kids. And many see school as a necessary evil, a place where we "do time" until we are sprung. These notions are reflections of the century-old doctrine of factory schooling. Thankfully, we are moving away from that model. Despite some significant examples, such as the ones cited above from Hiroshima, Los Alamos, and Redwood Falls, one aspect where we have yet to shift is in how schools relate to their communities.

If there ever was a time for schools to become actively engaged in community affairs, that time is now. Our society is in deep, deep trouble. While statistical studies show this country's overall crime rate is not rising, violent crimes are increasing, taking a greater share of the crime pie every year. Not only that, but violent crime is getting more violent and more savage. Rape is more prevalent, and the audacity and brutality of perpetrators is more severe. There is a tidal wave of family violence washing over the land. Television, motion pictures, comic books, video games, and popular songs continue to glorify violence, and these industries show little sign of changing. When Toys-R-Us announced in 1994 that they would no longer sell toy guns, industry analysts were aghast.

The effect of this violence on young people is devastating. Children are witnessing more and more violence, especially kids in economically and socially oppressed communities. The lives of nearly an entire generation of African Americans have been touched by murder. Toy guns are among the biggest money-makers for that industry. Handguns, knives, and other weapons go to school every day, and not just to the stereotypically "tough" inner-city schools.

Transforming our society into one that is nonviolent is not going to be easy. Yes, many of us have been working at this for years, and it is often hard to see any progress. Much of that work has been in the area of education. Many people are now working to bring the values, skills, and strategies of conflict resolution into the lives of young people and the adults who work with them. Since the late 1980s, there has been an explosion of interest in mediation and conflict resolution in K–12 schools.

Schools have a responsibility to respond to these problems. At minimum, schools must equip students with the tools they need to solve these problems. Metal detectors are not the answer. Ideally, schools will go beyond this to an active role in community problem solving—not just by adults. By actively participating in community affairs, young people will gain practical experiences by learning in vibrant, relevant ways while making this a better world.

Schools cannot turn their backs on what is happening. Society is deteriorating around us. The ultimate value of the pedagogy of action is that it contributes to positive change. Along the way it teaches young people in an exciting way about how to be empowered, proactive citizens. These are values embodied in conflict resolution education and the folding of paper cranes.

Fifty years after Hiroshima the United States finds itself sitting atop another bomb. If we listen well we can hear Sadako, and many other children who follow in her footsteps, telling us that we must focus our efforts on peacemaking. We can indeed fold ourselves into a nonviolent society.

16

A Powerful Youth Movement

I want to go on living even after my death....in spite of everything, I still believe that people are really good at heart.

ANNE FRANK

IT'S MONDAY AFTERNOON AND THE SCHOOL BELL has just rung at the Albuquerque Academy, a private grammar school in Albuquerque, New Mexico. Children spill out of the building, some heading off to basketball practice or ballet lessons. But not sixth-grader Aubrey White. She's off to preside over a meeting of the Children's Peace Statue Committee at nearby Arroyo del Oso Elementary School.

In 1989, several students in Arroyo del Oso's program for academically gifted students entered the national "Future Problem Solvers" contest. The topic that year was the arms race, so the children proposed a peace statue as a way to voice their opposition to war. Encouraged by two teachers, the children developed the concept into an actual project: erecting a statue in Los Alamos, New Mexico, the birthplace of the atom bomb, as a monument to peace.

Aubrey, who attended Arroyo del Oso before switching schools, became involved with the peace statue project in 1992. During her tenure as president of the committee, the project has run into a few glitches, but that isn't deterring Aubrey, who is learning leadership, patience, and perseverance. A vegetarian for three years, Aubrey is accustomed to standing up for her beliefs. "At lunch," she says, "everyone at my school goes, 'moo, look I'm eating a cow.' They try to pressure me, but I try not to pressure them

---

Children around the world have been inspired by the life of Sadako Sasaki. In Albuquerque, New Mexico, not far from the site of the dawn of the Nuclear Age at Los Alamos, children have initiated and sustained a peacemaking project to build another children's monument and Peace Garden.

because it's their decision, really." When Aubrey heard about the sculpture, it fit in with her opposition to killing and her desire to act on her beliefs. "Kids know how to get their point across," she says. "Kids will stand up and say what they don't like, and sometimes adults will listen because they see a kid is really committed."

The committee solicited designs from children around the country; the winning entry came from Noe Martinez, now eighteen, of Dallas, Texas. The group also approached the Los Alamos county council to request a place to erect the statue. The council offered eleven sites to choose from. Now, however, the committee is dealing with the very real-life problem of politics. In September 1994, local elections resulted in some changes in the council. The new members were concerned that a peace sculpture would invite anti-nuclear protesters. At a meeting that fall, the council voted to reject the children's request for a site for the peace statue. Several children who attended the meeting left in tears.

Fund-raising has proved more encouraging. A "one name, one dollar" campaign asking children to send letters with a dollar enclosed has garnered letters from 90,000 students from all fifty states and sixty-three countries, bringing the committee's total funds to more than $90,000. The children want to reach a million dollars in order to build the sculpture and a surrounding garden, then maintain the project for the next hundred years.

The children unveiled their statue on August 6, 1995, the fiftieth anniversary of the bombings of Hiroshima and Nagasaki. The Peace Statue was intended as a gift from the children of the United States to the City and County of Los Alamos, birthplace of the atomic bomb. When the request for permanent placement was brought before the Los Alamos City/County Council, the idea was tabled and the statue refused. For one year it was appropriately honored at the Albuquerque New Mexico Museum, and it is now on loan to the Plaza Resolana in Santa Fe. Most of the cranes that once graced it have blown away.

If there were bridges between continents, between consciences, between cultures, bridges that erect themselves when a conflict needs to be resolved, bridges that make understanding happen, the words *peace* and *war* would not exist. This is a dream of mine. I am aware that it is not physically or humanly possible. The dream brings me joy and hope.

A model dreamer is Sadako Sasaki, a twelve-year-old girl from Hiroshima,

Japan. When she was two the atomic bomb was dropped on Hiroshima. Ten years later she was diagnosed with leukemia or the "A-bomb disease." It is hard for a twelve-year-old to comprehend her own death, so she embraced hope instead. There is a Japanese legend that says if you fold a thousand paper cranes you will live forever. It is a legend, a folktale, a dream. It offered Sadako a simple and concrete way to come to terms with her innocent death. Sadako, with the help of family and friends, started folding. She folded more than a thousand cranes before she died. She demonstrated dedication to her dream of living beyond age twelve, her dream that she was not a victim to a war that she, as a child, did not start and could not prevent. She worked hard to see her dream through. It does not matter that it was physically impossible; she needed to believe and hope.

Children around the world have been inspired by her dedication. In Hiroshima, her classmates raised funds to build a peace statue of Sadako holding a paper crane. Today in Albuquerque, New Mexico, there is a group of children working to build a sister peace monument in Los Alamos, the birthplace of the atomic bomb.

In 1990, the third-grade class at Arroyo del Oso Elementary School started the Future Problem-Solving Program. They read about Sadako and decided to fold a thousand paper cranes. They wanted to be more active and involved with the community and world. Their New Mexico history tied them to Hiroshima and Sadako through the military-scientific laboratories near their homes. So they marched down to the bank with $11.80 to start their fund to build a children's monument to peace.

In the past few years the project has grown and so have the children. Children from all across the United States have donated their time and money. To get more children involved, the Los Alamos children began a nationwide contest to design the peace monument. They invited children to explore the question "What does peace look like?" The local chapters of the American Institute of Architects accepted the submission and chose two designs to be constructed in scale models. These were sent to Albuquerque to be judged in the final contest. Sixteen finalists were chosen and finally Noe Martinez's design was selected for construction. Noe Martinez describes his design:

> The Peace Garden is a remarkable, refreshing oasis in the desert of Los Alamos, New Mexico. The peace memorial unites people from

all over the different areas of the earth that will come to gather around this wonderful oasis....It is a symbol of (hu)man's innate desire to be at peace with each other. The fountain is the focal point of the oasis. It is a spherical, spraying fountain that reminds everyone of one of life's sources. The fountain is surrounded by an encircling bed of flowers that form the shape of the continents of the earth.

The most spectacular part of the Peace Garden is that children visiting can plant flowers from their homeland around the fountain. The flowers, plants, and trees will grow, "showing how peace on the earth is continuously expanding." In the same way that children crown Sadako's statue with paper cranes, children can interact with the Los Alamos peace monument. For children growing up in a war-torn world it will be a peaceful oasis, an idea as much as a place that symbolizes life, nourishment, and a safe haven. Walking through the desert we will find an oasis of life, a cradle in which to dream.

In 2002 other children and their families have taken the lead. Their goal is to commemorate this Children's Peace Statue on Hiroshima and Nagasaki Days each year in unity with the annual observance of Peace Days in Japan. The garlands of cranes created by this community and other communities will be hung on the statue at the commemorations. The peacemaking community hopes that the teaching about Sadako Sasaki and the folding of origami cranes will become integrated into the curriculum of every school until all nuclear weapons have been abolished. The ideal is to commemorate recognized "Peace Days" annually to unify global intentions toward the creation of peace on Earth and to inspire others to become involved in creating peace. The community is now participating in a global initiative to fold a million cranes for peace by August 6, 2002. From their web site (www.networkearth.org/world/peace) they write "Creating peace, in many ways, is like folding a crane. At first it seems impossible, but step by step, with patience, intent, and concentration, the Peace Crane emerges—beautiful and full of grace. Don't forget to make your prayer for peace as you fill the crane with your breath." For further information and to send your cranes, write to Cranes for Peace, P.O. Box 9509, Santa Fe, New Mexico 87504.

The vision and commitment of students have continued to grow. The

Chugoku newspaper (Hiroshima, August 7, 2001) reports, "The 'World Children's Peace Statue' erected through the fund-raising efforts of high schools students in Hiroshima, was unveiled August 6 in front of the Hiroshima Municipal Baseball Stadium in Nada Ward. The students raised 7 million yen [$65,000] by collecting contributions on the streets. The new generation is working together to send a message for peace.... About three hundred middle and high school students on the construction committee attended the ceremony. Junpei Teraoka,...a senior at Sotokju High school, called out to 'hand down the A-bomb experience to the next generation and appeal for nuclear abolition.' Eight students unveiled the statue.... A freshman at Yasuda Girls High who lives in Kuba, Otake, said, "I participated with a question, 'What is peace?' I found out that peace is what you achieve through your own actions."

17

Young Peacemakers

Sustaining a Peacemaking Community

> *Establishing lasting peace is the work of education; all politics can do is keep us out of war.*
>
> —Maria Montessori

YOU CAN SENSE SOMETHING DIFFERENT IN THE AIR when you approach a Peace Site school. Outside the building, flying on a pole, will be an Earth Flag and the United Nations flag, outward signs to the community that the school is a Peace Site. Walking up and down the halls you may see international flags, travel posters, maps, and phrases in different languages. You may see pictures, stories, poems, and thoughts about peace, friendship, kindness, and respect. But, most of all, there is something much deeper—a feeling, a sense of warmth and welcoming that makes everyone who enters feel happy to be there.

The Peace Site idea developed from the works of Louis Kousin and the inspirations of Lynn Elling, Board Chair of World Citizen, Inc. The mission is to "develop in people, particularly young people, a global perspective with a sense of world citizenship for a peaceful, healthy world, and the survival of the human family, which includes everyone across the oceans, as well as across the street."

I first met first-grade educator Glenda Peterson when we joined a group of Twin Cities citizens traveling by bus to the annual Nobel Peace Prize Forum to hear Walter Mondale and Harold Stassen. Glenda serves on the board of World Citizens, Inc., which fosters international Peace Sites and encourages communities to fold birds of peace as part of their peace work. Glenda is an exemplary model of leadership through service, and this essay exemplifies our belief in the power of purposefully creative places of peacemaking.

Just what is a Peace Site? It is any school, church, place of worship, business, park, home, or public space where people are committed to

— protecting the environment;

— promoting intercultural understanding and celebrating cultural differences;

— seeking peace within themselves and relationships with others

— reaching out in service to others; and

— working toward a better understanding of the United Nations and law with justice.

Students, staff, and families working together help everyone become more aware of the world around them. Projects that promote a peaceful, healthy world have pulled schools together and have made real differences in peoples' lives. Children have been and continue to be change agents for peace. The most significant impact of all is experiencing an attitude of peacemaking. Children understand "the citizenship of peacemaking." Peacemaking, like citizenship, is more than obeying the rules and being respectful and nonviolent. It's the public work of problem solving and conflict resolution.

Approaching the Peace Site idea from a global village perspective fulfills the need students have to live locally and think globally. Looking into the future, students become empowered to gain control of their lives and help create changes that will affect the future. By encompassing all areas of the curriculum in the global perspective, students will create a climate of cooperation and a commitment to global citizenship, responsibility, and understanding.

How does one begin? The Peace Site idea is planted by a seed, one person to take the information back to her site and share the concept and ideas at a meeting of interested staff and parents. PTA/PTSA and other parent groups have promoted and supported highly successful Peace Site programs. After some "think time," at a second gathering, discuss the possibilities and make the decision to become a Peace Site. Create a steering committee of staff, parents, and students to lead the project. Task forces will develop along with projects and activities.

Inform students, families, and the community of the decision to become a Peace Site. Create an interest survey asking for ideas and volunteers.

After tabulating the surveys, decide which activities are possible and form task forces to do specific work. Enjoy the togetherness, cooperation, and fun as your entire school works together at peacemaking.

One school formed a task force of teachers from all grade levels that spent time examining all areas of the curriculum for global concepts already being taught. Working together they blended the concepts into interdisciplinary global themes. The starting point was the local school and the community. The United States and its cultural ties to Europe; holidays around the world; China, Africa, Asia, Russia, and South America formed a framework for study for a year.

At the end of one school year, families were asked to log their summer travels and encouraged to keep journals. On a large map in the hallway, families flagged their travels. A summary of the information showed that families from that school traveled to forty-seven states, Washington, D.C., ten countries, and five islands. Asking families what they could share brought forth a tremendous response and a wealth of resources to tap throughout the year. Speakers, lyceums, and artists in residence all incorporated the global theme.

Putting existing technology to broader use by staff, students, and community is a major goal. Telecommunications such as "Global Kid Chat" and contacts with possible partner schools in other countries have produced wonderful results, as have video productions of school programs and activities and video letter exchanges. Sharing activities with the community via cable television and local newspapers has been highly successful.

Cooperative learning and sharing is a basic premise in the Peace Site program. Staff, students, and families create, develop, and work in areas of interest. Family fun nights with "Flavors of the World" and dancers from different areas of the world show a commitment to the global perspective.

Encourage community involvement in planning, executing, and disseminating project activities. After-school activities and community education classes featuring global languages, global music, around the world cooking, cultural studies, and ethnic dance instruction will further support the global theme. Family field trips offer interesting possibilities.

Young peacemakers have made significant contributions and commitments to protect the environment. Outstanding projects include collecting pennies for the rain forest and reading for the rain forest; cleaning up streams, lakes, and woods; stopping pollution; emphasizing recycling and pre-cycling; adopting a zoo animal or a raptor; planting flowers at a local park; being educated about the environment; and changing family lifestyles to support a healthy world.

Young peacemakers have promoted and continue to promote intercultural understanding and the celebration of cultural differences. Some highly successful family projects include creating peace quilts (each family creates a square of peace); designing shoe box floats celebrating each family's heritage; creating family heritage flags; enjoying family cultural nights; celebrating, highlighting, and enjoying the families in the school.

Young peacemakers seek peace within themselves and relationships with others. Anti-violence curriculums are available today. Conflict management and problem-solving strategies help students work toward these goals. It is not easy to be a peacemaker and to solve differences in nonviolent ways. A peace rug, a peace chair, a peace table, a peace place…whatever it takes to help young ones solve their problems…Some principals have noticed a dramatic reduction in discipline problems because of peace programs, and school discipline policies have been changed to reflect the peacemaking concept.

Young peacemakers reach out in service to others. This is probably the most heart-warming part of a peacemaking school. We can not begin too early teaching children to care about others. The satisfaction that comes from within is immeasurable. Some successful outreach projects include conducting canned food drives for food shelves; collecting warm clothing, particularly mittens, and giving them to children's homes; collecting books and distributing them to needy people; collecting and distributing good, used toys; making things for senior citizen and nursing homes; going to the homes and singing to the residents; making paper cranes to send to children and families who need the inspiration and hope. A big part of the Peace Site program is to find a partner school and help that school become a Peace Site, too.

The 1000 Cranes Project has been an integral part of the development of many Peace Sites. Inspired by the story of Sadako and the original 1000 Cranes Club, older children in our schools learned how to fold the peace birds and in turn taught younger ones. Imagine the possibilities—the camaraderie, the bonding of children as they learn together and share dreams of peace. "Crane fever" took hold and hundreds of children folded thousands and thousands of cranes. Strings of a thousand cranes each were sent to Hiroshima and the White House. Beautiful stories of friendship and kindness developed as the birds were folded and shared. Children found joy in folding the smallest birds and the most colorful. Thousands of birds hung through the hallways of schools. Many people shared the feeling of peace and joy when they stood under the canopy of birds.

To this day the crane, peace bird, means something special to the children, staff, and families of our schools. Tiny birds were given as mementos of one school's dedication ceremony. The crane/dove is becoming a traditional part of a number of Peace Site schools' graduation ceremonies. Younger children fold cranes in school colors, put them on ribbons, and place them around the necks of the graduating students. Then the graduating students walk through an arch made by the kindergarten (or youngest students). Students leave the school with best wishes. The same could be done to welcome students.

Staff members who leave at the end of the year receive a corsage made with the bird of peace and the school color ribbon. Wreaths of cranes, crane ribbons, and other visual symbols are daily peace reminders. Establishing traditions in our schools help carry the dream of peace.

Young peacemakers learn about the United Nations, its history and part in the ever-changing world. Young peacemakers question and encourage fairness and justice for all.

The day that your school is dedicated as an International Peace Site is a day of celebration. Creating that special day will be a joyful task. Select a date of historical significance, such as Dr. Martin Luther King Day in January, Earth Day in April, World Law Day in May, the anniversary of the bombing of Hiroshima in August, United Nations Day in October, Human Rights Day in December, or a date of significance for your school. Involve all your students, staff, and parents in the planning. Invite administrators, community leaders, other interested schools, and existing peace schools to observe and/or participate. Plan for a keynote speaker and students' visions of peace through written work, poetry, or song. Decorate with United Nations flags and symbols of the Earth. At the end of the ceremony, take everyone outside and as the Earth Flag and the United Nations flag slowly approaches the top of the pole and white birds of peace fly free into a blue sky, everyone will be touched by peace.

Remember that becoming a Peace Site is a beginning. There is always more work to do. You may choose to rededicate your school every year as a recommitment to peace. You may choose to take one of the five strands that are an integral part of the Peace Site idea and focus on it for the year. Over the years some schools have added other symbols outside their school such as markers, gardens, and Peace Poles.

In our community, Bloomington, Minnesota, we have dedicated five Peace Site schools and have formed a partnership. Working along with other peace organizations, the police department, Grandmothers for Peace, the United Nations Association, Hamline University, Kids for Saving Earth Worldwide, administrators, school board members, and other schools that are working on becoming Peace Sites, we have made plans for doing significant work in our community. In the spring of 1995, all of the schools will participate in an environmental project that will enhance the city park and create a peace place for all to enjoy.

Young peacemakers are the hope of our world, the future bright for peace and love. It is "the time of the dove" and the time of and for our children.

18

Two Hiroshima Stories

It is hard for me to believe that almost three decades have passed since my wife and I arrived in Hiroshima for the first time, but I have no doubt that what I learned there has affected everything I have done or felt since. Hiroshima, along with its pain, offers a special kind of illumination.

ROBERT JAY LIFTON
preface to *Death in Life: Survivors of Hiroshima*

MUSHROOM CLOUD

In the old Puritan worldview the child was evil incarnate: innately unruly and spoiled. As with witches, so with children: the devil and his works had first to be searched for and discovered and then beaten out of them. However, as far as I, a teacher in an international school, am concerned, it is not the child who is dangling by a thread over the fires of hell; it is I. Teachers everywhere mediate between opposing viewpoints on curriculum content in regard to subjects such as evolution and human sexuality. But teachers in the international environment must face the additional problem of parental worries about this very environment. What do we emphasize most: the culture of the host country or the history of our home country? How can we teach inches and feet in a metric world?

In the almost continuous discussions of what it means to teach in an international school, ethnocentrism and "adulto"-centrism prevail. The fact

---

This essay is composed of two articles that appeared in 1988 in *Hiroshima Signpost: The English Language Monthly*, a magazine written by foreign residents in Hiroshima and published by the International School. Walter wrote the first part, and Swiss educator Gauthier Loffler wrote the second part—one of many articles he wrote on his personal journey of peacemaking.

that the school is in Hiroshima City, which is also a potent symbol, compounds the issues; the parent body is often in disagreement about the atomic bombing and the nature and goal of peace education.

A perfect example of how two mature, reasonable adults can disagree about questions of human value is the debate over nuclear proliferation. Please do not misunderstand me. I am a teacher partly because of the dynamic human issues that can be raised in the school environment and that encourage children and adults to have reasonable arguments. Hiroshima International School is an excellent place to have such heated discussions. Here gum chewing and caffeine drinks are things of the past, and homework expectations are perennial. But one very special and highly delicate issue has raised its head on opposite—but forever historically linked—sides of the globe. The issue concerns the mushroom cloud. In both Hiroshima and Richland, Washington, idealistic and thought-provoking adolescents wrestle with the question of what their sports team should be called. The question is important, because unlike the eating-on-the-bus issue, this one has serious sociopolitical overtones in both communities.

Hiroshima International School has a problem: we have a junior high ball team without a mascot. The original members of the team want to establish a name and a tradition. In Richland, Washington, the team does have a name, which has great support among its community, but which also has thousands of opposing voices throughout the rest of the United States. Richland High is the home of the Bombers, whose emblem is the mushroom cloud formed in 1945 over Hiroshima. Richland is the home of the Hanford Nuclear Reservation, the major employer of the town's 30,000 residents and the primary developer of the nuclear weapons industry in the wartime days of the Manhattan Project (the code name for the development of the nuclear bomb used on Hiroshima). The Beavers changed their name to the Bombers at a time when the town was gushing with pride over its role in developing the atomic bombs that ended World War II. Today most of the townspeople think that a campaign by a small group of high-schoolers to change the emblem of the mushroom cloud is nothing less than an affront to civic pride, if not to historical fact. The mushroom symbol is everywhere, outlined on the floor tile of the entrance hall to the school, on a sign towering over the football field, on letter jackets and high school rings, and on the business card of every faculty member. It's a tradition.

In Hiroshima and Richland, kids are asking, "What's in a name?" While Richland has its Atomic Bowling Lanes and a main thoroughfare called Nuclear Lane, the concept of *heiwa*, or "peace," has not been sacrosanct in Hiroshima. In the city, we have the Peace Mannequin Company, Peace Plastic Surgery, the Peace Service Station, and even Peace Pachinko and Pinball Hall, not to mention Peace Park. For months, the HIS (Hiroshima International School) kids have been searching for a name, a symbol for their team, and as expected from imaginative pubescent thinkers, they've come up with a litany of strange suggestions. The Nosepickers and the Cockroaches were initial gags; the Fighting Cranes and the Seahawks got some play, only to be subjugated by the No-Names, the Losers, and the Hunks in Steel (or Satin). Inevitably, rather serious debate and propaganda for the A-Bombs, the Nukeheads, and the LB's (Little Boys) were heard.

I share the non-Puritanical notion about kids expressed by Jim, an English teacher of Richland, "Our kids are good kids. They're not warmongers. But there is almost a mob reaction going on here. Our job is to make them think."

Now our Critical Thinking class has a genuine issue to struggle with. After lots of discussion, most of our students agreed with the feelings of Richland's baseball coach, Scott Woodward. He remembered the year before when a group of Japanese high school students toured Richland and saw the local kids wearing their letter jackets with the mushroom cloud. Trying to explain the emblem to the Japanese students he said, "Left me feeling like I was standing outside without a fig leaf on." The HIS kids thought it would be offensive to Hiroshima residents to walk Hondori with a nuclear cloud imprinted on their sweatshirts, but then again, some argued it's just a symbol. They talked to Mr. Yaguchi, our beloved bus driver and a bomb victim. He thought the mushroom cloud emblem would be fine if it had three or four doves sitting on top, like partridges in a pear tree. The Dove Bombers?

I'll never forget in 1970 playing in a losing soccer game at the University of Miami before hundreds of screaming fans yelling, "Kill 'em, nuke 'em, kill 'em, nuke 'um." How did they know the Florida defensive back was from Hiroshima? Perhaps I glowed in the dark. No, "nuke 'em" had become a battle cry for the gridirons of the atomic age. Forty years ago the majestic mushroom cloud signified to those Richland folks the proud end to a terrible war. Today it embodies a symbol of world destruction of us all. We children of the nuclear age will proceed to choose a name, perhaps a wild animal, for our team. Personally I have hope we will choose the image of a dark, dead globe in the throes of nuclear winter. Then we would call our team, and all of us, The Losers.

30 YEARS OLD ON BOYS' DAY

A monument free of intrigues in the midst of the Peace Park celebrates its thirtieth birthday this coming May 5, Boys' Day. A party will be held for the weather-worn concrete statue with a child holding an iron paper crane on top of it. The monument's story inspires children all over the world to fold millions of paper cranes every year. The origami inspired by *Genbaku-no-ko-mno-zo* produces so many small, colorful paper birds that all the monuments in the Peace Park can be decorated all through the year with newly made bundles of folded paper. Day by day, red-and-blue-dressed tourist guides narrate the statue's story, which has been retold in many different ways: the story of Sadako Sasaki, who died of leukemia at the age of twelve, ten years after she had been exposed to the atomic bomb radiation on August 6, 1945.

MONKEY

Sadako's house stood along the Hakushima streetcar line, two hundred yards north of Hatchobori. On the morning of August 6, 1945, she was playing outdoors. Her parents, busy in their barber shop, could not keep an eye on their firstborn daughter for a while and Sadako was exposed to radiation. She wasn't hurt by burns, nor were her parents, who rushed out of the crushed and burning home just in time. Relatives in Kyushu were able to lend money to rebuild the barber shop. Soon Sadako-chan acquired a healthy sister and brother. Because her elder brother often teased her, she somehow lost cheerfulness early, clenching her teeth while helping her mother as much as she could.

In school Sadako was popular for her running abilities and on sports days held twice a year she made a name for herself by helping to win the popular end-of-the-day class relays. Her cheering classmates called her "monkey," which seemed to fit this girl perfectly, for she could run as if she were leaping through empty space. Sadako felt uneasy sharing the joy of having won loudly and in public. She enjoyed singing on her own. Often on her way home from school she heard herself singing a song from her childhood, her lips chanting: "Moon is shining, night is wonderful, come sing and dance with me, come-come-come."

During November 1954, Sadako caught a cold and developed an enlarged lymph node. The node was investigated by the Atomic Bomb Casualty Commission on Hijiyama Hill. Her parents had brought her up the hill to foreign doctors, although the research institute had incurred some hostility for its policy of examination without treatment. Sadako's parents learned that their daughter had a fatal disease. Before sending her to the Red Cross Hospital, her parents presented Sadako with her first kimono, sadly symbolizing her entry into maidenhood. The present was expensive, but the bills for medical treatment almost ruined the family.

PAPER CRANES

In the hospital she was rarely visited by her classmates, as rumors circulated that atomic bomb illnesses were contagious. Not knowing about her deteriorating health, she occasionally ran through the hospital corridors to visit other children and play with them. Sadako saw one of her playmates, a younger girl, dying of leukemia. She got a shock: "Will that happen to me too?" Her mother continued to console her, buying her rice cakes and candies. "You'll soon get better," Sadako-chan often heard from a mother withholding her tears.

It's not certain who told Sadako about the meaning of folding cranes. According to an old superstition, folding paper cranes helps to cure diseases. The real crane often serves as a symbol of love and long life. Sadako had started to fold paper cranes when her condition restricted her to bed. Although she soon learned to do it quickly and properly, the paper she used made it a tough task. The bedridden girl made use of the greased paper used to wrap her medicine (since at that time pills were not yet common and cheap enough for everybody).

She fixed on the saying that folding a thousand paper cranes would make one's wish come true. And Sadako-chan continued to fold them long after the goal of one thousand had been met. However, she suddenly refused medication for her steadily worsening pain because "it will slow down the healing process." Her death on October 15, 1955, was reported in all the local papers: "Another child died of leukemia, the atomic bomb disease." After her funeral, a private chart was found on which Sadako had written down the changing numbers and percentage of red and white corpuscles in her blood. The discovery that she had more than a presentiment of her young and seemingly useless death shocked many adults in the face of the determination of a twelve-year-old girl so bitterly fighting for her life. Her bereaved family still had to pay the bills for Sadako's transfusions for a long time. It forced the family to move to a smaller and less expensive house. Is it meaningless to fold paper cranes remembering Sadako?

THE JANITOR

Among those people who knew about Sadako Sasaki's existence only from the newspapers covering her brave death was twenty-six-year-old Ichiro Kawamoto. As the mid fifties politically were a time of intense ideological warfare that forced people apart while curbing almost all peace movements in Hiroshima as well as elsewhere, Kawamoto deliberately decided to pursue his own peace activities. Quitting his regular job and becoming a day laborer, he made himself find time to help poor hibakusha. The young man born in Peru, South America, often visited families who had lost children due to the atomic bomb's aftereffects.

The meeting with Mrs. Sasaki planted the idea in Kawamoto's mind to render Sadako's death a little bit meaningful by asking her former classmates to start a campaign for a monument for all children victimized by a war they had no responsibility for. After the children had agreed, Kawamoto asked Sadako's school principal to give official support. The poorly dressed day laborer was turned down, for he had no clear plan. Through leafleting and sending letters telling Sadako's story and asking for support, the children gradually received a lot of money. Seeing the campaign burgeoning, the school principal took over the responsibility for the project, which was renamed "Campaign for the Children's Peace Monument." The successful story and the many newspaper articles led as yet undecided supporters to join the dream Kawamoto Ichiro first had. The Sasaki family did its best to give their time to the various groups that asked the barber family for cooperation. By the end of 1956, enough money had been raised to appoint a famous Tokyo art professor to sculpt the monument, and the unveiling ceremony took place on May 5, 1958. It was followed by a film company shooting a semi-documentary about Sadako's life and her brave classmates erecting her a monument.

At the party thanking the movie makers, the unemployed Kawamoto, who had mainly given support to the Sasaki family during the three-year statue campaign, brought forward the idea of building a new children's peace group independent of dogma and without any political affiliations. Thus, *Orizuru-no-kai*, The Paper Crane Club, was founded and today members continue to visit and help forgotten hibakusha while also sharing the responsibility for folding paper cranes, which have become an international symbol for children wishing peace.

The Sasaki family now lives in Kyushu. They left Hiroshima in 1959 since the campaign had made many people wonder about a family who apparently capitalized on the death of their daughter. How else, they asked, than by being rich, is it possible to become so popular? When the Sasakis left Hiroshima they also had to give their second son up for adoption to more successful relatives.

Ichiro Kawamoto still lives in town, now a janitor at Jogakuin Junior High School. Among the many other activities he started was the successful campaign to preserve the Atomic Bomb Dome, since in the sixties many people wanted the crippled building to disappear forever.

When I recently visited the thirty-year-old A-bombed children's statue, halfway between the well-preserved former Prefectural Industrial Promotion Hall and the Cenotaph, inside the Peace Park, a blue-dressed tourist guide explained that the red-and-black-and-white "V" on the statue would stand for "victims." For me, it was like hearing "victory" and from far away I heard Sadako-chan's voice, whispering: "Why did they make war on me?"

Bibliography

Abrams, Jeremiah. 1990. *Reclaiming the Inner Child.* Los Angeles: Jeremy Tarcher.

Adler, Gerhard, ed. 1984. *Selected Letters of C. G. Jung.* Princeton: Princeton Univ. Press.

Akiba Project 84. 1984. *Hiroshima and Nagasaki through the Eyes of the American Journalists.* Hiroshima: Hiroshima International Cultural Found.

Andrews, V., R. Bosnak, and K. Goodwin, eds. 1987. Facing Apocalypse. Dallas: Spring Publications

Bachelard, Gaston. 1971. *The Poetics of Reverie,* trans. by Daniel Russell. Boston: Beacon Press.

Barefoot Gen, Project Gen, c/o Jim Peck. New York: War Registers League.

Bateson, Gregory. 1972. *Steps to an Ecology of Mind.* New York: Ballantine Books.

Berman, Morris. 1981. *The Reenchantment of the World.* Ithaca: Cornell Univ. Press.

———. 1989. *Coming to Our Senses: Body and Spirit in the Modern History of the West.* New York: Simon and Schuster.

Berry, Thomas. 1988. *The Dream of the Earth.* San Francisco: Sierra Club.

Cassirer, Ernst. 1944. *An Essay On Man: An Introduction to a Philosophy of Culture.* New Haven: Yale Univ. Press.

Chujo, Kazuo. 1984. *The Nuclear Holocaust* (A personal account). Translated by Asahi Evening News. Tokyo: Asaki Shinbu.

Coerr, Eleanor. 1978. *Sadako and the Thousand Paper Cranes* (hardcover, illustrated by Ronald Himler). New York: G. P. Putnam & Sons.

———. 1982. *Sadako and the Thousand Paper Cranes* (paperback). Tokyo: Yamaguchi Shoten.

Committee for the Compilation of Materials on Damage Caused by the Atomic Bombs in Hiroshima and Nagasaki. 1978. *Hiroshima and Nagasaki* (The physical, medical, and social effect of the atomic bombings). Tokyo: Iwanami Shoten.

———. 1986. *The Impact of the A-Bomb, Hiroshima and Nagasaki, 1945–1985*. (A recent abridged edition of the above book). Translated by Eisei Ishikawa M.D., and David L. Swain. Tokyo: Iwanami Shoten.

Cousins, Norman. 1987. *The Pathology of Power*. New York: Norton.

Del Tredici, Robert. 1968. *At Work in the Fields of the Bomb*. New York: Harper and Row.

DeMausse, Lloyd. 1974. *The History of Childhood*. New York: Peter Bedrick Books.

Dream Network Bulletin, vol. 14, no. 4, 1996. Moab, Utah.

Dunne, John. 1972. *The Way of All the Earth: Experiments in Truth and Religion*. New York: MacMillan.

Edinger, Edward. 1984. *The Myth of Consciousness: Jung's Myth for Modern Man*. Toronto: Inner City Press.

———. 1985. *The Anatomy of the Psyche: Alchemical Symbolism in Psychotherapy*. LaSalle, Ill.: Open Court Press.

———. 1999. *Archetype of the Apocalypse: A Jungian Study of the Book of Revelation*. Chicago: Open Court Press.

Enloe, Walter. 1992. "Peaceful Paper Cranes." In *Learning by Giving: K–8 Service Learning*, edited by Rich Cairns. St. Paul, Minn.: National Youth Leadership Council.

———. 1993. "The Thousand Cranes Club." In *Linking through Diversity*, edited by Walter Enloe and Ken Simon. Tucson, Ariz.: Zephyr Press.

———. 1994. "Sadako and the Thousand Cranes Club." In *An Instructional Guide to Teaching about the United Nations*, edited by James Muldoon and Mary Eileen Sorenson. New York: UNA-USA.

———. 1996. "Paper-Folding as Constructive Action." In *Creating Context*, edited by Walter Enloe. Tucson, Ariz.: Zephyr Press.

———. 1997. *Birds of Peace: Building Community and a Peaceful World*. San Francisco: Whitewing Press.

———. 1998. *Oasis of Peace: A Hiroshima Story*. St. Paul, Minn.: Hamline University Press.

———. 2002. *Lessons from Ground Zero: A Hiroshima and Nagasaki Story.* St. Paul, Minn.: Hamline University Press.

———. 2002. "Peace Trees." In *Tree Stories*, edited by Karen Shragg and Warren Jacobs. SunShine

Enloe, Walter, and Steve Leeper. *The Thousand Cranes Club*, Hiroshima Center for Conflict Resolution. Hiroshima: Hiroshima Shoten, Afton Press.

Enloe, Walter, and Randy Morris. 1998. *Encounters with Hiroshima: Making Sense of the Nuclear Age.* St. Paul, Minn.: Hamline University.

Enloe, Walter, et al. 1991. *Birds of Peace.* Twin Cities, Minn.: United Nations Association, Afton Press.

Erikson, Erik. 1964. *Insight and Responsibility: Ethical Implications of Psychoanalytic Insight.* New York: W. W. Norton.

———. 1980. "Elements of a Psychoanalytic Theory of Psychosocial Development." In S. I. Greenspan and G. H. Pollack, eds., *The Course of Life: Psychoanalytic Contributions toward Understanding Personality Development, vol. I, Infancy and Early Childhood* (pp. 11–61). National Institute of Mental Health.

Fox, Matthew. 1988. *The Coming of the Cosmic Christ.* New York: Harper and Row

Gandhi, Mohandes. 1968. *An Autobiography: My Experiments With Truth.* Boston: Beacon Press.

Garrison, James. 1982. *The Darkness of God: Theology After Hiroshima.* Grand Rapids, Mich.: Wm. B. Eerdmans.

Gilligan, Carol. 1982. *In a Different Voice: Psychological Theory and Women's Development.* Cambridge, Mass.: Harvard Univ. Press.

Hachiya, Michiko, M.D. 1956. *Hiroshima Diary* (the journal of a Japanese physician, Aug. 6 to Sept. 30, 1945). Translated by Warner Wells, M.D., Chapel Hill: Univ. of North Carolina Press.

Harada, Tomin. 1978. *Hiroshima Surgeon.* Translated by Robert and Alice R. Ramseyer. Los Angeles: Faith and Life Press.

Hersey, John. 1946. *Hiroshima.* New York: Bantam.

Hibakusha: Survivors of Hiroshima and Nagasaki. 1986. Tokyo: Kosei.

Hill, Michael Ortiz. 1994. *Dreaming the End of the World: Apocalypse As a Rite of Passage.* Dallas: Spring Publications.

Hillman, James. 1975. *Re-visioning Psychology.* New York: Harper and Row.

———. 1996. *The Soul's Code: In Search of Character and Calling*. New York: Random House.

Hiroshima Interpreters for Peace. 1989. *Hiroshima Handbook* (general reference book about Hiroshima, including a Japanese-English Dictionary of A-bomb related terms). Hiroshima: Hiroshima Interpreters for Peace.

Hiroshima. 1992. "Send Her a Thousand Cranes" is the first song on the jazz fusion band Hiroshima's album *East*.

Ibuse, Masuji. 1977. *Black Rain*. Translated by John Baxter. New York: Kodansha International.

Ikagami, Nagako. 1980. *The Twinkling Stars Know Everything*. Published by author.

Jung, C. G. 1971. Coll. Wks. 14, *Mysterium Coniunctionis*. Princeton: Princeton Univ. Press.

———. 1971. Coll. Wks. 18, *The Symbolic Life: Miscellaneous Writings*. Princeton: Princeton Univ. Press.

Jungk, Robert. 1959. *Strahalen aus der Asche (Children of the Ashes: The Story of a Rebirth)*. Bern: Alfred Verlag Ltd. (Sadako's story originally appears in the West).

Kaminski, Marc. 1974. *The Road from Hiroshima* (a narrative poem). Simon and Schuster.

Kaya, Dr. Fumiko. 1966. *The Mushroom Cloud*. Translated by Ryoji Kumagawa. Published by author.

Keen, Sam. 1983. *The Passionate Life: Stages of Loving*. New York: Harper and Row.

———. 1986. *Faces of the Enemy*. New York: Harper and Row.

Keeney, Bradford. 1994. *Shaking Out the Spirits: A Psychotherapist's Entry into the Healing Mysteries of Global Shamanism*. Barrytown, N.Y.: Station Hill Press.

Kernberg, Otto. 1975. *Borderline Conditions and Pathological Narcissism*. New York: Jason Aronson.

Kimura, Yasuko. 1974. *White Town Hiroshima* (has become a movie that is played every year in Hiroshima). Translated by Nobuko Ueno and Jerri Okada. Tokyo: Bunka Hyoron.

Kohut, Heinz. 1971. *The Analysis of the Self*. New York: International Univ. Press.

Kosaki, Yoshiteru, ed. 1985. *A-Bomb: A City Tells Its Story*. Translated by Kiyoko Kageyama, Charlotte Susu-Maho and Kaoru Ogura. Hiroshima: Hiroshima Peace and Culture Found.

———. 1986. *Hiroshima Peace Reader*. Translated by Akira and Michiko Tashiro, and Robert and Alice Ruth Ramseyer. Hiroshima: Hiroshima Peace Culture Found.

Lasch, Christopher. 1978. *The Culture of Narcissism: American Life in an Age of Diminishing Returns*. New York: W. W. Norton.

Leguin, Ursula. 1990. "The Ones Who Walk Away from Omelas." In *Reclaiming the Inner Child*, edited by Jeremiah Abrams. Los Angeles: Jeremy Tarcher.

Lifton, Betty Jean. 1987. *A Place Called Hiroshima*. Photos by Eikon Hosoe. Tokyo: Kodansha International.

Lifton, Robert Jay. 1967. *Boundaries: Psychological Man in Revolution*. New York: Simon and Schuster.

———. 1970. *History and Human Survival*. New York: Random House.

———. 1975. *Death in Life: The Survivors of Hiroshima*, New York: Simon and Schuster.

———. 1979. *The Broken Connection: On Death and the Continuity of Life*. New York: Simon and Schuster.

Lifton, Robert Jay, and Greg Mitchell. 1995. *Hiroshima in America: Fifty Years of Denial*. New York: Putnam.

Lockhart, Russell. *Psyche Speaks: A Jungian Approach to Self and World*. Wilmette, Ill.: Chiron Publications, 1984.

Macy, Joanna. 1983. "Despair Work." In W. McClinn, ed., *Mark Twain Himself: Humor, War and Fundamentalism* (pp. 225–41). Dubuque, Ia.: Kendall-Hunt.

———. 1988. *World As Lover, World As Self*. Berkeley: Parallax Press.

———. 2002. *Widening Circles: A Memoir*, Gabriola Island, B.C.: New Society Publishers.

Macy, Joanna, and Molly Young Brown. 1998. *Coming Back to Life: Practices to Reconnect Our Lives, Our World*. Gabriola Island, B.C.: New Society Publishers.

Mahdi, Louise C., et al. 1987. *Betwixt and Between: Patterns of Masculine and Feminine Initiation*. Chicago: Open Court Press.

Margalit, Avishai. 2002. *The Ethics of Memory*, Cambridge, Mass.: Harvard University Press.
Maruki, Toshi. 1981. *The Hiroshima Story*. Tokyo: A & C Black.
Matsuki, Suguru, ed. 1986. *Testimonies of Hiroshima and Nagasaki* (Lutheran survivors and their families). Translated by Earl Bergh. Hiroshima: Committee for Peace and Nuclear Disarmament.
Matsumoto, Yuko. 1971. *My Mother Died in Hiroshima*. Translated by Akira Matsuo. Hiroshima: Hiroshima Peace Culture Found.
May, Rollo. 1981. *Freedom and Destiny*. New York: W. W. Norton.
Merton, Thomas. 1964. *Gandhi on Non-Violence*. New York: New Directions.
Morris, Randy, and Walter Enloe. 1998. *Encounters with Hiroshima: Making Sense of the Nuclear Age*. St. Paul, Minn.: Hamline University Press.
Morrow, James. 1986. *This Is the Way the World Ends*. New York: Henry Holt.
Mutwa, Vusamazulu Credo. 1985. *Indaba My Children: African Tribal History, Legends, Customs and Religious Beliefs*. London: Kahn and Averill.
———. 1996. *Song of the Stars: The Lore of a Zulu Shaman*. Barrytown, N.Y.: Station Hill Press.
Nagai, Tetsyo. 1980. *The Bells of Nagasaki*. Tokyo: Kodansha International.
Nakazawa, Keiji. 1978. *I Saw It, I Saw It* (in comic form). Hiroshima: Educomics.
Nam, Paksu. 1986. *The Other Hiroshima* (Korean A-bomb victims tell their story). Translated by Greg Barrett, Bill Healy, Warren Hesse, Phil Hill. Self-published by author.
Noel, Dan. 1997. *The Soul of Shamanism: Western Fantasies, Imaginal Realities*. New York: Continuum Press.
O'Conner, Peter. 1986. *Dreams and the Search for Meaning*. New York: Paulist Press.
Oe, Kenzaburo, ed. 1980. *Atomic Aftermath* (short stories about Hiroshima and Nagasaki). Tokyo: Shueisha.
———. 1975. *Hiroshima Notes*. Tokyo: YMCA Press.
Ohara, Miyao, ed. and trans. *The Songs of Hiroshima* (an anthology of songs and poems in both Japanese and English). Hiroshima: Satsuki Shuppan.
Oliver, Mary. 1992. *New and Selected Poems*. Boston: Beacon Press.
Osada, Arata, ed. 1952. *Children of Hiroshima* (accounts of the bombing

written in 1950 by children who were elementary to high school students at the time). New York: Harper and Row.

Peace Declarations. 1995. Delivered by the Mayors of Hiroshima. Hiroshima: Hiroshima Peace Culture Found.

Perlman, Michael. 1995. *Hiroshima Forever: The Ecology of Mourning*. Barrytown, N.Y.: Barrytown Ltd. Press.

Raheem, Aminah. 1987. *Soul Return: Integrating Body, Psyche and Spirit*. Lower Lake, Calif.: Aslan.

Rhodes, Richard. 1988. *The Making of the Atomic Bomb*. New York: Simon and Schuster.

Roszak, Theodore, et al. 1995. *Ecopsychology: Restoring the Earth, Healing the Mind*. San Francisco: Sierra Club Books.

———. 1995. *The Memoirs of Elizabeth Frankenstein*. New York: Random House.

Sardello, Robert. 1992. *Facing the World with Soul: The Reimagination of Modern Life*. Hudson, N.Y.: Lindisfarne Press.

———. 1999. *Freeing the Soul from Fear*. New York: Riverhead Books.

———. 2001. *Love and the World: A Guide to Conscious Soul Practice*. Hudson, N.Y.: Lindisfarne Books.

Schell, Jonathan. 1982. *The Fate of the Earth*. New York: Alfred Knopf.

Sussman, Linda. 1995. *The Speech of the Grail: A Journey Towards Speaking That Heals and Transforms*. Hudson, N.Y.: Lindisfarne Press.

Takayama, Hitoshi. 1968: *Hiroshima in Memoriam and Today*. Tokyo: Published by author.

Takeda, Eiko. 1983. *Little Mary: The Blue-Eyed Doll*. Translated by Michael Toyama and J. Littlemore. Hiroshima: Yamaguchi Shoten.

Tarnas, Richard. 1991. *The Passion of the Western Mind*. New York: Ballantine Books.

The Day Man Lost. 1972. New York: The Pacific War Research Society, Kodansha International.

Thomas, Gordon. 1977. *Ruin from the Air: The Atomic Mission to Hiroshima*. London: Hamish Hamilton.

Tillich, Paul. 1948. *The Shaking of the Foundations*. New York: Charles Scribners' Sons.

Tunison, Nancy H. 1971. *Hiroshima No Pika* (Pika is the word used to describe the bomb's flash). Tokyo: Kagyusha.

von Eschenbach, Wolfram. 1961. *Parzifal: A Romance of the Middle Ages.* trans. by Helen Mustard and Charles Passage. New York: Random House.

Warden, John, ed. 1982. *Orpheus: The Metamorphosis of a Myth.* Toronto: University of Toronto Press.

Weart, Spencer. 1988. *Nuclear Fear: A History of Images.* Cambridge, Mass.: Harvard Univ. Press.

Whitmont, Edward. 1982. *The Return of the Goddess.* New York: Crossroads.

Yamaguchi, Yuko. 1978. *The Angry Jizo.* Translated by Beth Harrison and Hisashi Oda. Tokyo: Yamaguchi Shoten.

OTHER RESOURCES

On a Paper Crane: A Video

On a Paper Crane is an animated cartoon created in Japan to give children of the world a message: the abolition of all nuclear arms and the importance of peace. The story is as follows: Tomoko is a young girl living in Hiroshima. One day during her summer vacation, she visits the Hiroshima Peace Memorial alone. Shocked and exhausted, she strolls through the Peace Memorial Park and meets a mysterious girl. Her name is Sadako. She was exposed to the A-bomb radiation at age two and died ten years later. Today Sadako guides Tomoko on a spectacular adventure. For information on the English version write: Peace Anime No Kai Dokuritsu Eiga Center 7th Floor, Taiyo Building 3-16-2 Shimbashi, Minato-ku Tokyo, Japan 100 (fax, 81-3-3432-8633)

A Thousand Cranes: A Play in One Act

Quickly becoming a new children's classic, *A Thousand Cranes* tells the heart-touching and true story of the little girl who inspired millions with a simple but often neglected message—"Peace in the World." Twelve years after the bombing of her home Hiroshima, Sadako bravely struggles for long life by following the Japanese tradition of folding one thousand cranes as a symbol of hope. Although she does not survive, her spirit and the beauty of her message live on in the hearts and minds of today's children.

A Thousand Cranes: A Play in One Act by Kathryn Schultz Miller may be ordered from The Dramatic Publishing Company, 311 Washington St., Woodstock, IL 60098.

Ms. Miller is Artistic Director of ArtReach Touring Theatre, whose company tours nationally, performing *A Thousand Cranes* and other plays for children and adults alike. For information write ArtReach, 3074 Madison Rd., Cincinnati, OH 45309 or call (513) 871-2300.

Sadako Peace Club

Initiated in 1995 by peacemaker Michiko, this club publishes materials, including wonderful T-shirts, and a beautiful musical score and tape of an original song about Sadako. Write to Sadako Peace Club, P.O. Box 1253, Issaquah, WA 98027-1253, or fax 206-391-4797.

Sadako Project

The Center for Informed Democracy, led by peacemaker George Levenson, offers a plethora of materials including posters, crane buttons, books, and origami paper. It has a great video on paper-folding as well as the beautiful moving video *Sadako and the Paper Cranes,* based on Eleanor Coerr's picture book with illustrations by Ed Young. The video is narrated by the acclaimed actress Liv Ullmann and music is by the master George Winston. Write the Sadako Project, P.O. Box 67, Santa Cruz, CA 95063, or fax 408-426-2312 (for more information see earlier chapter in this book). Search the Internet for their Web site address.

Sadako Paper Crane Project

A project linking schools to build friendship and international understanding around Sadako, paper-folding, and communication. Write to Sharon O'Connell, 2423 East Lake Road, Skaneateles, NY 13152, or search the Internet for the Web site address.

International Children's Peace Statue

A new project initiated by Hiroshima International School to build a new monument for Hiroshima to the children of the world to celebrate the millions of cranes sent each year by school children around the world. To get involved write 1000 Cranes Club, Hiroshima International School, 3-49-1 Kurakake, Asakita-ku, Hiroshima shi, Japan 739-17, or search the Internet for the Web site address.